GREENHOUSE MANAGEMENT

Robert W. Langhans

Cornell University

SECOND EDITION

GREENHOUSE MANAGEMENT

A GUIDE TO STRUCTURES, ENVIRONMENTAL CONTROL, MATERIALS HANDLING, CROP PROGRAMMING AND BUSINESS ANALYSIS

Line Drawings by Virginia C. Langhans

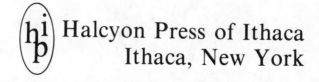 Halcyon Press of Ithaca
Ithaca, New York

To Kenneth Post
for instilling in me
his enthusiasm for floriculture

CONTENTS

PREFACE

This book presents technical information on the management of greenhouses. Whether plants are grown for profit, pleasure, research, or instruction, the manager must understand the forces at work in the greenhouse and the equipment that controls them. There are examples in this book of many factors that must be taken into account in the design, construction, and operation of the greenhouse. In addition, detailed drawings help illustrate most of the equipment discussed in the text. The advantages of each system are evaluated from both a practical and economic viewpoint.

The first section describes the structures necessary to a greenhouse operation. The location, design, construction, and maintenance of greenhouses, cool rooms, storage space, workrooms, and growth rooms are discussed. The importance of planning the entire greenhouse range in advance is emphasized.

The second section contains technical discussions for obtaining the environmental control essential for plant growth. The systems for controlling light, temperatures, humidity, and carbon dioxide levels are examined, and the instruments for measurement and control are described in detail.

Section III gives the relative advantages of various materials handling, watering, and fertilizing systems, as well as complete descriptions of the equipment used in each process. Safety precautions are emphasized in the chapter on pesticides.

The final section is a guide to managerial decision-making. Many examples are used to illustrate the calculations on which crop programming is based. The chapter on record keeping and business analysis explains the purpose of accurate records and demonstrates the techniques of analysis. The final chapter advises the greenhouse manager of some of his legal obligations.

The outline and emphasis of subject matter for this book has evolved over 10 years of teaching a course titled "Greenhouse Management". The students taking this course were seniors that had some background in economics, math, chemistry, and a real desire to manage a greenhouse. They had had good courses in plant culture, plant physiology, nutrition and agronomy. The need was for more information on structures, environmental control, materials handling, crop programming and business analysis, therefore the emphasis of these subjects in this book.

There is extensive use of line drawings, as they allowed me to emphasize particular points, especially fine details.

The use of the metric system in this book has been a problem. In practical greenhouse management, the metric system is not used. Most units of length, weight and volume are in English units and not metric, but tables of metric conversions are given in the appendix. Temperature and light measurements are given in both English and metric units.

The reference lists at the end of each section include most of the major works and is the material that was drawn upon.

The subjects covered in this book are changing rapidly and by the time this book is published and distributed, some subjects will be incomplete. For example, information on rolling benches and highly insulated thermal blankets is now available, but not covered extensively in this text. I welcome suggestions for material to be included and correction of any errors for the next revision.

A number of people have played different roles in this book. I wish to thank the 300 plus undergraduate students that took the "Greenhouse Management" course. Much appreciation is expressed to the teaching assistants that took responsibilities and added depth to the subjects. They include: Nancy Cannon, Rick Cerilli, Gil Hilen, Steve Koenigsberg, Kent Kratz, Ellen Paparozzi, James Stefanis, Ellen Sutter, David Weisser and Mike Wolfe.

A group of distinguished people also reviewed various parts of the manuscript. My appreciation is expressed to them for taking the time and making helpful suggestions: Ralph Freeman, Floricultural Specialist, Long Island, NY (the whole manuscript); Prof. Dana Goodrich, Agricultural Economics, Cornell University (Section IV, Crop Programming and Business Analysis); Dr. Harold Gray, President, National Greenhouse Co., Pana, IL (Section I, Structures); Dr. Allen Hammer, Professor of Floriculture, Purdue University (Section I, Structures); Jack Hildinger, Marketing Manager, Environmental Controls Products, Acme Engineering and Manufacturing Corp., Muskogee, OK (Section II, Environmental Control).

Lisa Turner edited the manuscript and Marian Rollins did the typing. I wish to express my appreciation for their fine efforts.

Last, but not least, Virginia Langhans, my wife, is thanked for she did all the art work and kept me encouraged.

R. W. Langhans, Ithaca, NY

SECOND PREFACE

The reception of this book has been very good and the original printing was quickly depleted. It has been about 5 years since I first sat down and started to write and it needed to be updated. I use the book in my "Greenhouse Management" course and the students helped find errors, noted missing discussions and asked about new subjects. It was rather amazing the number of additions to this 2nd edition, including thermal blankets, waste heat greenhouses, rolling benches, plant plugs, additional lamp background, measuring light, IR heating, computer controllers, fertilizer calculations, nutrient film technique, biological control, and electronic spread sheets to mention the major items. It clearly indicates the dynamics of the floricultural industry and emphasizes the importance of keeping up with technology. A book such as this serves as an excellent means of recording the changes that occur over the years.

Teaching the greenhouse management course has given me the opportunity to work with an additional fine group of undergraduate students. They always stimulate enthusiasm. The graduate students play a very important role in this course. Their discussion and particiation make this course especially enjoyable. Doug Cox, Gary Keever, Cathy Klein, Idris Mohamed Ahmed, William Miller, Larry Rupp, and Randy Woodson are added to the distinguished list of T.A.'s.

For general interest this is a venture my wife and I have undertaken. We are the publisher, editor, artist and layout people. The printing is done by Cayuga Press of Ithaca and the binding by Vail-Balu of Binghamton, New York. This has the advantage of reducing the time lost in communication between the editor and author and gives me the opportunity to place the tables and figures where I think they should be.

The typing of the revision was done by Elaine Depew and I thank her.

I would like to thank my publisher, illustrator, book distributor and wife for the multiple roles she plays in making this book fun.

R. W. Langhans
Ithaca, NY
11/82

SECTION I

Structures

1

GROWING STRUCTURES

Growing plants out of season, when the outside conditions are unsuitable, is the basic reason for building greenhouse structures. Primary considerations are satisfactory plant growth and economics. If the plants are not productive or the costs are higher than the returns, the structure is not satisfactory.

Years of development have produced many types and forms of greenhouses and this evolution is still occurring. Shapes that were rejected a few years ago are again coming into vogue with the changing energy picture. We will review the basic forms and put their utilization into the present day perspective. Although next year this perspective may change, the basic principles remain constant.

The first commercial growing structures were cold frames, which were eventually heated with decomposing manure to form hot beds. The hot beds were dug out to improve working conditions and called pit houses. The houses were raised and became the present-day greenhouse. At the turn of the century new structural materials became available: glass, metal framing, and galvanized pipe. Efficient boilers and better heating systems were developed.

Greenhouses, as we know them today, were built in the vicinity of large cities so they would be close to the market, as transportation was a limiting factor. Labor was relatively inexpensive and automation was not an important consideration. Greenhouse men worked long hours and controlled by hand all of the functions of the greenhouse — ventilation, heating, watering, and yearly removal of soil from the benches. The start of World War II and the ensuing labor shortage promoted automation in the greenhouse, which included coal stokers or oil or gas burners for the boilers, automatic vents, steam sterilization of the soil, and automatic watering. Transportation after World War II was greatly improved and proximity to the market lost its attraction. Other factors such as land, light, and cheap labor became more important. As mechanical ventilation began to replace natural ventilation, an excellent low-cost summer cooling system was developed. This was a boon for greenhouse operators in the south, where summer growing had been just about impossible because of the heat.

The early 1950s were a time of great excitement for the greenhouse industry. The wooden greenhouse gave way to aluminum structures. Using sheet polyethylene, a greenhouse operator could quickly and inexpensively put up acres of polyethylene-covered structures. More recently, rigid plastics, especially fiber glass, became available for covering greenhouse structures.

Today the greenhouse operator has many structural options and great freedom of choice as to location. The rise in energy costs and the possibility of shortages have created some new limitations that affect both heating and transportation.

SITE AND LOCATION

The factors determining the choice of location are climate, markets, labor, transportation, heating fuel, and taxes. There should be a reasonable means of transportation to the appropriate market. If the operation will be large, the availability and skill of the work force will be important considerations. An operation located in almost any area of the United States except southern Florida and southern California will have to check on the availability of heating fuel. Some states and communities encourage new agribusinesses by offering tax benefits.

Waste heat from a number of sources including electrical power plants, natural gas compressor stations and heat from fermentation of alcohol all could be potential sources of heat. These heat producers are usually near areas of high population centers, thereby, additionally reducing transportation.

After the general location has been decided upon, the actual site must be selected. Things to be considered in site selection are topography, drainage, water supply, pollution, light, and wind.

Topography. Before the twentieth century, greenhouses were commonly built on the south side of hills to capture the maximum winter light. Movement up and down the hillside was difficult and slow, but labor was relatively inexpensive. Today labor is more expensive and most automated equipment works best on level ground, so a flat piece of land is advisable.

Drainage. Improper water drainage can cause years of aggravation. Consider for example a five-acre piece of land with three acres of greenhouses and one acre of buildings roads and paved parking area. Eighty percent of the land is covered, and when it rains, the remaining acre will have to absorb all of the water that was formerly absorbed by five acres. The drainage patterns and capacity of the area will be radically changed and, to avoid problems, they should be carefully studied. Most counties have engineers who are familiar with the area and will help design proper drainage facilities.

Water Supply. A greenhouse operation uses a great deal of water, which has been estimated at one quart per square foot of covered ground per day. A one-acre greenhouse uses approximately 10,000 gallons of water per day. The quality of the water is also important. For example, a high level of salt can cause major problems with plant growth, and can also damage a steam or hot water heating system. It is costly to remove salts from water. (Chapter 18 reviews this subject in greater detail.)

Pollution. Greenhouses built downwind from chemical factories or power plants that were polluting the air have had serious problems. Care should be taken to avoid such situations.

Light. Light is most important for plant growth and the site should be free of obstructions. If the site is in a valley and the sun sets below the hills at two o'clock every day, the variety of plants that can be grown will be limited. Trees, buildings, and other obstructions may cause shadows and should be carefully studied.

Wind. Many locations with ideal light and drainage conditions seem to have the disadvantage of high prevailing winds. Winds during the winter months drastically increase the heating cost. Wind shelters should be considered. The local weather bureau can usually give figures on the average wind force for each month of the year. Average wind speeds over 15 mph should be avoided.

Planning

After all the factors have been checked and the exact site located, the next step is to plan the layout of the entire greenhouse range. If the initial program calls for only one greenhouse, though eventually there will be 50 greenhouses, plan and lay out the whole project at the start. This will ensure that the roads will be wide enough, the boiler will be in the best location, and the circulation of material and labor around all 50 greenhouses will be smooth and easy. Many greenhouse ranges show the lack of overall planning. Each year another greenhouse is built, each at a different angle, each a different size, and when finally completed, circulation and transportation are awkward. Plan the whole site before the operation starts.

COLD AND HOT FRAMES

Cold frames are used during the spring and they accommodate the expansion of the greenhouse operation during the spring rush. They make an excellent structure for holding and hardening of bedding plants and other plants for outdoor sales. Hot frames are heated cold frames, and the basic structures of the two are similar. Plastic houses are rapidly replacing cold and hot frames because they are easier to use during periods of low outside temperatures and inexpensive versions are available.

Construction

A sash (usually glass) is placed on a frame that holds it above the plant (Fig. 1.1). The sash is movable to allow for ventilation and the frame tilts to the south to capture the most light.

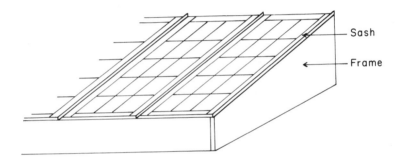

Figure 1.1   Sash and cold frame.

Sashes are usually 3 by 6 feet, for over this size they are too heavy to handle (Fig. 1.2). The slope is six inches higher on the north side than the south. The dimensions of the frame are 5 feet 11 inches wide and in multiples of 3 feet in length (Fig. 1.3).

The most common material used to construct the sash and frame is wood. California redwood resists rot and with proper maintenance should last for many years. Other woods will rot quickly unless they are specially treated.

Heating

Hot frames are heated with electric heating cables placed on the ground as shown in Figure 1.4. Some frames are heated with steam or hot water pipes (Fig. 1.5.).

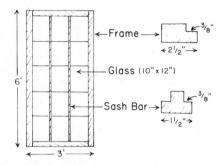

Figure 1.2   The dimensions of a sash.

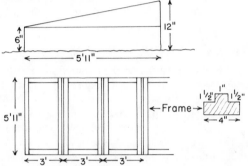

Figure 1.3   The dimensions of the frame.

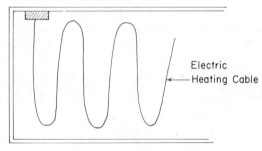

Figure 1.4   Installation of electric heating cable in a hot bed.

Figure 1.5   Heating pipes in a hot bed.

Ventilation

To prevent the frames from becoming too hot when the sun is shining the sashes are slid down to let the hot air leave and in warm weather are removed completely as shown in Figure 1.6. Some frames have been automated with a mechanical greenhouse ventilator system.

Figure 1.6   Moving of frame for ventilation.

FOUNDATIONS AND CURTAIN WALLS

Care should be taken to insure a proper foundation is made for any structure larger than a cold frame. In some areas the ground freezes for several feet, and if the foundation is not deep enough the thawing and heaving process will lift up, break, and disrupt the structures. Local building contractors have information on the depth and kind of foundations that are needed for a particular location. The minimum depth of the foundation is 18 inches to ensure that the soil will be firm enough to carry the load. Be careful in filled areas.

Footings

The footing is the base or foot of the wood or steel upright that goes into the ground. Commonly, a series of holes are dug, the posts placed into the holes, and the holes filled with concrete. The posts are lined up before the concrete has hardened. Another method, used for aluminum houses, is to pour concrete footings and place bolts upright in the concrete. The posts are then bolted onto the footings after the concrete has hardened (Fig. 1.7.).

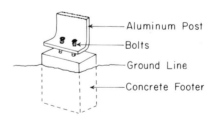

Figure 1.7   Aluminum post bolted to a concrete footing.

Curtain Walls

In most greenhouses, the curtain walls are two- to three-foot high, solid walls on the sides and ends. The walls are constructed from a variety of materials usually concrete, cinder block, or asbestos cement. Abestos cement is probably the material most commonly used.

The best construction is a poured concrete wall at or below the soil line and deeper than the frost line with the abestos cement wall placed on top to form the curtain wall as shown in Figure 1.8.

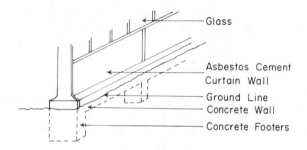

Glass

Asbestos Cement
Curtain Wall

Ground Line

Concrete Wall

Concrete Footers

Figure 1.8   Asbestos cement curtain wall below glass structure and above the footings and foundation wall.

Floors

There are a number of materials that can be used for the greenhouse floor, gravel, blacktop and cement to mention a few. The choice will be dependent on cost and use. Paths and walks, especially if they will convey light vehicles should be 4 inches of concrete. A solid floor of concrete is expensive and water drainage is more complicated.

Some greenhouse operators are growing directly on the floor and heating the floor. The heat pipes are placed in the floor and covered with 4 inches of porous cement.

    1 cubic yard of porous cement:

        2800 lbs. of 3/8 inch aggregate (no sand)

        5.5 sacks of cement

        22 gallons of water

This mixture allows free drainage of water and yet carries the load of a light vehicle (600 lbs per sq. ft. vs. 2500 lbs. per sq. ft. for regular concrete).

PLASTIC GREENHOUSES

Plastic greenhouses have been responsible for the greatest expansion of covered structures, so that today there are thousands of acres covered with plastic. Plastic is inexpensive and can cover almost any form. The greatest liabilities of plastic are poor durability and reduced light transmission. Most plastics become brittle in sunlight and discolor under ultraviolet radiation. When plastic is compared to glass, its life is short. Polyethylene with ultraviolet (UV) inhibitor will last two years, fiber glass with a Teflon coating will last ten years, and glass will easily last 40 or 50 years. Plastic does not allow as much light to pass through as glass does.

Types of Plastic

There are a number of plastic materials that have been used for greenhouse coverings. They can be divided into two general groups: sheet and rigid. The rigid plastics are manufactured in set sizes, most commonly in 4 by 8 foot panels, and they do bend, but not with the flexibility of sheet plastic, which comes in a wide variety of sizes up to 40 feet wide by 100 feet long.

Sheet Plastic. There are four types of sheet plastic materials: polyethylene, polyvinyl, polyvinyl floride, and polyester.

Polyethylene is manufactured in thin sheets, usually 4 to 6 mils thick with lengths and widths up to 40 feet by 150 feet. To reduce the detrimental effect of sunlight, an ultraviolet inhibitor is added. Monsanto 602 and 603 are good examples of polyethylene films with UV inhibitors that increase the film life up to 3 years. Polyethylene is by far the most common plastic material used for greenhouse covering in the United States.

Polyvinyl is manufactured in 4 to 6 mil thickness, but only in narrow widths. It has greater UV resistance than polyethylene, but unfortunately has an affinity for dust and must be periodically cleaned. It is the most common covering material used in Japan where apparently the dust problem has been solved.

Polyvinyl floride (Tedlar) is an extremely weatherable film, but is costly and manufactured only in narrow sheets. It is commonly used to cover inexpensive solar collectors.

Polyester (Mylar) is very resistant to breakdown by UV and has excellent light transmission, but is expensive and not commonly used.

Rigid Plastics. The four types of rigid plastic materials most often used for greenhouse coverings are polyvinyl chloride, fiber glass, acrylic and polycarbonate.

Polyvinyl chloride (PVC) is inexpensive when compared to the other rigid plastics, but ultraviolet causes a darkening of the material in a year or so which results in reduced light transmission.

Fiber glass is inexpensive enough that it can be considered for a greenhouse covering. It is made of polyester resin reinforced with glass fibers. Light transmission through fiber glass is good. The surface of fiber glass panels wears and the glass fibers come through the surface giving it a fuzzy look called "wicking" or "blooming". This fuzziness also collects dust and will reduce light transmission. To avoid this problem, the surface can be resurfaced with polyester resin, but this has not proven very practical. Long-lasting surfaces on fiber glass have been achieved by coating with Tedlar (polyvinyl floride). The manufacturers of Tedlar-surface fiber glass claim that it has a life of 15 to 20 years. The major drawback of fiber glass is that it is flammable and when it starts to burn it burns very rapidly. Fire insurance for fiber glass structures is more expensive than for other materials.

Acrylic (Plexiglass) is expensive for greenhouse coverings, scratches easily, and is combustible. Ultraviolet light does not break it down, light transmission is excellent, its strength is good and comparable to glass. The material has recently been manufactured in double sheets (SDP-16, Exolite). The two sheets are separated by ribs spaced approximately every 16 mm. Each sheet is 1.5 mm thick, the panel is 16 mm thick, 47.25 inches wide and can be obtained in lengths from 8 to 16 feet. The expansion and contraction of the material caused by temperature changes is large and special installation precautions are needed. The double sheets have an insulation value of 2 layers of glass (approx. R 1.7). Many installations of this material have been made on the sides and end walls of greenhouses.

Polycarbonate is a similar material to acrylic and similar double sheet panels are manufactured (SPD-Polycarbonate, Exolite). This material is scratch-resistant with slightly lower light transmission. A thinner panel (4 and 6 mm) and less expensive is manufactured (Qualex). These panels have particular use in doors or other areas where there is a high risk of breakage.

Light Transmission

Light transmission through plastic film has always caused some confusion, especially to the reader of advertising brochures. None of the plastic materials transmits as much visible light as glass. Many reports give light transmission of plastics in relation to glass, for example, new polyethylene film transmits 88% of the light that comes through glass. If glass allows 80% of available light to pass through it, then the polyethylene film really allows only 70.4% of the light to pass through, or in other words, a 30% reduction. Another term that is used imprecisely is diffused light. Diffused light means scattered in different directions. For example a manufacturer's photograph will show a lack of a shadow under a particular plastic panel and imply more light is allowed through the cover. Actually, the light is being diffused as it passes thru the cover in all directions and some of the light is being directed away from the surface; therefore, there is a reduction in light (Fig. 1.9). Light intensity measurements made in glass and polyethylene greenhouses are shown in Table 1.1.

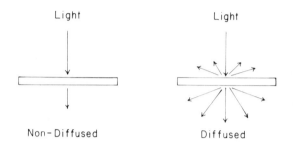

Figure 1.9   Diffusion of light through plastic and glass.

Table 1.1   Light intensity measurements made in Ithaca, NY, on September 17, 1970, in a glass house and two plastic houses (R. Sheldrake).

| | | | At pot level | |
Location	footcandles (lux)	percentage of outside light	footcandle (lux)	percentage of outside light
Outside	9,800 (105,840)	100	—	—
New glass house	7,600 (82,080)	78	7,200 (77,760)	73
New UV polyethylene house	7,200 (77,760)	73	6,900 (74,520)	70
Year-old UV polyethylene house	6,800 (73,440)	69	6,500 (70,200)	66

There is no question that light levels are lower in a plastic structure. This will be a problem, however, only during the darker winter months. Plastic houses are normally used for fall and spring crops, or in geographic areas where the light intensity is naturally high year round.

There is a light or energy loss of approximately 4.5% for each surface that light passes through (upper and lower surface) plus a possible loss in the body of the material. This means the best transparent material will have only a maximum of 91% light transmission. Glass falls into this category. Most other materials absorb some of the light energy in the body, therefore, the light transmission is less.

The light level in a greenhouse is very important. The Europeans have shown that a 1% loss in light translates into a 1% loss of dry weight of the plants. During the dark winter months, light levels are extremely critical.

Plastic houses are commonly used for fall and spring crops or in geographic areas where the light levels are high year round.

It is very difficult to measure the light level in a greenhouse. First the light will be variable in different locations in the house, the light will be variable in one location over time because of shadows. A glasshouse with 24 inch sash bar spacing is equivalent to 7% opaque structure. A plastic house with 48 inch bar spacing has 4% opaque structure. Maximum light penetrates any surface only when the light source (sun) is perpendicular to that surface. The rays of the sun are rarely perpendicular to even half of the surface. To compare one covering material with another, the best judge would be a measure of plants growing in the two structures.

The term foot-candle is used commonly in the industry to indicate light intensity. This is not the best term to use, because it does not describe the radiation that is useful for the plant. Visible light is used by the plant in photosynthesis, therefore, researchers use the term Photosynthetically Active Radiation (PAR). This measures the amount of light that can be used by the plant and is reported as micro moles per meter squared per second (μmol/m²/sec). The range using foot-candles to describe a dark winter day to a bright summer day would be 500 to 10,000 ft-c. The same range in PAR would be 100 to 2000 μmol/m²/sec.

Thermal Transmission

Thermal or heat transmission through plastics is an interesting phenomena as can be seen in Table 1.2. Polyethylene is very transparent to infrared, whereas glass is in the same category as fiber glass.

Table 1.2.   The thermal transmission of infrared (IR) through various materials.

Material	% transmission of IR
Polyethlene	71
Vinyls	12
Mylar	16
Fiber glass	1
Glass	1

Construction Plastic Houses

The rigid and sheet plastics are flexible enough to cover any conventional style of greenhouse, including houses with straight sides and the rounded forms such as the quonset and gothic (Fig. 1.10).

Each of these styles has its advantages. The conventional style requires no special equipment for construction as everything is straight. The advantages of the quonset style are its simplicity and strength, but special bending equipment for pipe and metal is needed. The gothic style has the assets of the quonset plus added height on the sides, but again special

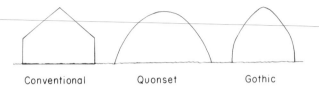

Conventional   Quonset   Gothic

Figure 1.10   General forms of plastic houses.

bending equipment is needed to form the curves. Most plastic houses are limited in size by the maximum width of a single plastic sheet because both sides of the plastic are attached at about ground level (Fig. 1.11).

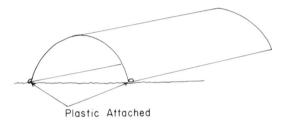

Plastic Attached

Figure 1.11   Plastic attached at side of greenhouse.

Handling of the plastic for greenhouse construction has been vastly simplified. Originally the plastic was attached to the wooden greenhouse frames with lath and nails or staples. Polyethylene expands and contracts over the range of conventional temperatures (0° to 100°F) by 3 to 4 percent. This means a change of 3 to 4 feet is possible for every 100-foot length of plastic. If the plastic was put on tightly in warm weather, then during cold weather the plastic would be very tight. The return of warm weather, however, would cause stretching, sagging and flopping in the wind. The manufacturers recommend putting the plastic on when the outside temperature is 55°F. When quonset type structures are used, wire cables are placed over each brace or bow to hold the plastic in place. This method makes changing the plastic a rather easy job (Fig. 1.12).

Air-inflated Plastic Houses

William Roberts at Rutgers University worked on a scheme using two layers of plastic in order to achieve some insulation value, to reduce condensation, and to keep the plastic rigid. The plastic sheets are attached together on the ends and sides of the greenhouse (Fig. 1.13). A small squirrel cage fan that can move 10 to 20 cubic feet of air per minute (CFM) with a 1/20-hp motor blows air in between the layers and keeps them inflated (Fig. 1.14).

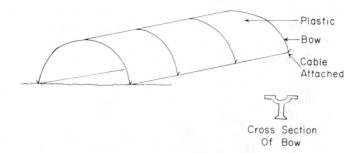

Figure 1.12   Plastic sheet held in place on a quonset greenhouse.

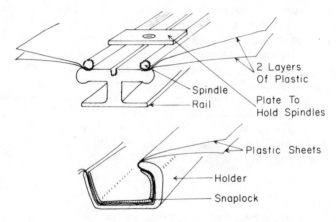

Figure 1.13   Two methods for attaching a double layer of plastic.

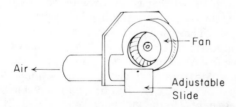

Figure 1.14   Squirrel cage fan to inflate double plastic layer.

To avoid overinflating the plastic, the area between the plastic sheets should have a static pressure of approximately .2 to .3 inches of water. This pressure can be measured with a manometer, either a purchased one or a simple one constructed and installed as shown in Figure 1.15.

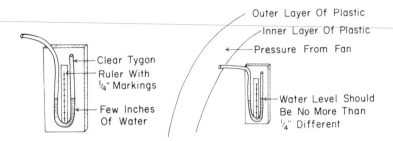

Figure 1.15 Homemade manometer and manometer installation in air-inflated plastic wall.

The air-inflated plastic structures are thermally insulated (30 to 40% fuel savings over a single layer) and do not flap in the wind. Condensation on the inside of the plastic film is greatly reduced, snow will slide easily from the surface, and replacement is relatively simple.

There are thousands of acres of air inflated double poly houses in the United States. Although the second layer of plastic reduces light, the benefits outweigh the light loss. There is a reduction of condensation on the inner layer of plastic which will increase the light level. The life of the plastic is increased because there is less flapping. Installation is greatly simplified because only the edges must be held in place. The heat loss during the heating season is significantly reduced over the single layer.

GLASS STRUCTURES

Glasshouses are considered permanent and are most used for year round growing in the United States.

Properties of Glass

Glass is a silicate material that is mixed with various substances to improve its light transmission and strength. Glass is produced in various grades and thicknesses. The best and most expensive glass is grade A, but B is a satisfactory grade for use in the greenhouse. It may contain some foreign matter and a few small bubbles but not enough to reduce light or to outweigh the price differential. Glass is sold as single, double, and triple strength. Glass of single thickness or strength is one-twelth of an inch thick (12 panes (lights) to the inch) and weighs 19 to 21 ounces per square foot. Double strength, used in greenhouses, has about 8 lights to the inch (1/8 in.) and weighs 26 to 29 ounces per square foot. Glass is shipped in boxes that contain about 50 sq ft per box. If the lights were 12 in by 12 in there would be 50 lights in the box and if the individual panes were 20 in by 24 in there would be 15 lights in a box. A box of double strength glass weighs about 87.5 pounds (92 pounds with the crating).

Triple strength is not common. Greenhouse glass costs in the neighborhood of $.50 to $.60 per square foot.

Design Concerns

The architect is concerned with the dead and live loads on the structure. The dead load is the weight of the structural material itself, the frame, glass, and so on, and is relatively easy to calculate. There are books available that give dead weights and breaking and bending weights of various types of building material. *National Design Specifications for Stress Grade Lumber and Its Fastening,* a book by the National Forest Products Association, and *Steel Construction Manual,* by the American Institute of Steel Construction, give most of the necessary information.

The live loads on a structure are more difficult to compute for they include snow, wind, and plants, if hanging baskets and overhead shelves are supported on the structure.

Wind. In most areas, the design should take into account a maximum wind load of 80 mph, which is a pressure of 16.4 lb/sq ft. Wind loads are difficult to measure because the pressure is not always in a uniform direction on the side and top of the structure. An area of reduced pressure is formed on the leeward side of the structure and causes an increased pressure inside the structure pushing up. Therefore, the anchoring of a structure is also important for wind considerations (Fig. 1.16). For example, tornadoes, with winds of 200 mph or greater, do not blow buildings down, but rather blow them up. Buildings explode because of the pressure difference between the inside and the outside. Greenhouse manufacturers consider a safe design one that can withstand a pressure of 15 lb/sq ft in a horizontal direction.

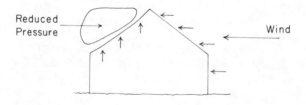

Figure 1.16 Direction of forces caused by wind blowing on a structure.

Snow. Most greenhouses are designed so that snow will normally slide off the roof, and the heat in the greenhouse will melt off a heavier snow. Unheated greenhouses can be broken down with snow loads. A greenhouse should be designed to hold at least 10 to 12 pounds of snow per square foot, or approximately 20 inches of snow. Usually a design consideration of snow and wind combined is a rating of 15 lbs/sq ft.

Plant loads. Plant loads on a greenhouse must be considered. A few hundred hanging baskets in addition to a foot of snow and a 30 mph wind can put too much stress on a greenhouse structure. Every winter a few greenhouses are stressed to the point of breaking and fall down. A safe design for snow and plant load would allow 15 lb/sq ft.

Building loads. As a rule of thumb, building in areas where snow loads or winds can be a problem, the architect uses 45 lbs/sq.ft.

Styles of Houses

There are four basic styles of glass greenhouses: even span, uneven span, ridge and furrow, and lean-to (Fig. 1.17). The even span greenhouses, where the roof angles are the same, is the most common. This greenhouse is the easiest and most economical to build because of its simplicity and the uniform pieces.

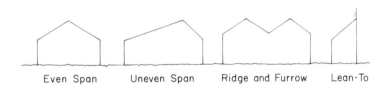

Even Span   Uneven Span   Ridge and Furrow   Lean-To

Figure 1.17   Four basic styles of glass greenhouses.

In the uneven span greenhouse, the roof angles are not the same. This greenhouse was most popular at the turn of the century and was built on the south side of hills. The wide span faced south to capture as much of the winter sun as possible. This type of structure is regaining its appeal since fuel costs have risen.

Ridge and furrow greenhouses save construction costs because some of the walls are eliminated. Heating costs are also lower because of reduced surface area. The ridge and furrow greenhouse is also labor efficient because it is easy to move within the structure. These greenhouses do have reduced light caused by more shadows from the heavy gutters. Most large greenhouse ranges today use the ridge and furrow style.

The lean-to structure is mostly used for special situations and is not recommended for commercial application because of reduced light.

Framing and Skinning

A number of types of materials are used in framing greenhouses: wood, pipe, steel, and aluminum. Each material has its advantages and disadvantages. The skinning is the covering of the frame and includes the sash bars that hold the glass and ventilators made of wood or aluminum.

Wood framing. Wood framing is not frequently used for large commercial greenhouses. The amount of wood framing needed to hold the weight of the structure is large and causes extra shading. The life of wood, under greenhouse conditions, is short compared to that of metal. The most commonly used wood for greenhouse construction is California redwood and if treated it will have a life in the greenhouse of up to 15 years. Other construction lumber such as fir and pine lasts less than 7 years under greenhouse conditions.

Wood preservatives. Wood preservatives can be used to lengthen the life of wood by improving its resistance to decay and insects. Creosote and pentachlorophenol should not be used in the greenhouse under any circumstances. These products produce fumes that are phototoxic. Preservatives such as copper chromate acid, chromated zinc chloride, chromated copper arsenate (Osmose K-33, Green Salt), ammonical copper arsenite (Chemonite) and fluorchrome arsenate phenol (Tantalith, Wolman Salt, Osmosalts) are nontoxic. Fluorchrome arsenate phenol is subject to leaching under very moist conditions. The other salts are very resistant to leaching. The water soluble salt treated wood is also recommended because there are less painting problems with this product than the oil-base preservatives.

Wood preservatives are applied in three ways, pressure, dipping and painting. Application by pressure is done at a factory, but is the best method, and painting the poorest. Pressure treatment can increase the life by 10 times that over untreated wood. The cost of the pressure treated lumber will be about 50% more than untreated, but the extended life makes it economically worthwhile.

Pipe framing. Pipe frame houses are constructed up to 40 feet wide. They have columns (Fig. 1.18). Columns are desirable if overhead shelving or hanging baskets are used, but undesirable if automatic black clothing for photoperiod control is needed or tractors are used to till the soil. The pipe is cut to proper lengths and special fittings are used to hold the frame together (Fig. 1.19). A greenhouse framed with secondhand galvanized pipe will be much cheaper than one using new pipe.

Steel framing. Steel framing uses flat steel side posts and rafters that are trussed with flat steel to support the loads. The pieces are held together with gussets. This design eliminates the needs for columns for greenhouse widths up to 50 feet; greater widths require columns. This type of construction requires special cutting equipment and other tools, and is usually done by a professional greenhouse manufacturing company (Fig. 1.20).

Aluminum framing. Aluminum is not as strong as steel, and therefore, the members are deeper and heavier to achieve the same strength. The aluminum frame is maintenance-free as it does not rust and does not have to be painted. Most of the aluminum used in greenhouse construction is extruded to special specifications. It is expensive to produce the extrusion dies and usually only greenhouse manufacturing companies make these parts. The basic framing procedures are similar to those of the steel frame house: extruded aluminum members are cut to proper lengths and gusseted together.

Steel or galvanized nuts, bolts, and screws must not come in contact with aluminum or electrolysis will occur which will cause corrosion of the two dissimilar metals.

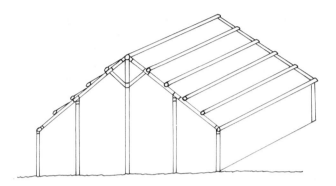

Figure 1.18   Pipe frame greenhouse.

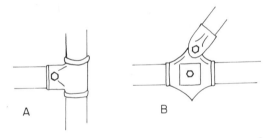

Figure 1.19   Fittings used in pipe framing.

Skinning. Skinning is the covering or glazing of the greenhouse (Figs. 1.21 and 1.22). Sometimes aluminum sash bars are used as skinning structures over a steel frame. A rubber or plastic gasket must be placed between the iron and the aluminum to avoid corrosion.

Aluminum sash bars are stronger than wooden sash bars and are usually spaced further apart, up to 24 inches. Less shading and the lower maintenance make the aluminum sash bars more popular. On the liability side, aluminum transfers heat faster than wood, and more fuel is required to heat an aluminum-skinned greenhouse than a wooden-skinned one.

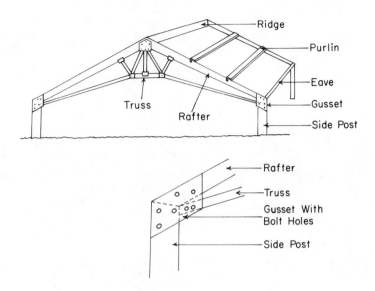

Figure. 1.20   Steel frame greenhouse.

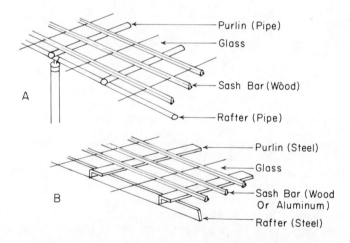

Figure. 1.21   Skinning of (A) pipe frame and (B) steel frame greenhouse.

Ventilation Mechanisms

The ventilators of a greenhouse are usually continuous along both sides of the top ridge and on the sides below the eaves (Fig. 1.23). The vents are opened and closed either by a rack and pinion mechanism or by an arm and rod. Turning the main pipe shaft operates the arm and rod, which push open the vent (Fig. 1.24). One hundred feet of vent is about the limit of the arm and rod system.

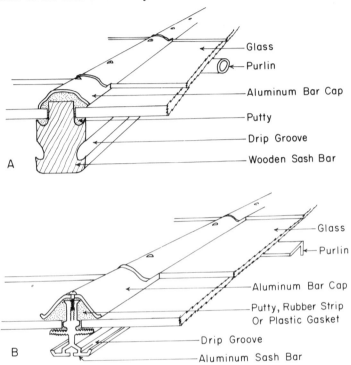

Figure 1.22 Skinning with (A) wooden and (B) aluminum sash bars.

The rack and pinion is also operated by turning the main pipe shaft, which turns the pinion along the rack and opens the vent (Fig. 1.25). This system will handle up to 200 feet or so of continuous ventilators.

The force to turn the main pipe shaft is provided through a gear reduction system and can be powered either by hand (Fig. 1.26) or by electric motor (Fig. 1.27). The longer the run of ventilators the greater the gear reduction. The electric motor is reversible, that is, it will work in either direction, to open and close the vents.

Maintenance

Conditions in a greenhouse are very conducive to rust and rot, but a well-maintained glass greenhouse will last 50 years or more. To avoid rapid deterioration, especially of steel and wood, the members must be

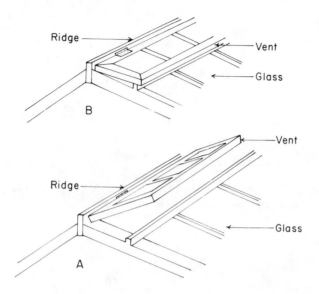

Figure 1.23 Top ventilators (A) opened and (B) closed.

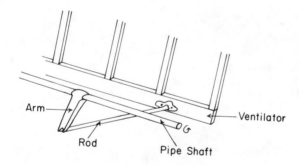

Figure 1.24 Arm and rod vent opening mechanism.

clean and coated with a protective layer of paint. Before any member in the greenhouse is repainted, it should be scraped to remove any rust, scale, or foreign debris, such as algea, in order to obtain a good painting surface. Metal surfaces after they have been cleaned should be primed with a metallic zinc paint, because of its rust-inhibiting properties. Wood surfaces should be primed with a zinc-free paint because zinc is less tolerant to moisture than other pigments such as lead and titanium. To reduce the movement of water through exterior walls from the inside,

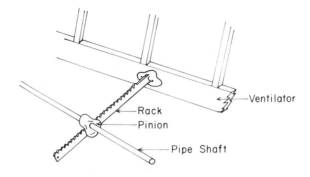

Figure 1.25   Rack and pinion vent opening mechanism.

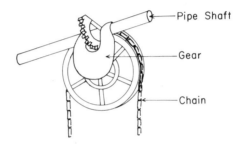

Figure 1.26   Hand chain pull to open and close the vent.

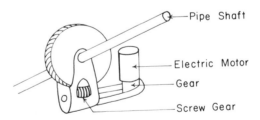

Figure 1.27   Motor driven vent mechanism.

which results in paint blisters and peeling, use a coat of aluminum paint with a varnish vehicle on the interior surface. The paint used should be carefully inspected and proven to not contain phytotoxic materials, such as phenols and xylenes, which are added to improve penetration, and mercury to inhibit mold growth. These paints may give off fumes and cause phytotoxicity. There have been examples of fumigation action from paint in a greenhouse for a year or more. The safest method is to buy the paint from a greenhouse manufacturing company. It has been demonstrated many times that the "best buy" was the best quality paint.

If a greenhouse has received regular maintenance, it should last for 40 or 50 years without reglazing. Bar caps that secure the glass have helped tremendously in preventing the putty from deteriorating and keeping the houses tight (Fig. 1.22).

Glass that is 40 to 50 years old will appear wavy and uneven, because the glass has actually settled, getting thicker at the bottom. Growers have claimed great improvements in plant growth after reglazing a greenhouse, which they attribute to the new glass and added light. When reglazing a greenhouse all of the glass is removed, the sash bars (if wood) are scraped and painted, and new lights or glass is set in place.

NEW STRUCTURES

There will continue to be innovations in greenhouse design. Over the past twenty years some innovations have been rapidly accepted, aluminum greenhouses, polyethylene covered greenhouses, and fiber glass covered greenhouses, for example, while others, air-inflated greenhouses and tower greenhouses, have not been as universally accepted.

Orientation. The present concerns in greenhouse design are to reduce heat loss and to improve the capture of winter sunlight. The orientation of the greenhouse can have an influence on the amount of winter sun collected. To collect the greatest amount of sun, the orientation should be east-west as shown in (Fig. 1.28). A greenhouse with a north-south orientation will not receive as much sunlight (Fig. 1.29). However, the plants growing in an east-west greenhouse will not receive as uniform light as those growing in a north-south greenhouse. The plants on the

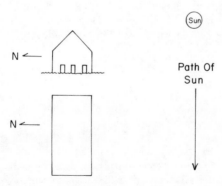

Figure. 1.28 East-west orientation of a greenhouse.

north side of an east-west greenhouse always get less light then plants on the south side. Shading especially in ridge and furrow houses with an east-west orientation will be greater than a north-south orientation. The question that must be answered is which is the most important — more total solar radiation or more uniform light.

An experiment run in England during the 1970's, compared light and crop growth between a single span greenhouse oriented east-west and 2 multispan (ridge and furrow) greenhouses oriented east-west and north-south. During the winter months, the east-west oriented houses had higher light levels and produced more crops of tomatoes, lettuce and chrysanthemums. The single span also produced more than the multispan with a similar east-west orientation. There were less or no differences during spring, fall and summer.

Figure 1.29 North-south orientation of a greenhouse.

It appears that the uneven span greenhouse with the long slope oriented to the south has some advantages for improved sun collection because more surface faces the sun (Fig. 1.30). If the north wall has a reflective surface, even more sunlight is collected in the greenhouse. (Fig. 1.31).

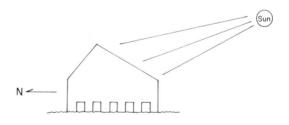

Figure 1.30 Uneven-span greenhouse facing the sun.

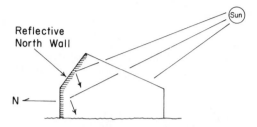

Figure 1.31   Uneven-span greenhouse with a reflective north wall.

If at the same time the north wall was insulated to reduce heat loss, there would be a fuel savings. The proper angle of the north wall to reflect the most sun, the proper angle for the south sloping roof to allow the greatest amount of sunlight to enter should be calculated. The calculation of the angle of the sun depends on latitude, season, and time of day. In the northern United States the angle varies from 25° at noon on December 21 to a maximum angle of about 75° at noon on June 21 (Fig. 1.32).

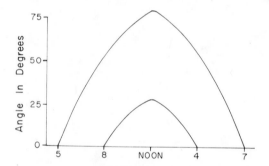

Figure 1.32   The path of the sun in the northern hemisphere.

The penetration of sunlight through glass is greatest when the sun is at right angles to the glass surface. If the sunlight is at less than a right angle, some of the light will be lost by reflection (Fig. 1.33).

Angle of incidence. The transmission of sunlight through glass is greatest when the sun is at right angles to the glass surface (angle of incidence would be 90°). If the sun is at less than a right angle (angle of incidence less than 90°), some of the light will be lost by reflection (Fig. 1.33). Light losses at various angles of incidence are shown in Table 1.3. If the sun is at an angle of 25° and the slope of the roof of a greenhouse is 25°, the angle of the sun to the glass will be 50°, 40° less than perpendicular (Fig. 1.34). The angle of incidence is 50°, therefore, the

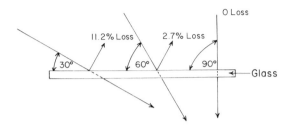

Figure 1.33 Light penetration through a glass pane.

reflected loss of sunlight is 3.4% (Table 1.3). As the angle of the sun decreases, the reflective loss becomes greater and less light enters the greenhouse.

To reduce reflection under low angles of incidence, the slope of the greenhouse roof would have to be 65° (Fig. 1.35). This design would be poor, because the house would be high, the sash bars would be long and the large roof surface would increase the heat loss and wind load.

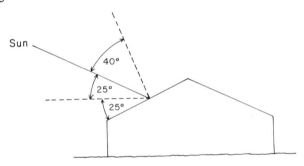

Figure 1.34 Relationship of the sun's rays to the greenhouse roof.

Table 1.3.   Reflective loss.

Angle of incidence (°)	Light lost (%)
90	0
60	2.7
50	3.4
40	5.7
30	11.2
20	22.2
15	30.0
10	41.2

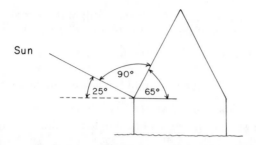

Figure 1.35 Relationship of the sun's angle to a 65° greenhouse roof.

Calculating slopes, heights and sash bar lengths.

Using a hand-held calculator with sine, cosine and tangent keys, it is easy to calculate the various slopes, heights, and length of sash bars on a greenhouse roof. First we need to know several dimensions. A, B, and C are angles in degrees and a, b, and c are the lengths in feet (Fig. 1.36).

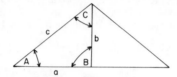

Figure 1.36 Dimensions of a greenhouse roof.

Calculate the sash bar length. To determine the length of a, b, or c, if two of the dimensions are known, use $c^2 = a^2 + b^2$. For example, if a = 10 feet and c = 11 feet then b = $\sqrt{21}$ or 4.5 feet.

If the length of the sash bar (c) is desired and the width of the house (2a) and the slope of the roof (A) are known, use cosine A = $\frac{a}{c}$. (Cosine — the ratio of the side adjacent to a given angle to the hypotenuse.) For example, if a = 10 feet and A = 26°, then .8987 = $\frac{10}{c}$ or c = 11.13 feet.

Table 1.4 shows the sash bar lengths for various greenhouse roof slopes and widths.

Table 1.4.   The length of sash bars in feet.

Width of greenhouse (ft)	Slope of roof		
	26.5°	32°	45°
20	11.12	11.79	14.15
25	13.9	17.73	17.67
40	22.44	23.58	28.28
50	27.8	29.48	35.34

Calculate the greenhouse width. If the width of the greenhouse (2a) is desired, and the length of the sash bar (c) and slope of the roof (A) are known, use cosine $A = \dfrac{a}{c}$. For example, c = 15 feet and A = 30°, then

$.8660 = \dfrac{a}{15}$ or a = 13 feet. The width of the house would be 26 feet.

Calculate the slope of the roof. If the angle or slope of the roof (A) is desired and the width of the house (2a) and the height of the roof (b) are known, then use tangent $A = \dfrac{b}{a}$. (Tangent — the ratio of the side opposite a given angle to the side adjacent to the angle.) For example, if the house is 20 feet wide (a = 10 feet) and the roof is 5 feet high (b = 5 feet), then tangent $A = \dfrac{5}{10}$ or A = 26.6°.

If the height of the roof (b) and the length of the sash bar are known, then use sine $A = \dfrac{b}{c}$ (Sine — the ratio of the side opposite a given angle to the hypotenuse.) For example, if the sash bar is 12 feet, (c = 12 feet) and the roof is 5 feet (b = 5 feet), then sine $A = \dfrac{5}{12}$ or A = 24.6°.

Spacing of structures. To avoid having one greenhouse shade the next, they should be separated by a proper distance, which can be calculated using the dimensions in (Figure 1.37). To determine the distance first solve for y, when the height of the greenhouse (h) and the minimum angle of the sun are known. For example, if this greenhouse is 30 feet wide and 15 feet high and the angle of the sun on December 21st is 26°, then

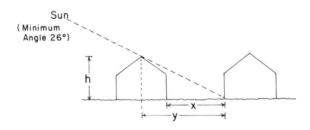

Figure 1.37 Dimensions for calculating the proper spacing of greenhouses.

tangent $A = \dfrac{h}{y}$

tangent $26° = \dfrac{15}{y}$

.4877 y = 15

y = 30.75 ft

From Figure 1.34 we note that half of the width of the greenhouse needs to be subtracted $30.75 - \dfrac{30}{2} = 15.75$ feet. There will be no shadow cast by the southern greenhouse onto its northern neighbor if they are 15.75 feet apart.

Windbreaks. It has been shown that a 15 mph wind can double the heat lost from a glass greenhouse as compared to a no wind situation. The loss from a plastic house would be less. This loss can be reduced by windbreaks. Plant materials such as deciduous and evergreen trees make good wind barriers, but are slow to reach a reasonable size and require relatively large land areas. They must be far enough away so they cast no shadows. A plant barrier 30 feet high will provide wind protection 300 yards downwind. Wind fences can be constructed that are also very effective. A 12 foot high fence placed 50 feet from a 15 foot high greenhouse, will provide effective wind protection. The barrier or fence should have a porosity of 50 to 60% for best results.

2

BENCHING

Greenhouses are expensive to operate; greenhouse space, therefore, must be used to the maximum. It is not practical to use all of the ground area for growing plants, for there must be access to each plant. The growing area between the aisles is called the bench. The type of bench, width, height, and placement in the greenhouse, depend on the crop and on personal preference. The choice of benching material is governed by economics and the desired degree of flexibility.

PLACEMENT OF BENCHES

There are two general possibilities of bench placement in a greenhouse: longitudinal and peninsular. The longitudinal arrangement of benching is particularly useful for ground bench growing, especially if the benches are full of soil. Watering, steam sterilization, and harvesting of cut flowers are easier to perform on longitudinal benches (Fig. 2.1). Peninsular benching lends itself particularly well to pot plant growing and it provides sales areas. The large central corridor allows for easy manuevering of carts or people, and the pot plants need be carried only a short distance to be placed on or removed from the bench (Fig. 2.2).

Figure 2.1   Longitudinal bench arrangement.

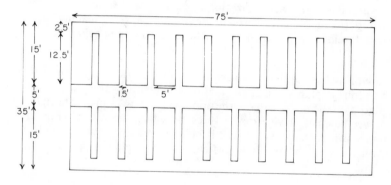

Figure 2.2   Peninsular bench arrangement.

EFFICIENT USE OF SPACE

The ratio of the square feet of bench space to the total floor area of the greenhouse expressed as a percentage, is the benching efficiency.

Let us look at a few examples. The first employs a longitudinal benching arrangement in a greenhouse 35 feet by 75 feet that contains 2625 sq ft of floor area (Fig. 2.1). If we use 3-foot wide benches and 2.4-foot wide aisles and allow 3 feet at the ends of the benches, the greenhouse has a benching efficiency of $[6 \times 69 \times 3] \div [35 \times 75] \times 100 = (1242 \div 2625) \times 100 = 47\%$.

If we widen the benches to 4 feet, the aisles will be narrowed to 18 inches (about minimum), and the benching efficiency would go up to $[6 \times 69 \times 4] \div [2625] \times 100 = (1656 \div 2625) \times 100 = 63\%$.

If we make the 4-foot wide benches 2 feet longer, allowing a 2-foot turn-around at the end of each bench (a minimum distance), the benching efficiency would be increased to $[6 \times 71 \times 4] \div [35 \times 75] \times 100 = (1704 \div 2625) \times 100 = 65\%$.

To improve the efficiency still more we could use five 5-foot wide benches and still have the minimum 18-inch walks. This would improve our benching efficiency to $[5 \times 71 \times 5] \div [35 \times 75] \times 100 = (1775 \div 2625) \times 100 = 68\%$. Our benching efficiency would be increased, but moving around would be more difficult.

In the first example, there was 1242 sq.ft. of bench area as compared to 1775 sq.ft. in the last example. A difference of 533 sq.ft., which is actually a 43% increase in bench area.

Peninsular benching allows for more efficient utilization of space. For example, we use 5-foot wide benches and 18-inch aisles with a 5-foot wide center aisle. This design has 10 aisles and 11 peninsula benches in our 35-foot by 75-foot greenhouse (Fig. 2.2). The benching efficiency would be $[22 \times (15 \times 5) + 20 (1.5 \times 2.5] \div [2625] \times 100 = (1725 \div 2625) \times 100 = 66\%$.

The efficiency of space utilization in the greenhouse can be improved by using tiered benches, growing hanging baskets, placing shelves overhead, temporarily widening benches and rolling benches.

Tiered Benches

Tiered benches can be used to grow plants that do not require high light such as foliage plants and African violets. Sometimes fluorescent lamps are placed on the under sides of the upper benches to improve the light on the lower benches. Two or even three tiers have been used (Fig. 2.3). Drainage is a problem with tiered benches. The upper benches must not leak on the ones below. It is difficult to move plants on and off the benches.

Figure 2.3   Tiered benches.

Hanging Baskets

A number of systems have been devised to hang plants in the greenhouse. Commony the hanging baskets are suspended from the frame of the greenhouse, over the aisles to avoid dripping on the benches. Care must be taken not to overload the frame of the greenhouse (Fig. 2.4). Shading of the plants underneath is also a problem.

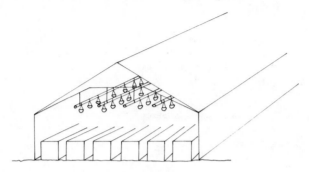

Figure 2.4 Hanging baskets suspended from a greenhouse frame.

Overhead Shelving

Wooden planks (12 in by 2 in) are placed on special brackets attached to the columns or suspended from the truss of the greenhouse frame (Fig. 2.5). Pot plants can then be grown on top of the shelves. Shading and drip from the overhead shelves are concerns and care must be taken not to overload the greenhouse frame.

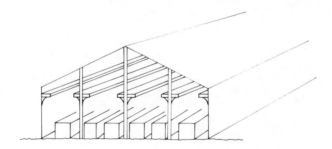

Figure 2.5 Overhead shelving on brackets attached to the columns.

Temporary Bench Wideners

Temporary bench wideners are constructed by pulling out braces across the aisles from the existing benches and placing wooden planks on the braces filling the aisles. This system is used when spacing of the plants is important and bench space is short (Fig. 2.6). This system does make spraying and other processes very difficult.

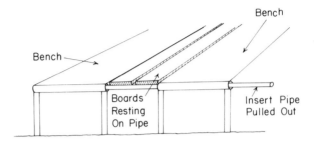

Figure 2.6   Temporary bench wideners.

Rolling Benches

Rolling benches, a recent innovation from Europe, has tremendous potential for increasing the space efficiency of a greenhouse. In most greenhouses, it eliminates all except one aisle per greenhouse. Space efficiency goes from 65% to 90%. Some installations are made right on top of the existing benches, others construct special frames (Fig. 2.7). The bench itself rests on 2 — 1¼ to 1½ inch pipes that run the length of the bench and roll between the frames and the bench. There is little friction and turning one of the pipes with a crank will easily move a 100 foot long bench full of plants.

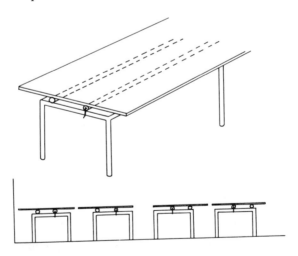

Figure 2.7   Rolling benches.

The improved benching efficiency of a greenhouse is very large. Using our example, 35 by 75 foot greenhouse and in the poorest case, we had six-3 by 69 foot benches and in the best case, we used five-5 by 71 foot benches, but with six-1.5 foot aisles. A rolling bench configuration would be six-5 by 71 foot benches plus one-4 by 71 foot bench, which would allow for one-2 foot wide aisle. The increase in bench area would be 1101 sq.ft. more than the poorest case above and 568 sq.ft. better than the best case above. The benching efficiency would be 89%.

A rolling bench system has also been put at ground level and used for growing cut flower crops.

CONSTRUCTION

The crops to be grown determine whether rasied or ground benches will be used, and economic factors, longevity and the cost of construction, influence the choice of materials.

Ground Benches

Ground benches are usually preferred for cut flower crops. It is easier to remove and sterilize the soil in ground benches, and the working height is usually more convenient for harvesting flowers, disbudding, and tying.

Ground benches can vary from simple marks in the soil to fully watertight benches. Most commonly ground benches are made with asbestos cement sidewalls with drainage below the soil (Fig. 2.8). The sides can also be made of poured concrete, concrete blocks, or wood.

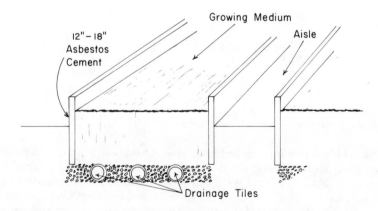

Figure 2.8 A ground bench with asbestos cement sides and drainage tiles.

Raised Benches

Raised benches are preferred for pot plant crops. The height of the bench should be comfortable to work at, usually 30 inches above ground level. The two major concerns with raised benches are the supports and benching material. A raised bench must be strong enough to support at least 25 lb per sq ft.

Support. The bench can be supported by a number of different materials including wood, pipe, and concrete blocks. If wood is used it should be treated to reduce rot as the supporting members are usually wet from the drainage of the bench. To reduce rot and give more stability to the bench, a concrete block or poured concrete footing should be used for each supporting leg. At least 2 by 4 dimension lumber should be used for the supporting loads and the legs spaced about 4 feet apart (Fig. 2.9).

A concrete block support is shown in Figure 2.10. The height of the bench is determined by the number of blocks and usually 6- or 8-inch blocks are used.

A pipe support frame is shown in Figure 2.11. Galvanized pipe should be used to reduce rusting. Usually one-inch pipe is used for the support legs. Heavier crops or wider benches may need additional supports.

Bench material. The selection of bench material is quite varied and includes snow fence, welded wire, wood boards, expanded metal, concrete forms, and asbestos cement. Cost, longevity, and flexibility are major considerations in selection of the right materials.

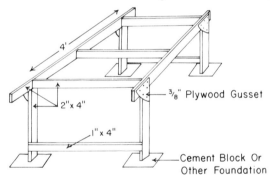

Figure 2.9   Wooden support for a raised bench.

Snow fence can be installed and removed quickly for a combination cut flower and pot plant operation. This material is readily adaptable. Redwood lath snow fence is the best material to use. The dimensions of the lath are ⅜ inch thick by 1½ inches wide, and the length varies from 4 to 6 feet. The laths are tied together with three strands of wire and can be rolled out very easily. It has a relatively short life (Fig. 2.12).

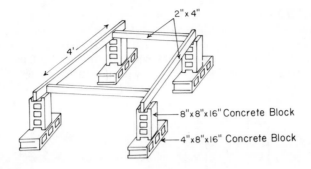

Figure 2.10 Concrete block support for a raised bench.

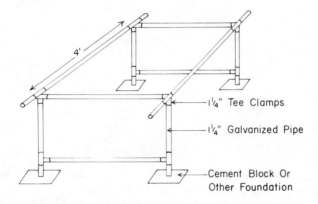

Figure 2.11 Pipe support for a raised bench.

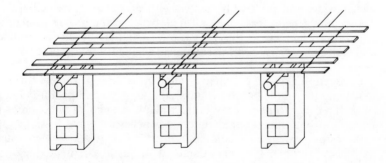

Figure 2.12 Snow fence used as a benching material.

Welded wire (one-inch square or smaller mesh) has been used successfully as a benching material (Fig. 2.13). It is usually stapled to the wooden support for added strength. It is inexpensive, flexible, and durable compared to the other benching materials. This material sags with weight and is difficult to use with pots three inches in diameter or smaller.

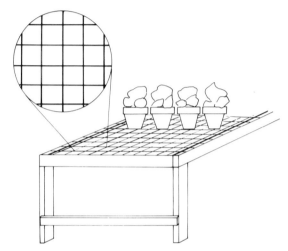

Figure 2.13   Welded wire used as a benching material.

Expanded metal is much stronger than welded wire. It is made in panels 6 feet long and 3, 4, or 5 feet wide. The expanded metal should be galvanized to resist rusting. It is expensive, and its life is quite long (Fig. 2.14). This material does not sag with weight and small pots can be used.

Wood boards used for benching should be at least one inch thick, 6 inches wide, and preferably treated with preservative (see Chapter 1). There should be at least one-half inch between the boards to allow for expansion when wet. If the crack is too small the boards will swell shut and stop drainage. Wood will rot and an average life expectancy is 5 to 10 years.

Concrete makes an excellent benching material. Concrete forms are made and the whole bench including the supports can be poured at one time. If a new greenhouse structure is planned and a lot of benching will be built at one time, poured concrete benches are quite feasible.

Asbestos cement is a combination of asbestos and cement that is extremely durable. It is manufactured in flat or corrugated sheets of various sizes (4 feet by 8 feet is most common) and thicknesses (⅜ inch, ½ inch, and ¾ inch are most common). The corrugated sheet has greater strength than the flat and is more commonly used. The uneven corrugated surface does have a disadvantage for holding pots. To overcome this problem many growers fill up the corrugations with sand or fine gravel (Fig. 2.15). If flat asbestos cement is used the supports will have to be wider to support the ends and edges as asbestos cement can be easily broken (Fig. 2.16).

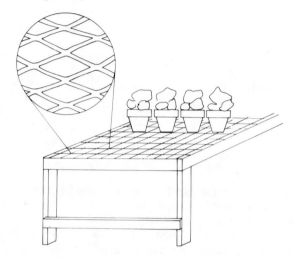

Figure 2.14   Expanded metal used as a benching material.

Figure 2.15   Sand or gravel fill in the corrugations to produce a flat surface.

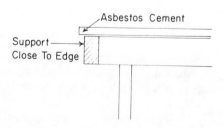

Figure 2.16   Supports to the edge of flat asbestos cement to avoid breaking.

Sides. If pot plants are to be grown, bench sides are not needed. If soil is to be held by the bench, then 6-inch sides are normally added. The sides can be made of wood or asbestos cement (Fig. 2.17).

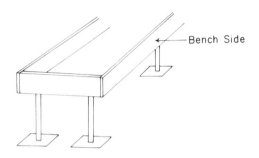

Figure 2.17   Asbestos cement or wooden sides for a bench holding soil.

Drainage. Benches must be designed to drain off excess water. The lath, welded wire, and expanded metal benches will not have any drainage problems. Wood, concrete, or asbestos cement benches may have drainage difficulties. Wooden benches, if the cracks are wide enough, will have adequate drainage. Concrete benches should be formed so there is a V in the bottom to channel the water to drains (Fig. 2.18). If the concrete bench is made in strips, cracks left between the strips will drain the water.

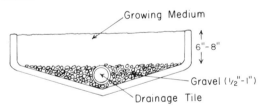

Figure 2.18   V-bottom concrete bench.

Flat asbestos cement can present a drainage problem if the benches are used to hold soil. One-half inch holes drilled on one-foot centers and a layer of ½- to 1-inch gravel placed on the bottom of the bench will improve drainage (Fig. 2.19).

Corrugated asbestos cement benches usually do not have drainage problems. The corrugations run the short way and when the sides are installed a space is left between the sides and the bottom sheet to allow for drainage (Fig. 2.20).

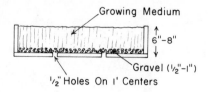

Figure 2.19 Improving the drainage from a flat asbestos cement bench.

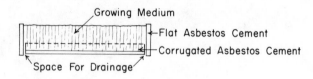

Figure 2.20 Drainage from a bench constructed with corrugated asbestos cement.

3

COLD STORAGE

Cool temperatures are used to slow the growth of cut flowers or potted plants, to store young plants and rooted cuttings for later planting, to allow for development of flowers on many bulb crops such as tulips, and to vernalize lilies. There are very few greenhouse operations that do not need a cold storage room. For a number of months of the year in many parts of the country, the outside air temperature is low enough for a naturally ventilated cold storage facility. Most cold storage facilities, however, are mechanically refrigerated to produce cold temperatures the year around.

LOCATION

The location of the cold storage facility is dictated by the frequency of its use. If the storage is used for bulbs, where the plant material is put in and removed a few months later, the storage does not have to be close to the working area. If the cold storage is for cut flowers where there is daily use, then proximity to the packing, grading, and shipping areas is of prime importance.

SIZE

The size of the cold storage room is sometimes difficult to determine without previous experience of the number of plants or containers to be stored. A good estimate can be calculated from crop programming and the anticipated size of the crop. It may be more economical to build two or more smaller cold storage rooms than one large room. Two cold storage rooms give greater flexibility, and one may be turned off when not in use.

Shelving in the cold storage room will allow more material to be held. Access to the material and movement around the room is important, so the room should not be completely full. In fact, all containers and boxes should be stacked so there is air movement around them, and not placed tightly against the wall.

REFRIGERATION EQUIPMENT

When the pressure of a liquid refrigerant is reduced it absorbs heat and vaporizes. When the vapor is compressed back to a liquid the heat previously absorbed is given off. This is the principle of refrigeration.

The vaporized refrigerant is compressed by the compressor, which is driven by a motor, and the vapor passes to the condensor where it loses heat (via air or water cooling) and condenses. The liquid refrigerant under pressure moves to the expansion valve, which allows the liquid refrigerant to pass into the evaporator (cooling coils), an area of reduced pressure. The liquid refrigerant is now under reduced pressure and, as it absorbs heat, vaporizes. The cycle is repeated and the vaporized refrigerant with the absorbed heat passes back to the compressor (Fig. 3.1).

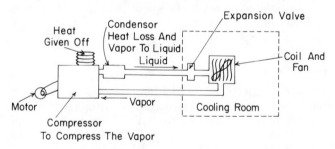

Figure 3.1 Schematic of a refrigeration system.

The capacity of the refrigeration unit is measured in Btu of heat removed by the condensor per hour. (A Btu, or British thermal unit, is the quantity of heat needed to raise the temperature of one pound of water one degree Fahrenheit.) For large units, rerigeration is measured in tons. One ton is equivalent to 12,000 Btu/hr.

Condensor and Compressor

The compressor is run by an electric motor that compresses or pressurizes the vaporized refrigerant. The vapor then loses its heat in the condensor and liquifies. The heat is removed from the condensor by either air or water cooling (Table 3.1).

Table 3.1.   Approximate typical capacities of condensor units

Hp of compressor motor	Type of cooling of the condensor[1]	Btu removed per hr[2]
1/3	air	2900
	water	3400
1/2	air	4400
	water	5300
3/4	air	6500
	water	8000
1	air	8500
	water	10500
2	air	17000
	water	22000

[1]Based on 90°F (32°C) air and 70°F (21°C) water temperature.
[2]Based on 36°F (2°C) refrigeration temperature and cooling coil temperature of 21°F (–6°C)

Note that water-cooled condensors are more efficient than air-cooled condensors. Water-cooled condensors, however, use large quantities of water, and some means of cooling and recirculating the water is necessary. Water cooling is usually found in larger installations.

Freon is the most common refrigerant, although ammonia (NH_4), methyl chloride (CH_3Cl), sulfur dioxide (SO_2) have been used.

Evaporative Cooling Coils

The refrigerant can be passed through pipes in the cold room, similar to those used in the perimeter heating system of a greenhouse (Fig. 3.2). The major problem with this system is stratification of the temperatures in the room, which can be very troublesome. Cold air settles to the floor unless there is some means of stirring the air.

The most common method of absorbing heat from the cold-room air is by cooling coil units. The air in the room loses its heat as it passes through the coils. Fans on the units move the air. The capacity of the fans should be great enough to move about one-third of the volume of the room per minute (Fig. 3.3).

Control

The most common control is a pressure switch in the vapor line that turns the compressor motor on and off as determined by the pressure in the line. The line pressure is controlled by the expansion valve, which opens and closes to allow the liquid refrigerant into the cooling coils to evaporate and increase the pressure. The operation of the expansion valve is controlled by a thermostat set at the appropriate refrigerator temperature (Fig. 3.4).

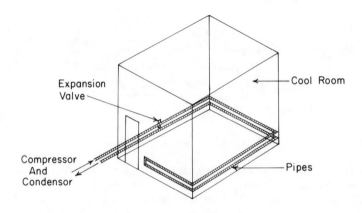

Figure 3.2   Perimeter cooling coil system.

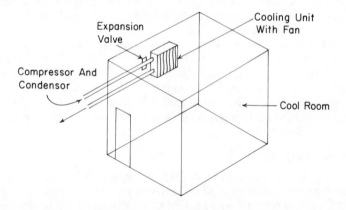

Figure 3.3   Cooling coil units in a cold room.

Defrost

The temperature of the cooling coil is usually 15 degrees F (8°C) lower than the desired air temperature. If the desired temperature of the cold room is 40°F, (4°C) then the coil temperature would be 25°F (–4°C).

Water vapor in the air condenses and freezes on the cooling coils at that temperature. If this action is allowed to continue, the area between the coils will fill with ice and frost and the fan will not be able to blow air through the coils. There are three methods to remove frost from the coils: allowing the fans to blow continuously, melting the frost with water, or recirculating hot gases.

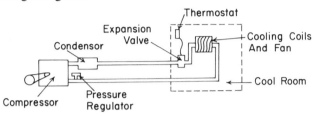

Figure 3.4   Control equipment for a refrigeration system.

Fan blowing is a simple system that turns off the refrigeration, but allows the fan to continue to blow. This system works only when the temperatures are above 32°F (0°C). The fan blows warm air (above 32°F (0°C) over the frost. The disadvantages of this system are that it is slow and temperature control in the cold room is disrupted for an extended period.

The water system operates by turning off the refrigeration at regular intervals and allowing water to run over the coils to melt the frost. This system is slow and wastes water.

To remove frost by the circulation of hot gases, a special line is run directly from the compressor to the cooling coils. Periodically by appropriate valving the expansion valve is turned off, and the hot compressor refrigerant gases bypass the condensor and go directly to the cooling coils, which heat and melt the frost. This system is more expensive than the others but is quick and automatic. Most refrigeration units use this system.

VAPOR BARRIER

A vapor barrier for cold rooms is very important because a moisture connection between the inside and outside makes any insulation almost useless. Cold rooms are ideal places to get condensation to form in the walls, for the inside temperature is cold (35°F[1°C]) and the outside room temperature is warm (70°F[21°C]). If for example the relative humidity in the outside room was at 50%, the psychometric chart in chapter 9 tells us that 70°F(21°C) air at the same relative humidity contains more water vapor than the 35°F (1°C) air. Water vapor will diffuse from a high concentration to a low concentration. Therefore, the water vapor will move from the outside to the inside. We also know there is a temperature gradient between the outside and the inside. At a particular point in the wall the temperature will be 58°F (14.4°C). At that point, the water vapor of the incoming 70°F (21°C) air will be at 100% relative humidity and at the next point closer to the inside, the air temperature will be cooler (57°F [13.8°C]). Condensation of the water vapor will occur at that point and there will be free water (Fig. 3.5).

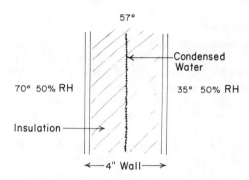

Figure 3.5 Condensation of water in the wall of a cold room.

Water is an excellent conductor of heat. Water condensed in the wall means a faster heat loss and even more condensation of water. If, for example, the wall when dry had an R value of 10, the wall saturated with water would have an R value of about 1. (R value is the resistance of a material to heat transfer).

To avoid this problem a vapor barrier should be constructed on the outside wall. Common materials used for vapor barriers are metalic foils, plastic sheets, asphalt-impregnated paper, and aluminum or asphalt paint.

CALCULATION OF REFRIGERATION REQUIREMENTS

To determine the refrigeration requirement, which is the number of Btu needed to maintain the storage room at the set temperature, we need to know the heat exchange rate of the walls, floor, and ceiling, the heat of respiration, the field heat of the plant material to be stored, and the service load.

Service Load

The service load is that heat created by the electric lights and the fan motors, and the heat loss through the opened door and the cracks around the door. Experience has shown that the service load can be estimated as 10% of the sum of the other factors, unless there are some special losses such as very frequent opening and closing of the door.

Field Heat

Field heat is the residual heat contained in the material that is put into the cold room. The assumption is that each degree Fahrenheit of differential per pound of material is equivalent to one Btu. If the mass of material to be cooled weighs 1000 pounds, the temperature is 70° F (21°C) and the desired temperature is 35°F (1°C) then field heat is 1000 (70 − 35) = 1000 (35) = 35,000 Btu.

Heat of Respiration

Heat is generated by the plant material through the process of respiration. The Btu produced depend on the storage temperature and the plant material. The heat of respiration of many fruits and vegetables has been measured, but unfortunately not those of floricultural crops. We will, therefore, have to assume the heat of respiration of our floricultural crops will be similar to other known crops (this assumption should be fairly valid).

Bulb crops. For the bulb crops (tulips, hyacinths, lilies, gladiolus, irises, etc.) the information for onions should be very representative (Table 3.2).

Table 3.2   The heat of respiration per ton of onion bulbs at various temperatures (from USDA Handbook #66).

Storage temperature in °F (°C)	Btu/T/day	Btu/T/hr
32 (0)	660–1100	27.5– 45.8
50 (10)	1760–1980	73.3– 82.5
70 (21)	2080–4180	128.3–176.2

The ranges given for the heat of respiration are due to the stage of maturity of the bulb and its moisture content. To be conservative we will use the higher values. Figure 3.6 shows the graph for the heat of respiration for floricultural bulbous material.

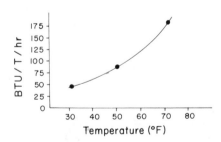

Figure 3.6   Heat of respiration for floricultural bulbous material.

Leafy crops. For leafy materials (cut flowers of all types, cuttings, and plants), the information for spinach should be very representative (Table 3.3).

Table 3.3.   The heat of respiration per ton of spinach at various temperatures (from USDA Handbook #66).

Storage temperatures in °F (°C)	Btu/T/day	Btu/T/hr
32 (0)	4240	176.7
40 (4.5)	7850	327.1
50 (10)	17940	622.5
60 (15.5)	38000	1583.3

It is interesting to note the much higher heat of respiration from leafy plant material in a more active state of growth as compared to bulbs in a less active state. Figure 3.7 shows the graph for heat of respiration for leafy floricultural plant materials.

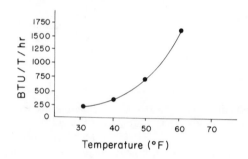

Figure 3.7   Heat of respiration for leafy floricultural plant material.

If we had a ton of tulips to hold at 40°F (4.5°C), the heat of respiration would be 62 Btu/hr (interpreted from Figure 3.6). If we had a ton of chrysanthemum plants to hold at 40°F (4.5°C), the heat of respiration would be 327 Btu/hr (interpreted from Figure 3.7).

Heat Exchange Rate

There is a temperature gradient between the storage room and the outside $(t_o - t_i)$. The rate of heat gain by the storage room depends on the gradient and the type of construction material. The resistance (R) of a material to heat transfer describes its insulation value. In Btu terms an R value of 5 means one square foot of material will allow .2 Btu/hr/degree differential to pass through. The higher the R value, the better the insulation value. Table 3.4 gives representative R values for construction materials used for refrigerated rooms.

Table 3.4.   R values for some common construction materials.

Material	R value
Structural material	
wood (1″)	1.09
plywood (⅜″)	.47
concrete block (8″)	1.11
concrete block (12″)	2.27
Asbestos cement (¼″)	.21
Insulation material	
Rigid	
wood fiberboard (1″)	3.21
polystyrofoam (1″)	4–5
polyurethane foam (1″)	6–7
Bat or blanket	
cellulose fiber	3.85
Glass wool	3.70
Wool fiber	4.00
Loose fill	
Cork (1″)	3.22
Perlite (1″)	2.78
sawdust (1″)	2.22
vermiculite (1″)	2.18

As a general rule, a refrigerator should have an R value of 8–10 for the floor, 16–20 for the walls, and 20–24 for the ceiling, if the refrigeration temperature is to be above 30° F (–1° C). This figure is based on experience and is a compromise between higher costs of insulation and higher heat loss.

Calculation of Refrigeration Size

It is expensive to design a refrigeration unit that is too large, and foolish to design a unit that is too small to do the job. Designers should plan for the maximum expected conditions.

It is important to determine the use of the equipment. If the storage unit is to precool lilies or tulips the requirements and outside conditions will be much different than if the storage room is to be used for holding cut pompon chrysanthemums from a year-round program.

Room heat exchange. The refrigerated cold room in our example will be constructed within a building heated to 70°F (21°C). The size of the room will be 10 feet by 20 feet by 7 feet high. The three layers of the floor are 4 inches concrete with 2 inches of polystyrene plus 2 inches of concrete; the side walls have 3 inches of polyurethane insulation between two layers of ⅜-inch plywood; and the ceiling has 4 inches of poly- urethane between two layers of ⅜-inch plywood. If the storage is to be used for precooling tulips from October through January, then the temperature conditions will not be severe. The outside conditions will be the heated room temperature of 70°F (21°C). The desired storage temperature would be 40°F (4.5°C). Therefore the following calculations will determine the room heat exchange:

Floor	R
4" concrete (4 × .08)	.32
2" polystyrene (2 × 5.0)	10.00
2" concrete (2 × .08)	.16
	10.48 total resistance

$$\text{Conductance is } \left(\frac{1}{R} = \frac{1}{10.48}\right) \text{ .095.}$$

Area of the floor is (10 × 20) 200 sq ft. If we assume an average soil temperature of 55°F (13°C) then the gradient between the inside and outside of the floor would be $(t_o - t_i = 55 - 40)$ 15°. Therefore, the heat gain through the floor in Btu/hr is area × conductance × temperature differential. (200 × .095 × 15) = 285 Btu/hr.

Walls	R
⅜" plywood	.47
3" polyurethane (3 × 6)	18.00
⅜" plywood	.47
	18.94 total resistance

Conductance is .053.

Area of the walls is [(10 + 20 + 10 + 20) × 7] 420 sq ft. The outside temperature is 70°F (21°C), and the differential (70 – 40) 30°. Therefore, the heat gain through the walls is (420 × .053 × 30) = 667.8 Btu/hr.

Ceiling	R
⅜" plywood	.47
4" polyurethane (4 × 6)	24.00
⅜" plywood	.47
	29.94 total resistance

Conductance is .04.

Area of the ceiling is 200 sq ft. The outside temperature in the roof of the building is commonly 10°F (5.5°C) higher than the set temperature, therefore 80°F (27°C) is used for t_o. The difference will be (80 – 40) 40°. Therefore, the heat gain through the ceiling is (200 × .04 × 40) = 320 Btu/hr. The total heat exchange for this cold room is (285 + 667.8 + 320) 1272.8 Btu/hr.

Lily bulb storage. The 1400 cubic feet of space in this refrigerated room could be efficiently packed two-thirds full with 460 cases of lilies. A case of 200 lily bulbs contains about 37.5 pounds of bulbs, and packing material, water, and case, weigh about 12.5 pounds.

To compute the field heat we assume the case of lilies to be at a temperature of 70°F (21°C) and we want to cool it to 40°F (4.5°C). The temperature will have to be lowered 30 degrees. The 460 cases weigh 50 pounds each for a total of 23,000 pounds. Therefore (23,000 × 30) 690,000 Btu will have to be removed from the cases of lilies to reduce their temperature from 70°F (21°C) to 40°F (4.5°C). This is a large amount of heat, and a decision must be made as to how quickly it must be removed. A good compromise is one week. Therefore, the rate of removal of field heat will be

$$\frac{\text{Btu removal}}{\text{time}} = \frac{690,000}{(7 \times 24)} = \frac{690,000}{168} = 4,107 \text{ Btu/hr.}$$

The heat of respiration of lily bulbs at a 40° temperature, according to Figure 3.6, is 62 Btu/T/hr. There are (460 × 37.5) 17,250 pounds of lily bulbs in the 460 cases or 8.6 tons. The heat respiration will be (8.6 × 62) 533 Btu/hr.

The total Btus required for this cold storage are:

room heat exchange	1273
field heat	4107
heat of respiration	533
	5913 Btu/hr
service load	591
	6504 Btu/hr.

The size of the refrigeration unit to cool this room should be 6500 Btu/hr, or a half ton unit.

Cut flower storage. If cut pompon chrysanthemum flowers are to be held the storage room will have different requirements, although they are calculated in the same way. The physical dimensions and construction of the room are the same as the example above, but the unit will be used during the summer when the outside air temperatures are higher. We will use for this example an outside air temperature, in the room, of 90°F (32°C). Heat exchange through the floor is (200 × .095 × 15) 285 Btu/hr; through the walls (420 × .053 × 50) 1113 Btu/hr; and through the ceiling (200 × .04 × 60) 480 Btu/hr. The total heat exchange for this room is 1878 Btu/hr.

When the cut flowers are brought into the cold room the field heat must be removed quickly (for our purposes, within 12 hours). Six 12-oz bunches of pompons will be placed in a container of water in the refrigerated room; each container will cover 4 square feet of floor area, and this refrigerated room will hold 50 containers. The plant material will be cycled every 48 hours.

The field heat will just be from the plant material (the water in the containers can be ignored), which weighs about 225 pounds. The pompon chrysanthemums will come directly from the field and be at 95°F (35°C). Therefore, the field heat to be removed in 12 hours will be [225 × (94 – 40) = 225 × 55] 12,375 Btu, or 1031 Btu/hr.

The heat of respiration for leafy floricultural crops from Figure 3.7 is 327 Btu/T/hr, and 225 pounds of chrysanthemums produce

$$\frac{327 \times 225}{2000} = 37 \text{ Btu/hr.}$$

The total refrigeration requirement is

room heat exchange	1878
field heat	1031
heat of respiration	37
	2946 Btu/hr.
service load	294
	3240 Btu/hr.

The size of the refrigerator unit to cool this room should be 3240 Btu/hr, or a quarter-ton unit.

Under the conditions stated above the refrigeration unit would operate at capacity for 12 hours until all the field heat was removed, then run at approximately two-thirds capacity for 36 hours. The cycle would then be repeated when a new cutting was added. These should be the maximum conditions and for most of the year the refrigeration unit will operate less frequently.

Estimated Costs of Operation

To estimate electrical costs, engineers figure the refrigeration unit will operate 12 hours per day year round. To estimate the cost of electricity for the chrysanthemum cold storage above, we find in Table 3.1 that a one-third horsepower motor driving a water-cooled compressor produces 3400 Btu/hr. It requires 400 watts to run a 1/3 hp electric motor. If the cost of electricity was $.05/KW, then the cost would be (.05 × .4 × 12) $0.24 per day, or (30 × .24) $7.20 per month or (365 × .24) $87.60 per year. There are other costs that should be included such as maintenance and replacement.

4

WORKROOMS

Employees spend many hours in the workroom or head house of most greenhouse operations, and yet it is often the least planned, darkest, most uncomfortable area in the whole range. The head house is used for many different purposes depending on the type of operation. The major uses are potting, grading, packing, shipping, plumbing, welding, electrical work, office work, and eating. There are some general considerations for all workrooms which include lighting, temperature control, noise control, ease of movement, and location of restrooms.

If employees are doing detailed work such as reading scales, writing numbers, judging flower qualities, and pricking off seedlings, a minimum of 50 foot-candles of light should be used. Even the quality of the light is important. Cool white fluorescent lamps produce a bluish cast and warm white fluorescent lamps produce more red and warmer colors. If flowers are to be judged for quality, warm white fluorescent lamps are better.

If the operation is such that the employees are doing the job for a number of hours during the day, the temperature should be comfortable. Fans or air conditioning for summer and heat for the winter are important.

It has been shown that excessive noise can cause fatigue and poor health. Locate the workroom or muffle the noises so there is none to bother the employees. Background low volume music has been shown to be restful.

The work area should be planned so people and material can be easily and quickly moved. Having to step over something routinely or to move material the long way around is wasteful of labor and discouraging to the employees.

Restrooms should be located close to the work area. Many states have laws about restrooms that dictate the number per number of employees, ventilation, lighting, showers, and so forth.

TYPES OF WORKROOMS

Potting

A number of schemes have been devised for the potting operation. It can be located right in the greenhouse, in the corridor, or in the head house. If potting is done in the greenhouse, the empty pots are placed on the bench, and filled with soil, and the greenhouse employees plant the cuttings or small seedlings. The major advantage is that the potted plants do not have to be moved. The disadvantage is the discomfort for the employees, especially in the summer when the greenhouse can be very warm.

The potting operation can be placed in the greenhouse corridor connecting multiple greenhouses, which is more comfortable because the pots, soil, and plant material are brought to the potter. On the other hand, the potted plants must be transported to the greenhouse and the conditions of the greenhouse corridor are not always controllable, especially during the summer when it may get too warm.

The most common area for the potting operation is the head house. Automated equipment such as rollers, conveyors, automatic pot fillers, waterers, and stacking equipment can be permanently installed there. The temperature and light conditions can be controlled and it is the most comfortable for the employees. The disadvantage is that the potted plants have to be transported to the greenhouse. The need for automation is determined by the size and the consistency of the operation. If the potting operation pots just 4-inch chrysanthemums on a year-round basis then machinery for pot filling, watering, and conveyors to move the plants to the greenhouse can be devised. If the potting operation is sporadic, for poinsettias in the fall and lilies in the spring, then a highly automated system may not be justified.

The movement of material, including pots, soil, plants, and potted plants, into and out of the potting area should be well planned.

Grading and Packing

The cut flower operation needs a room where the flowers can be brought to be judged for their quality, graded, and bunched. The room should be centrally located because all of the flowers come to this area. The refrigerated room should be close because the cut flowers are frequently held in a cold room before grading, and almost always after grading. The flowers are usually graded by people. Roses are about the only flowers presently being graded by machines. In the hand grading operation, the flowers are laid on tables and the grader picks up each stem. The tables should be at a comfortable height for each operation. The distance the grader must move to place the flowers in the various grades should be short, and the light for seeing the flowers should be good. After the flowers are graded, they are collected and given to a packer who counts the number of stems and bunches the flowers for market. This operation is done rapidly; table height, lighting, and ease of movement should be considered.

Shipping

In the shipping room the crops are boxed and placed in containers for sending to the market. They can be either cut flowers or potted plants. In many operations the grading and packing room serves as a shipping area and the crop is packed for shipping after the grading operation is completed. The shipping room requires access to the refrigerator and a loading area for trucking.

Maintenance

There are a number of repairs done around the greenhouse that involve plumbing, welding, carpentry, and electrical work. Most of these operations require special, expensive equipment, and a workroom to accommodate it should be designed. Its size will depend on the size of the greenhouses and the amount of repairs the greenhouse operator wishes to perform. Some managers prefer to contract out all of the mechanical repairs while others prefer to do as many as possible themselves.

5

STORAGE ROOM

There never seems to be enough storage space for the greenhouse operation. The storage room is one that many managers either do not plan for or do not think they can afford to construct. Storage space is important, not only for the convenience of having something on hand when needed, but because it allows a manager to take advantage of discounts by buying in large lots or at off times. The materials are protected until needed if properly stored.

There are some definite types and requirements of storage areas depending on the materials to be stored. The most commonly stored items are dry goods, soils, fertilizers, and pesticides.

DRY GOODS STORAGE

Dry goods include paper, boxes, foil, containers, cloth, pots, and anything else that is dry and has a long life. Both free water and water vapor can destroy much of this material. Hence good protection including heat and ventilation is necessary. Shelving should be used to improve the space efficiency. The storage should be designed to use materials handling equipment, fork lift trucks, elevators, and so forth.

Some type of inventory system should be used to account for the materials removed. This will ensure that each item will be reordered before it is completely used up. An inventory system will also indicate whether a particular item is being used. If not, it may be best to sell or throw out the unneeded material to open space for something more valuable.

SOIL STORAGE

The value of soil storage space depends on the type of operation. A cut flower operation may have no need for a covered soil storage area, while a pot plant or bedding plant operation will need one. It is a poor procedure to store peat moss, perlite, vermiculite, and soil out of doors. A heavy rain or snow can completely shut down the soil mixing operation. The components should at least be stored under a shelter to keep them dry.

The size of the storage area can be computed by knowing the number of bales of peat moss, bags of perlite or vermiculite, and cubic yards of soil needed for a season's operation. The soil storage room should have doors wide enough for trucks to go in and out and for conveyors to load and unload.

The location should be such that wheeled vehicles can get to the storage. Neither heat nor water are needed. Electricity would be worthwhile to illuminate the area for easier loading and unloading.

The media mixing area should be large enough to move vehicles with supplies in and the media out. Storage of the media can be in bins. For many operations, the media is mixed as needed, thereby eliminating double storage. The media mixing area will need heat, electricity, and water.

FERTILIZER STORAGE

Many fertilizer salts have an affinity for water so a primary consideration for the fertilizer storage area is that it be dry. Many operations handle tons of fertilizer a year and use as many as ten different types. The area should be large enought to handle at least a six-month supply and close to the greenhouse or fertilizer injection station where the fertilizer will be used. If the operation mixes its own fertilizer salts then scales, containers, and water should be conveniently located for the mixing operation.

PESTICIDE STORAGE

Pesticide storage is perhaps the most important, because the materials are dangerous. Many of the chemicals are poisonous and they give off poisonous fumes when burned. Therefore, the pesticide storage should be in a separate, unconnected, building, so that a fire will not send smoke all through the greenhouse. The building should be locked so that unauthorized people and children do not get into the bags, boxes, and bottles of pesticides.

The building should have shelves to store the pesticides efficiently. A weighing area with scales and a mixing area with water to mix and wash would be useful. The storage should be heated to keep liquids from freezing. The formulations of liquid pesticides contain enough water that freezing and thawing will cause separation and disruption. (See Table 19.4). The building should be ventilated.

The pesticide storage area should be well identified. Gas masks, respirators, special clothing, and emergency equipment should not be stored in this building.

Federal and State governments now have strict rules and regulations about the use and storage of pesticides.

6

GROWTH ROOMS

Propagation, either the germination of seeds or the rooting of cuttings, is probably the most critical stage in plant development. Experience has shown that environmental conditions during propagation have a great influence on the ultimate growth and quality of the plant. Most genera of plants can be successfully propagated indoors under artificial light if accurate and consistent control of light and temperature can be obtained. This chapter is concerned with lighting in various types of growth rooms.

The artificially lighted area for plant propagation can be a lamp over a greenhouse bench or a special light, and temperature controlled room. Any of the arrangements described in this chapter, can be used for germinating seeds, rooting cuttings, or starting rooted cuttings in the pot.

LIGHTING FOR PLANT GROWTH

Light can be obtained from a number of artificial sources including incandescent, fluorescent, and high intensity discharge (HID) lamps. The intensity and quality of the light and the heat and size of the lamps are concerns in designing a growth room.

The efficiency of visible light output, that is, the intensity of light for a given amount of electricity, is highest for HID lamps. The HID is three times, and the fluorescent twice, as efficient as the incandescent lamp.

The energy for photosynthesis comes from visible light, which is a small part of the electromagnetic spectrum (Fig. 6.1). The capacity of chlorophyll (the photosynthetically active material in the plant) to absorb energy from light depends on the wave length of the radiation (Fig. 6.2). The intensity of artificial light in the visible wave lengths varies with the type of lamp. (Fig. 6.3).

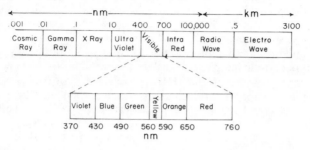

Figure 6.1   Visible light in relation to the electromagnetic spectrum.

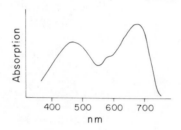

Figure 6.2   The absorption curve of chlorophyll.

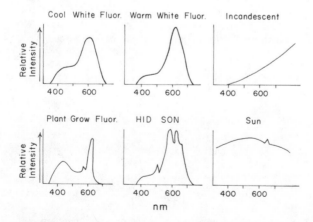

Figure 6.3   The spectral distribution of the sun and various types of lamps.

Most research on the effects of the various fluorescent lamps on plant growth has shown little difference among them except for a slightly larger growth response with cool white fluorescent lamps. The reason is that cool white fluorescent lamps produce more visible light than warm white fluorescent which in turn produce more than the plant-growing fluorescent lamps. Although the plant-growing lamps have a spectral distribution that closely parallels the absorption band of chlorophyll, they do not produce as much as visible light. Plants apparently respond more to intensity than to quality.

The incandescent lamp produces a lot of heat. About 85% of the electrical input to the lamp is converted to infrared radiation. The other types of lamps, fluorescent and HID, are relatively cooler.

The size and shape of the fluorescent lamp is well suited for use in growth rooms. Its light is produced over a large area, while the incandescent and HID are point sources (Fig. 6.4). The length of fluorescent lamps varies from 6 inches to 8 feet. The depth of the fluorescent lamp is much shallower than the HID lamp. The diameter of a fluorescent lamp varies from ⅝ to 2⅛ inches. The height of an HID lamp varies from 12 to 15 inches and a 100-watt incandescent lamp is about 4 inches high (Fig. 6.5).

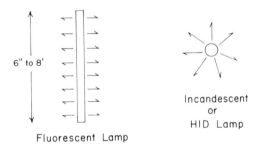

Figure 6.4   Light distribution from fluorescent and point-source lamps.

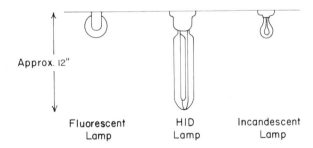

Figure 6.5   The depths of the three common lamps when installed.

Lamp Coding

Incandescent. There are many variations of incandescent lamps manufactured including shape, bases, filament design, voltage and wattage.

Most incandescent lamps use coiled tungsten wire as the filament. Electric current is passed through the wire and because of resistance to the flow of electricity, it gets hot and glows (incandesces). The wire gets so hot that some of the metal evaporates and condenses on the glass surface, and we see a blackening of the lamp. The lamp life is primarily determined by the length of time it takes to evaporate enough metal to weaken the wire to the breaking point. The temperature of the wire is very critical and is primarily controlled by the voltage. The lamps are designed to burn at specific voltages, 120 volts is the most common in the United States. If a 120 volt lamp is operated in a 230 volt electrical system, its life will be extremely short, but bright. Conversely, if a 230 volt lamp is operated in a 120 volt electrical system the light output will be reduced and the life extended. It is possible to get very long life from lamps by reducing the voltage, but with reduced light output and altered light quality. The filament wire in a low voltage lamp is short and thick as compared to a high voltage lamp which is long and thin.

The small lamp sizes, usually 40 watts and less are vacuum types. The higher wattage lamps are usually filled with a mixture of argon and nitrogen gases. If oxygen was present, the filament would burn up immediately. This happens when the glass bulb is broken and air enters.

The two basic incandescent lamp shapes are pear (A) and the long neck pear (PC). The diameter of the lamp is given as a number, which represents the number of 1/8 inch increments. For example, A-19 is a pear-shaped lamp 2-3/8 inches in diameter. Most lamps are made of soft or lime glass with a safe operating temperature of 700°F with inside frosting. Lamps can also be obtained clear and with various combinations of frosting and coated necks. Pyrex glass lamps are used for reflector lamps and other special uses. There are numerous types of bases, but medium bases are the most common.

Incandescent lamps are purchased by wattage, i.e., 40W or 60W. The lumen output from the lamp increases as the wattage increases as shown in Table 6.1. The efficiency of the lamp also increases as the wattage increases as can be seen by the lumens per watt in Table 6.1.

Fluorescent. Fluorescent lamps are produced in many combinations of lengths, colors, and wattage. The code on the lamps have the following sequences: F96T12/CW/VHO. F — fluorescent; 96 — length of the lamp in inches; T — tubular; 12 — diameter in 1/8 inches, i.e., 12 equals 1-1/2 inches; CW — cool white; VHO — very high output.

The common color variations are CW — cool white; WW — warm white; D — daylight; CWX — deluxe cool white; and W — white.

Table 6.1.   Total lumen output and lumens per watt for various wattages of incandescent lamps.*

Lamp wattage	Total Lumens	Lumens per watt
15	125	8.3
25	235	9.4
40	455	11.3
60	870	14.5
75	1190	15.8
100	1750	17.5
150	2880	19.2
200	4010	20.0

*The lamp type was A-19 120 volt. The information was obtained from General Electric Commercial and Industrial Lamp Catalog-9200 General Electric Company, Lighting Business Group, Nela Park, Cleveland, OH 44112.

There are three electric loadings used to drive the lamps. These are regulated by the ballasts. The standard, uses less than 10 watts per lamp foot and a F48T12/CW requires 40 watts. The next loading is called "high output" (HO), uses about 15 watts per lamp foot and a F48T12/CW/HO requires 60 watts. The highest loading is called "very high output" (VHO), uses about 25 watts per lamp foot and a F48T12/CW/VHO requires 110 watts. The higher the loading the greater the light output, but the shorter the lamp life (Table 6.2).

Table 6.2.   Lamp life, initial lumens, lumen output at 40% useful life and lumens per watt for two sizes of fluorescent lamps driven by three wattages.*

Lamp type	Watt	Lamp life	Initial lumens	Lumens at 40% of lamp life	Lumens per watt
F48T12/CW	40	18,000	3,150	2,805	78.8
F48T12/CW/HO	60	12,000	4,300	3,740	62.3
F48T12/CW/VHO	110	9,000	6,250	4,875	56.8
F96T12/CW	75	12,000	6,300	5,800	84.0
F96T12/CW/HO	110	12,000	9,200	8,005	83.6
F9612/CW/VHO	205	9,000	14,000	10,600	68.3
F96PG17/CW/VHO[1]	215	9,000	16,000	12,800	74.4

*The information was obtained from General Electric Commercial and Industrial Lamp Catalog — 9200. General Electric Company, Lighting Business Group, Nela Park, Cleveland, OH 44112.

[1]PG17 — Power Groove — 2-1/8 inches. This lamp has increased surface because of its greater diameter and by the dimples in the lamp.

The fluorescent lamp is sensitive to temperature. A temperature of around 80°F is best. Temperatures lower or higher reduce both light output and lamp life. Fluorescent lamps are not recommended for refrigerators because of the reduced light output.

SINGLE, FIXED BENCH

The simplest and most common adaptation of greenhouse space for plant propagation is to hang a fluorescent lamp fixture over a greenhouse bench (Fig. 6.6). It is simple to install and relatively inexpensive. Light intensity below the fixture will vary from 700 to 280 foot-candles (7560 to 3024 lux) depending on the distance of the bench from the source (Fig. 6.7). The disadvantage of this system is usually temperature control. Temperatures should be between 70°F (21°C) and 80°F (27° C) for the germination of most plants, and greenhouse temperatures are rarely that high, especially at night.

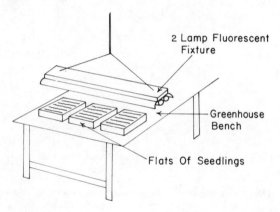

Figure 6.6 Two-lamp fluorescent fixture over a greenhouse bench.

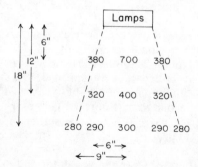

Figure 6.7 Light intensity in ft-c below a 4-foot long, 40-watt cool white 2-lamp fluorescent fixture.

TIERED BENCHES

A tiered bench system can be constructed in the greenhouse or in a special room (Fig. 6.8). In the greenhouse the temperature problem will be the same as for a single bench. A special room can have better temperature control. The tiered design has the advantage of good utilization of space, but the disadvantages of difficulty in moving the plant material, limited size, and heat build-up.

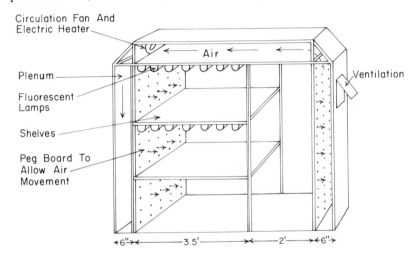

Figure 6.8 Tiered growth room. A third tier could be set up on the base.

To reduce the heat problem during the day the ballasts for the fluorescent lamps are placed on the outside of the unit so that heat emitted will not affect the inside air temperature. A vent on the outside as shown in Figure 6.8 can be automatically or manually operated during the day to allow cooler air to enter and warmer air to leave. A circulation fan moves the air around the unit through the plenum and into the chamber through the small holes in the walls. The fan rating should be about 100 cubic feet per minute (cfm) for the unit shown in Figure 6.8.

If the lights are not on for 24 hours, the temperature will be lower than desired at night. To overcome this problem an electric strip heater can be placed in the roof plenum area. The size of the electric heater should be the same as the electric load to the fluorescent lamps. For example, in the unit sketched in Figure 6.8 there are 14 fluorescent lamps using 110 watts per lamp or a total of 1540 watts, and a 1.5-kilowatt heater should be used at night.

The fan runs continuously and the ventilator and electric heater are controlled by thermostats.

The light level used in these units varies from 800 to 1500 foot-candles (8640 to 16,200 lux). Eight-foot 110-watt cool white fluorescent lamps are commonly used. The height of the lamps above the shelf will vary between 1.5 and 2 feet and the spacing of the lamps is as shown in Figure 6.9.

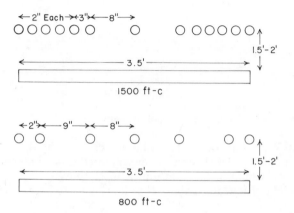

Figure 6.9   The spacing of fluorescent lamps to obtain 800 or 1500 ft-c at bench level.

Space in the unit shown in Figure 6.8 could be increased by using the bottom shelf, but experience has shown that it is very difficult to move flats in and out of this area. The shelves are spaced two feet apart; the first shelf is two feet from the floor, the second four feet from the floor, and the roof six feet. The shelves have a maximum width of 3½ feet, if they are to be loaded and unloaded from just one side. Eight-foot fluorescent lamps are used, giving the units a depth of 8 feet. The unit shown in Figure 6.8 has dimensions of 6½ feet by 8 feet by 6½ feet and a lighted shelf area of 56 square feet.

This type of unit uses the equipment to the maximum and allows for easily handling of the plant material in and out of the room. For greenhouse operations with large numbers of seedlings or cuttings or starting of plants, this system is best.

MOVABLE BENCHES AND MOVABLE LIGHTS

The movable design obtains maximum use of the lamps by moving either the plants under the lights or the lights two times a day over the plants (Fig. 6.10). The installation costs of the ballasts, lamps, fixtures, and wire in a movable arrangement are more than costs for the other systems, but because more plants can be lighted with one lamp unit, it becomes economical.

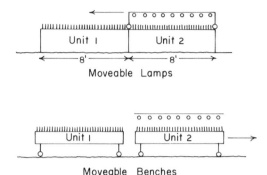

Moveable Benches

Figure 6.10 Sketch of the two movable system.

The movable units are 8 feet wide, determined by the length of the fluorescent lamps. The length will depend on the available space. About 25 feet is maximum if the light unit is to be moved.

The height of the lamps above the plants is 1.5 to 2 feet, and the range of light intensity is 800 to 1500 foot-candle (8640 to 16200 lux). Spacing of the lamps is shown in Figure 6.11.

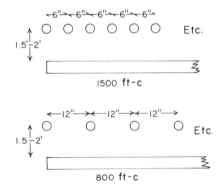

Figure 6.11 Spacing of 110-watt cool white fluorescent lamps to achieve 800 to 1500 ft-c at bench level.

The movable units are usually placed in large rooms or buildings that already have some means of temperature and ventilation control. It is necessary to move the units every 12 hours from one side to the other.

Calculating the cost of lamp operation.

To determine the cost of operating the lamps, we must know the on time in hours per day, the wattage of the lamps and ballast, and the cost of electricity. For example — the lamps are operated 16 hours per day, there are 13 — 110 watt fluorescent lamps and the electric costs are $0.05 per KW. Then — no. of hrs of operation × total KW of the lamps × cost of electricity = cost/day, or, 16 × 13 × .110 × .05 = $1.14/day or, 365 × 1.14 = $417.50/year.

REFERENCES

American Institute of Steel Construction. 1965 *Steel construction manual,* New York, NY.

Ditchman, J. P. 1955. Light for plant growth. *General Electric Application Engineering LS 168,* Nela Park, OH.

Duncan, G. and J. Walker. 1971. Preservative treatment of greenhouse wood. University of Kentucky Extension Report AEN-6, University of Kentucky, Lexington, KY.

Dunn, S., and C. J. Bernier. 1961. The Sylvania Gro-Lux Fluorescent lamp and phytoillumination. *Sylvania Lighting Product Bulletin 0-230,* Danvers, MA.

General Electric. 1966. Fluorescent lamp spectral data. *General Electric Lamp Information 211-3066,* Nela Park, OH.

General Electric. 1956. Lamps and Spectrum. *General Electric Large Lamp Division LS 135,* Nela Park, OH.

Gray, H. 1956. *Greenhouse heating and construction.* Florists' Publishing Co., Chicago, IL.

Harnett, R., T. Simms and G. Bowman. 1979. Comparison of glasshouse types and their orientation. Experimental Horti *31*:59-66.

Layer, John. 1971. Refrigerated farm storage. *Cornell University Information Bulletin 16.* Cornell University, Ithaca, NY.

Lord & Burnham. *Greenhouse parts and supplies catalog.* Lord and Burnham Co., Irvington-on-Hudson, NY.

National Forest Production Assoc. *National design specifications for stress grade lumber and its facing.*

National Greenhouse Co. *National greenhouses — greenhouse parts, supplies, accessories catalog.* National Greenhouse Co., Pana, IL.

Ross, D. S. and R. A. Aldrich. 1976. Production operation analysis, pp. 386-397 *in* J. Mastalerz, ed., *Bedding Plants,* Pennsylvania State University. State College, PA.

Rough Bros. 1977. *1977-78 greenhouse catalog.* Rough Bros. Cincinnati, OH.

Taft, L. R. 1926. *Greenhouse construction.* Orange-Judd Co., New York.

Tavernetti, J. R. 1948. Construction of farm refrigerators and freezers. *California Agricultural Experiment Station Circ.* 387:18, Berkely, CA.

The Electric Council. 1975. Grow electric-growing rooms. Warwickshire, England.

Walker, J. and G. Duncan. 1973. Greenhouse structures. University of Kentucky Extension Report AEN-12, University of Kentucky, Lexington, KY.

————————————. 1974. Painting greenhouses and equipment. University of Kentucky Extension Report AEN-14, University of Kentucky, Lexington, KY.

Wright, R. C., D. H. Rose, and T. M. Whiteman. 1954. The commercial storage of fruits, vegetables and florists and nursery stock. *U.S.D.A. Handbook No. 66,* Washington, DC.

Wright, W. J. 1949. Greenhouses-their construction and equipment. Orange-Judd, NY.

Sylvania. 1977. Incandescent lamps. Sylvania Engineering Bulletin 0-324.

SECTION II

Environmental Control

7

HEATING

The feasibility of growing crops in greenhouses has followed the efficiency and economics of heating systems. When coal and coal boilers became economical, greenhouse construction boomed. Efficient heating systems meant that night temperatures could be controlled to keep out frost during the coldest winter weather. The first flower crops grown in the greenhouse during the winter were cool crops such as violets, but the diversity of crops quickly expanded as fuel costs decreased and boiler efficiency improved. Today tropical species such as foliage plants and orchids are commonly grown in northern greenhouses.

Heating systems have become very efficient, but the greenhouse itself is a difficult structure to heat. The greenhouse design admits the maximum amount of light during the day, which in turn means poor conservation of heat at night. With the energy crisis of the 1970s and high fuel costs, many operators are looking for ways to improve the efficiency of heating and the insulation of their greenhouses.

COMPUTING THE HEATING REQUIREMENT

To estimate the heating requirement (H) we must first consider how and at what rate the heat leaves the structure. Heat leaves the greenhouse through the walls, floor, and roof, in other words the surface. The amount of surface area (A), therefore, is needed for the calculation. (The heat lost thru the floor is minimal and therefore the area of the floor is not included in the calculations.)

Calculating the Greenhouse Surface

Let us use as an example a conventional even span greenhouse, 75 feet long and 35 feet wide. The sidewalls are seven feet high, and the height of the ridge is 16 feet (Figure 7.1). The side surface is computed by $A = He \times 2 (W + L)$; or $7 \times 2 (35 + 75) = 1540$ sq ft. The top surface includes the roof and the end areas above the eave. The length of the sash bars (SB) is needed for this calculation and can be measured or computed from the other measurements. To calculate SB when we know W and Hr, we use the formula for right triangles: $(SB)^2 = (W/2)^2 + (Hr)^2$; or $(17.5)^2 + (9)^2 = 19.5$ ft. The roof area is $2 \times SB \times L$; or $2 \times 19.5 \times 75 = 2925$ sq ft. The surface area of the ends above the eaves is $W \times Hr$; or $35 \times 9 = 315$ sq ft. The total greenhouse area is the sum of these three products: $1540 + 2925 + 315 = 4780$ sq ft of surface.

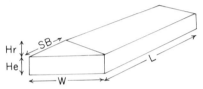

Figure 7.1   Measurements of a greenhouse: W = width, L = length, He = height to eave, Hr = height from eave to ridge, SB = length of sash bar.

If the structure is a quonset type, for example, 100 feet long and 20 feet wide, the surface area is determined as follows (Figure 7.2). The roofline, or circumference (C), can be measured directly or calculated by assuming that it is half a circle. The circumference of half a circle is calculated by

$$\frac{2\pi r}{2}; \text{ or } \frac{2(3.14) \ W/2}{2} = \frac{62.8}{2} = 31.4 \text{ ft.}$$

The roof area is then $C \times L$; or $31.4 \times 100 = 3140$ sq ft. The end areas can be considered two half circles, equal to πr^2; or $3.14 (100) = 314$ sq ft. The total area of the quonset greenhouse includes these calculations: $3140 + 314 = 3454$ sq ft of surface.

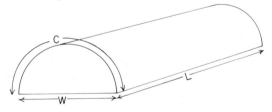

Figure 7.2   Measurements of a quonset greenhouse: W = width, L = length, C = circumference.

Design Temperature

The rate of heat loss is dependent on the material and the temperature gradient between the inside and the outside. Glass is a poor resistor to heat loss and has an R value (R_g) of 1.1. This means that one square foot of glass will transmit 1.1 Btu per hour per degree (F) of temperature difference between the two sides. The inside temperature (t_i) is the desired temperature in the greenhouse at night. The outside temperature (t_o) or design temperature is the average coldest temperature of a particular geographic location. (The outside temperature will not exceed the design temperature more than 1% of the time.) Table 7.1 lists design temperatures (t_o) for some locations in the United States.

Table 7.1.   Design temperatures

Location	Design temperature in °F (°C)
Miami, Florida	45 (7)
San Francisco, California	35 (2)
New York, New York	5 (-15)
Seattle, Washington	20 (-6.5)
Bismark, North Dakota	-22 (-30)

Source: ASHRAE, 1977, Handbook and Product Directory: Fundamentals.

Quick Heat Calculations

A formula to determine the heat loss from the greenhouse is $H = U_g \times A(t_i-t_o)$, where H is Btu required to heat the greenhouse per hour, U_g is the transmission coefficient of glass, A is the surface area of.
the greenhouse in square feet, t_i is the desired night temperature of the greenhouse, and t_o is the design temperature for that location. Let us use as an example a glass-covered greenhouse 75 feet long and 35 feet wide with a surface area of 4780 square feet, a desired night temperature of 60°, and a design temperature of -10°. Therefore, H = 1.1 × 4780 (60 – -10) = 1.1 × 4780 × 70 = 368,060 Btu/hr. This method gives a quick estimate of the Btu requirement for that greenhouse, which can be used for calculating the boiler size and radiation surface.

Heat Calculations

When a more precise heating estimate is needed, a number of additional factors must be considered. Wind velocity, a more accurate measurement of the heat transmission of glass at different temperatures, the construction of the sidewalls, and the condition of the greenhouse structure must be taken into account.

The basic heating estimates assume a wind speed of less than 15 miles per hour. If the average wind speed for the location of the greenhouse is greater than 15 MPH, a factor must be added because more heat will be required (Table 7.2).

Table 7.2.   The wind factor (W) to be used for wind velocities over 15 mph.

Velocity in mph	W
15	1.0
20	1.04
25	1.08
30	1.12
35	1.16

An alternate wind factor (W) 10% higher should be used for glass houses if the indoor temperature (t_i) will be 70°F (21°C) or above, or if the heating units blow on the glass or if 40% or more of the input Btu are radiated overhead rather than toward the perimeter of the greenhouse. The reason for the 10% adjustment is that the laps in the glass are usually frozen closed at temperatures below 15°F (-9°C). More Btu will be required to heat the greenhouse than the original factors indicate.

The resistance of glass to the transmission of heat is not a constant, but varies with temperature (Table 7.3). Glass will transmit 66.6 (60 × 1.1) Btu per hour per square foot at a temperature differential of 60°, but will transmit 79.1 (70 × 1.13) Btu at 70°.

Table 7.3   The transmission of heat (U_g) through glass at various temperature differentials.

t_i-t_o °F(°C)	Ug
50 (10)	1.09
55 (13)	1.10
60 (15.5)	1.11
65 (18)	1.12
70 (21)	1.13
75 (24)	1.14
80 (27)	1.15

Most greenhouses are constructed in such a way that the glass walls do not go all the way to the ground, but rest on sidewalls or curtain walls generally made of asbestos cement, poured concrete, or concrete blocks. The heat loss (R_w) through these surfaces is less than that through glass (Table 7.4).

Heat is also lost from greenhouses in other ways that must be accounted for. There is exfiltration via cracks and laps in the glass, which will vary according to the age of the structure. The construction of the greenhouse, either metal or wood, and the covering, glass or plastic, are relevant, because metal transmits heat faster than wood and plastic is tighter and has less exfiltration than glass. Table 7.5 gives ex-

Table 7.4. The transmission of heat (U_w) through various curtain wall materials.

Material	U_w
⅜" corrugated asbestos cement	.94
4" poured concrete	.76
6" poured concrete	.67
8" poured concrete	.60
4" concrete blocks	.58
8" concrete blocks	.46

perience factors (C) derived from many years of observation that should be incorporated into the computation of the heating requirement of various types of structures.

Table 7.5. The type and condition of the greenhouse (C).

Description of greenhouse	C
Glass, metal frame and bars	1.08
Glass, steel frame and wood bars	1.05
Glass, wood frame and bars	
tight house	1.00
fairly tight house	1.13
loose house	1.25
Fiber glass, wood frame	0.95
Fiber glass, metal frame	1.00
Plastic, single layer, metal frame	1.00
Plastic, double layer, metal frame	0.70

We will use an example similar to that for our first general heating estimate, a fairly tight wooden glass greenhouse, 35 feet by 75 feet, with a 3-foot high 4-inch poured concrete curtain wall. The average wind velocity during the winter period given by the weather bureau for this particular location is 20 miles per hour. The design temperature is $-10°$ F ($-23°$C) and the desired night temperature is $60°$F ($15°$C). The heating system will incorporate normal perimeter heating pipe. The formula would be: $H = WC(U_wA_w + U_gA_g) (t_i-t_o) = 1.04 \times 1.13 (.76 \times 660 + 1.13 \times 4780) (70) = 1.04 \times 1.13 (502 + 5401) \times 70 = 485,604$ Btu/hr. The figure 485,604 is used to determine the size of the boiler or unit heaters needed to maintain a $60°$F ($15°$C) night temperature under the stated conditions of outside temperature, wind, and greenhouse conditions. If the conditions are poorer, i.e. higher winds or lower outside temperatures, the inside greenhouse temperature will be lower than $60°$F ($15°$C). These conditions happen relatively few times and for just a few hours each year. To design for the maximum conditions possible in any one geographic location would in most cases be too expensive.

Calculating Monthly Btu Usage

During the times when the outside environmental conditions are not as severe as described above, the Btu usage will be much less. To estimate the average Btu requirment for a monthly heating period, use the heating requirement (H) and the average temperature for each month (local weather bureaus or heating oil distributors can supply this figure). With these two factors, an estimate of the Btu used can be calculated.

Let us use the example greenhouse above (35 feet by 75 feet) and calculate the Btu requirement for the month of January in an area where the average temperature is 30°F (–1°C). The formula is

$$H_a = \frac{H\,(t_i - t_{oa})}{(t_i - t_o)},$$

where H_a is the average Btus per hour, H is the Btu/hr. used to determine the heat required, t_i is inside temperature, t_o is outside design temperature, and t_{oa} is average outside temperature.

$$\frac{485,604\,(60 - 30)}{(60 - -10)} = \frac{485,604 \times 30}{70} = 208,116 \text{ Btu/hr.}$$

To convert this information to actual amount and cost of fuel used, use the following formula:

$$F = \frac{H_a\,(N)}{E\,(h_v)},$$

where F is gallons of fuel, H_a is the average Btu requirement per hour, E is the efficiency of coverting the fuel to energy, h_v is Btu per gallon of fuel, and N is the number of hours. In our example, there are 744 hours in the month of January, No. 6 oil can usually be used at an efficiency of 70%, and there are about 150,000 Btu per gallon. Therefore,

$$F = \frac{208,116 \times 744}{.7 \times 150,000} = 1475 \text{ gallons of No. 6 oil.}$$

If No. 6 oil costs $0.80 per gallon then the fuel cost for the month of January would be $0.80 × 1475 = $1180. Usage for each month of the year. can be calculated and an accurate heating cost can be estimated. It is worth making a monthly fuel estimate. If the actual use is more than or less than the computed use, then some investigation should be made to determine the reason. There may be a colder or warmer month; there could be heat leaks, misset temperatures, faulty burners, or other mechanical problems.

Lowering the Night Temperature

These calculations can also be used to determine the fuel savings that can be accrued by lowering the night temperature. Using the above example, let us drop the temperature 2°F. The Btu usage per hour then becomes:

$$\frac{485,604 \times 28}{70} = 194,242 \text{ Btu/hr}$$

and the number of gallons becomes:

$$\frac{194,242 \times 744}{.7 \times 150,000} = 1376 \text{ gallons of No. 6 oil}$$

and the fuel cost for the month of January would be:

$$\$0.80 \times 1376 = \$1100$$

A 5°F lowering of the temperature would reduce the heating cost to $983 or a 17% reduction. The danger in this practice is there probably would also be an increase in the croping time of the plants, which could be more costly than the fuel savings.

FUEL

The type of fuel used is dependent upon a number of factors, including cost, availability, air pollution laws, and convenience. Cost would seem to be the major criterion, for although in some areas of the United States coal is the cheapest fuel, it is not now commonly used in greenhouses. All types of fuel have been used for heating greenhouses and the operator has many options.

Wood

Charcoal was the first reported source of heat for greenhouses. Wood burning as a heat source until just recently was not very common. In some areas of the United States, where lumbering is a major industry, wood chips, sawdust, and slab wood are relatively inexpensive, and are used as a source of fuel. The major problems with this source include special equipment to handle the wood and ash and the pollution from the smoke. Wood produces approximately 7000 Btu per pound or half the output of coal.

Coal

Coal was for years the major source of energy for heating greenhouses, especially in the northeast where the greenhouse industry started. With inexpensive gas and oil, the inconvenience of handling coal and pressure from government agencies to reduce air pollution have caused the florist industry over the past 15 years or so to convert away from coal.

Coal is generally the cheapest fuel, but has a number of inconveniences such as storage, handling, and pollution, especially when compared to the other main sources, gas and oil. There are two types of coal, soft or bituminous and hard or anthracite. Very little soft coal is used because it is difficult to avoid pollution problems with the smoke. It also produces very high levels of soot, and the boilers and burners must be cleaned frequently, even daily. Anthracite causes less pollution, but there are some sources of anthracite that contain sulphur, which burns with the coal and must be removed from the smoke. Sulphur removal adds to the costs of installation and maintenance.

With modern equipment, coal is usually crushed into small pieces and fed by a stoker into the furnace, and the ashes are automatically removed, a great advance over the hand fired and cleaned equipment of 30 years ago.

In terms of heat production, 12 pounds of coal are about equal to one gallon of oil; coal provides approximately 12,000 Btu per pound.

Oil

There are a number of different weights of oil used for heating. Crude oil when distilled produces gasoline, kerosene, deisel fuel, and No. 2 through No. 6 heating oil. The grades are determined by the number of seconds necessary for a certain quantity of oil to flow through a standard orifice at a given temperature. The thicker or more viscous the oil, the higher the grade. No. 6 oil, in fact, must be heated before it will flow freely. The cost of oil is also in order of viscosity, i.e. No. 2 is generally more expensive than No. 6. Most large greenhouse operations burn No. 6 oil, whereas small operations burn No. 2 or perhaps No. 4. The special preheating equipment required to handle No. 6 oil is costly and difficult to handle. Interestingly enough, No. 6 contains more Btu per gallon then No. 2, 150,000 as compared to 140,000.

Gas

There are two forms of heating gas, natural and propane. Propane is expensive and used very little for heating greenhouses. Natural gas, in areas where it is available, is used in preference to coal or oil in spite of the fact it is more costly. Gas is much more convenient than coal or oil because it has no storage or special handling requirements. Gas burns so completely that for all practical purposes only carbon dioxide and water are left; the smoke is no problem and the burners and boilers are usually clean and require no special maintenance. It is apparent, however, that natural gas may be one of our first natural fossil fuels to disappear so the cost will go up and the availability rapidly decrease. Growers will be forced to consider other sources of fuel.

Comparison of Fuel Costs

To compare the costs of various fuels the following formula can be used:

$$\text{Cost/Unit Fuel A} = \text{Cost/Unit Fuel B} \frac{\text{Burning efficiency Fuel A}}{\text{Burning efficiency Fuel B}}$$

$$\times \frac{\text{Btu/unit Fuel A}}{\text{Btu/unit Fuel B}}$$

For example, let us compare natural gas with bituminous coal. The cost of natural gas is $0.50 per therm or 100,000 Btu. What would be the equivalent cost of one ton of bituminous coal? The burning efficiency and Btu/unit are given in Table 7.6.

$$\text{coal} = .5(\frac{.6}{.75}) \times (\frac{25,000,000}{100,000}) = \$100/\text{ton}.$$

If you are paying $0.50/therm for natural gas and coal is less than $100/ton, then coal would be the cheaper fuel to burn.

Table 7.6.   The output efficiency of boilers using various types of fuels and the number of Btu/unit of fuel.

Fuel	% efficiency	Number of Btu/unit
Electricity	100	3,413/KWh
Natural gas (methane)	75	100,000/100 ft³ (therm)
Propane	75	87,959/gal
Kerosene	70	130,637/gal
#2 Oil	70	139,400/gal
#4 Oil	70	145,600/gal
#5 Oil	70	150,700/gal
#6 Oil	70	153,600/gal
Hard coal* (anthracite)	60	26,000,000/ton
Soft coal* (bituminous)	60	25,000,000/ton
Hard wood*	60	24,000,000/cord

Source: Handbook and Products Director: Fundamentals, Amer. Soc. Heating, Refrigeration, Air Conditioning Engineers, Inc., NY. 1972.

*estimated — the exact number depends on the source, moisture, etc.

WASTE HEAT

There are tremendous amounts of heat from electrical generating plants, natural gas pumping stations and industrial plants that are discarded into the air or taken away by water. For example, an average size electrical generating unit uses about 3 billion Btu/hr. One billion Btu are converted into electricity, 1 billion Btu are discharged up the smoke stack and 1 billion Btu are removed by the cooling water. Other processes are even more inefficient. The question is how to capture this waste heat and put it to use in the greenhouse.

There are examples of waste heat heated greenhouses using different systems of distributing the heat. The Sherburne greenhouse complex of about 4 acres uses warm water from the cooling towers of the Sherburne Power Plant of the Northern States Power of Minneapolis, Minnesota. The warm water passes through large coils at one end of the greenhouses and fans behind the coils blow air through the coils and around the greenhouse. Bryfogle, Inc., a 4-acre greenhouse complex in Washington-ville, Pennsylvania, obtains heat from the cooling tower water of Pennsylvania Power and Light's Montour Steam Electric Station. The warm water is passed through a flooded floor and the heat radiates to the plants above. The largest installation to date is in Yorkshire, England. The Drax Power Station supplies warm water for a 20-acre greenhouse growing tomatoes (to be expanded to 80 acres in the next few years). This venture is a cooperatively owned operation by Express Dairy Foods, Ltd. and the Central Electricity Generating Board of England. The heat is extracted by heat exchangers (water to air) and the warm air blown around the greenhouse.

At least three thorough analyses of waste heat for greenhouses have been performed: The Celanese Greenhouse Study of Edmonton, Alberta, Canada; Using Power Plant Discharge Water in Controlled Environment Greenhouses, Tennessee Valley Authority, Muscle Shoals, Alabama; and Waste Heat Greenhouse Research, Cornell University, Ithaca New York.

There are a number of liabilities that must be overcome. The very large expenditures of money to "get started" usually stops the small operator. The unreliability of the generating equipment, i.e., it breaks down and/or is shut down for maintenance, usually for one month a year and usually during the heating season. This requires a backup heating system. The temperature of the water in those units using cooling towers is in the range of 90° to 100°F, therefore, great quantities of water are needed with large exchange surfaces. Some electric generating stations (for example, all those in New York State) use the once-through cooling system. The water is extracted from a river or large lake and is returned to the same source with the temperature raised a few degrees. During the winter, the return water may be a few degrees above freezing. Heat pumps would be needed in these situations, but then the expense becomes, at this economic stage, too high.

Maginnes in Saskatchewan, Canada, used successfully the waste heat from the turbine engines used to pump natural gas. There are numerous gas pumping stations across the U.S. and Canada that have real potential. The fermentation process produces excessive heat. In Decatur, Illinois the Archer Daniel Midland Company heats a greenhouse with the warmed water from a corn fermentation process. The alcohol is used for gasahol.

SOLAR

No matter what the primary source of heat, solar is extremely important. We still don't have a good calculation or confirming measurement for the total solar impact on a greenhouse.

For the commercial greenhouse, it does not appear that an active system of solar collection and storage is economically feasible even for greenhouses in the south. There does appear to be real merit in utilizing passive solar collection. There are many winter days even in the north when the solar input is sufficient enough to keep the heat off and in fact even heat up enough to cause the ventilation system to remove the heat. It is ironic in those situations, because a few hours later as the sunlight decreases, heat must be added. The basic philosophy of passive solar collection is to let in as much light as possible to heat up the mass and reduce the heat loss when the sun is not shining. Thermal blankets (page 101) when used in a greenhouse can reduce heat loss at night up to 90%. So the heat (in the mass of soil, plants, benches, etc.) when the blanket is closed does not radiate to the cold sky.

We have recently investigated the question: Can plants integrate or average temperature? We have found that a plant grown at a constant night temperature of 60° F will be the same as one grown with an average temperature of 60° (i.e., ramped from 70° to 50 during the night). Similar results appear to be true for day temperatures. This means that undulating temperatures can be used to grow plants. There would be no ventilation during the day unless the temperature was very high (100° F). The sun would gradually raise the temperature in the morning and fall towards night, a thermal blanket pulled at night would greatly reduce the night heat loss and the temperature allowed to decay to a point so as to average the desired night temperature. This principle should be a real boon to greenhouses in the south and other areas of high solar radiation.

To put solar energy into proper perspective for greenhouse heating, let us use the greenhouse in our previous examples and, from the heating requirements calculated for the month of January, a requirement of 208,116 Btu per hour, or for the whole month 154,855,504 Btu. Lets use a solar intensity of 3000 foot-candles (32400 lux) for six hours each day (a generous estimate for most areas in the United States). From Figure 9.1 it can be seen that 3000 ft-c (32400 lux) produces approximately 75 Btu per square foot per hour, therefore, in our example, the greenhouse with 2625 square feet of floor area would receive (75 × 2625) = 196,875 Btu per hour from the sun. Multiplying this by the number of hours of light per day and by the number of days per month gives (6 × 31 × 196,875) = 36,618,750 Btu per month, or approximately 24% of the heating load for the month of January. There are many problems to solve such as the efficiency of collection and storage, but this calculation does give an order of magnitude. If we were to use solar collectors rather than the greenhouse, we would need four times the area of the greenhouse to collect enough solar energy to heat this greenhouse.

BURNERS

Coal Burners

Coal Burners have a stoker, which is an enclosed screw system that slowly takes the coal from a hopper or storage bin to the fire. By the action of the same stoker system, the spent ashes spill over the side of the burner and are removed. (Figure 7.3).

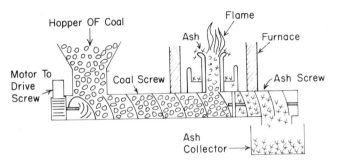

Figure 7.3 Coalstoker

Oil Burners

There are two types of oil burners, the gun and the rotary. Each has its advantages with the gun type being the more common. The gun burner sprays a mixture of oil and air into the fire chamber where it is ignited with an electric ignitor (Fig. 7.4). The rotary burner sprays the oil in a circular motion on to vanes in the fire chamber where it is then ignited with an electric ignitor (Fig. 7.5).

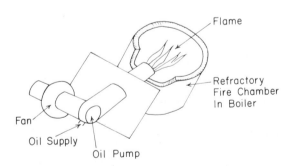

Figure 7.4 Gun type oil burner.

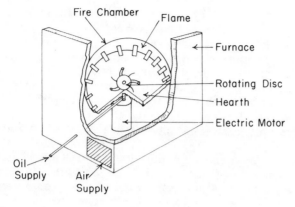

Figure 7.5   Rotary type oil burner.

Gas Burners

Gas burners are perhaps the simplest for they are like the burners used in a cooking stove except larger (Fig. 7.6).

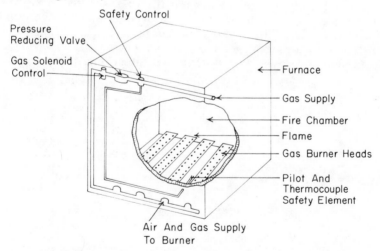

Figure 7.6   Gas burner.

BOILERS

The first heated greenhouse burned charcoal in the middle of the house to obtain heat. Then a stove was placed at one end of the greenhouse with a tube or smoke stack extending the length of the greenhouse and exiting at the far end. This design was used to extract as much heat as possible.

Engineers began to design systems to transfer heat (Btu) from the flame of the burning fuel to a remote point. Water has some very excellent capabilities. It picks up and releases heat rapidly, holds a lot of heat for its volume (1 Btu per pound per 1°F), and changes its state. It takes a great amount of heat or energy, about 960 Btu per pound for water to go from a liquid to a vapor. When the vapor or steam condenses the same amount of heat is released. Water, therefore, is a very efficient mechanism for heat transfer. If we burn the fuel and heat the water to form steam, this can efficiently transport heat through pipes to the greenhouse where exposed pipes in the greenhouse will radiate heat. The hot water or steam is produced in a boiler. A boiler is nothing more than a large container for holding water, usually with a burner in the bottom as the source of heat. Boilers are generally rated on their output of Btu or on horsepower. Very large boilers use a horsepower rating; and one horsepower = 33,475 Btu per hour.

Types of Boilers

There are many types and sizes of boilers. They run from small unit heaters for heating residential homes to very large units for heating large greenhouses and factories and to generate electricity. They all use the same basic principles. A burner of one of the types discussed above, is the source of heat. The heat from the burning fuel is transferred to the water in one of two ways. Either the heat, flame, and gases, pass through tubes (fire tubes) that are submerged and surrounded by water (Fig. 7.7) or they pass around tubes filled with water (water tubes) (Fig. 7.8).

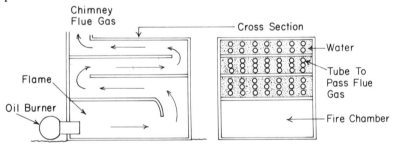

Figure 7.7 Four-pass fire tube boiler.

The fire tube boiler is generally recommended because it has a large steam or water storage capacity that can withstand rapid temperature changes, which are common in greenhouse operations.

Terms

There are a number of terms used in boiler technology that should be explained. A low pressure boiler is one that runs with less than 15 pounds of steam pressure and generally the farthest distance the steam can be

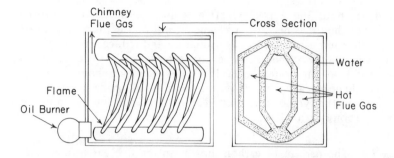

Figure 7.8 Water tube boiler.

moved from the boiler is 300 feet. For greater distances a high pressure boiler should be used, which is usually more costly. A package boiler is purchased and shipped fully equipped and "ready to go," only the electricity, water, fuel supply, and piping need to be attached. The build-up boiler is actually put together or constructed on the site. Package boilers are the most common in greenhouse operations.

Boilers are equipped with safety equipment and electronics that must be maintained. These are specific and when either purchasing new or working with a older boiler the instruction manual is most helpful.

BOILER EFFICIENCY

Not all of the heat energy produced is converted into useful heat. Some of the heat is lost up the chimney, incomplete combustion and from the boiler itself. Table 7.6 is a general estimate of the efficiencies of the various types of fuels. The efficiency of individual boilers can be determined by noting the ratings of input and output Btu or horsepower. The percentage differences between the input and output describes the efficiency under ideal conditions. For example, a boiler input specification may show 1,500,000 Btu/hr. and 1,200,000 output Btu/hr. This boiler would be 80% efficient. Remember this is at maximum efficiency and efficiency lowers when the boiler is not working at full capacity. The percentage efficiency given in Table 7.6 are probably more reasonable estimates on an overall year round efficiency. These percentages are important in estimating the amount of a fuel used to heat the greenhouse (page 85).

The efficiency of an individual boiler can be monitored by measuring the stack temperature, the oxygen, carbon dioxide and carbon monoxide. The objective of a boiler is to transfer as much heat from the gas to the water. It has been calculated that the best efficiency is when the stack temperature or flue gas is about 150°F(65°C) above the temperature of the water in the boiler. For example, if it is steam, the stack temperature should be about 360°F (182°C). If it is not, the burner needs to be adjusted or the tubes need to be cleaned. Soot on the tubes, caused by incomplete combustion, serves as insulation and reduces efficiency. To properly adjust the burner it is necessary to measure the oxygen, carbon dioxide and carbon monoxide levels. The oxygen level should be 1-2%, there should be no carbon monxide and the carbon dioxide level will vary according to the type of fuel used. Table 7.7 gives a few examples of proper carbon dioxide levels.

Table 7.7   The percent of carbon dioxide in the flue gas to determine boiler efficiency.

	Natural gas	No. 2 oil	No. 6 oil
Efficient	10%	12.8%	13.8%
Inefficient	8%	9.0%	12.0%

Boiler Water

Boiler water care is critical for the proper maintenance and efficiency of the inside of the boiler. Scale formation, pitting, corrosion of the pipes and mud formation are problems caused by improper care. These problems are found in large systems where there is a great deal of make-up water added to the system. The water is lost by leaks or steaming, both common in greenhouse operations.

Scale formation is caused by deposits of calcium, magnesium and silica. It has been reported that a 1/16 inch scale deposit will increase fuel consumption by 5%. Pitting and corrosion are caused by high oxygen levels in the water. Mud is caused by excessive and dirty make-up water or by precipitation of the water treatment chemicals. All of these problems can be prevented by proper water treatment. Each situation is different and it is best to hire a professional boiler consultant to make recommendations for the treatment of the boiler and the water supply.

A water meter should be located on the boiler make-up water line to keep track of the amount of new water added to the boiler. This will show if there are large leaks in the heating system. A water softener is often used on the make-up water to reduce the levels of calcium and magnesium. Chemicals are added to the make-up water to reduce the oxygen level, foaming and precipitation of various impurities. To remove the impurities, called mud, the boiler is periodically blown down. The frequency of blowdown and quantity of water removed is a function of the amount of make-up water and the amount of impurities in the boiler. A measurement of the suspended solids, total dissolved salts and the gallons of make-up water per hour determine the blowdown schedule.

DISTRIBUTION OF HEAT IN THE GREENHOUSE

Hot Air

There are a few methods to get the energy from the burning fuel to the greenhouse. In some cases small boilers or furnaces are placed right in the greenhouse. These generally heat air, which is then distributed by fans. Small house furnaces have been used successfully as heating units in greenhouses (Fig. 7.9).

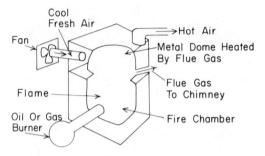

Figure 7.9   Hot air furnace.

The Modine unit heaters are usually fired by gas but can also be hooked directly to a central hot water or steam system (Fig.7.10). They have the advantages of being relatively inexpensive and portable. The disadvantage is that the distribution and uniformity of heat in the greenhouse are generally not as good as with a conventional radiant pipe system. The units are used in three ways: to produce vertical discharge, to produce horizontal discharge, and in conjunction with the fan-jet ventilation system (Fig. 7.11).

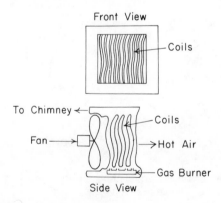

Figure 7.10   Modine type heater.

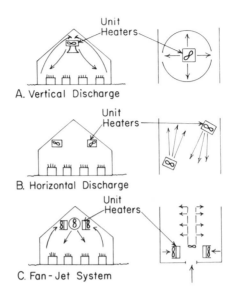

Figure 7.11   Distribution of air by unit heaters.

The fan-jet system, because of the mixing of air, is probably the most uniform of the hot-air heating systems (see Chapter 8). The vertical and horizontal distribution systems can blow very hot air onto the plants and cause excessive drying of the plant material. Careful observations of the air discharge patterns will help. Continuously running fans will also reduce the excessively high temperatures. An example of the temperature variation from a vertical discharge unit is shown in figure 7.12.

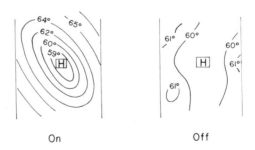

Figure 7.12   Distribution of heat in a greenhouse with a vertical discharge unit heater on and off.

Many greenhouses, especially plastic ones are heated with hot-air units. Many use either one or two horizontal discharge units to heat the houses (Fig. 7.13). They seem to work satisfactorily. The biggest problem in the plastic houses has been that many self-fired units were not designed to allow enough outside air in for the burners and either the efficiency of the burners was greatly reduced or in some cases an actual deficiency of oxygen and incomplete combustion occurred.

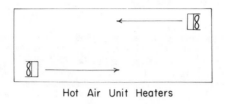

Hot Air Unit Heaters

Figure 7.13   Air circulation with two horizontal discharge unit heaters.

Central Boilers with Radiant Pipes

The most common means of heat distribution is through pipes in the greenhouse, like radiators in a residential house. The easiest and most convenient place to put the pipe is on the perimeter of the greenhouse. Fortunately, this arrangement probably gives the most uniform temperature. This can be seen in Figure 7.14.

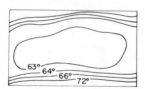

Figure 7.14   Temperature pattern in a greenhouse heated by perimeter pipe.

Air patterns caused by heating a greenhouse are rather interesting, as seen in Figure 7.15, and can be affected by winds, as shown in Figure 7.16. Air patterns in the greenhouse will be affected if additional heat pipe is placed overhead as shown in Figure 7.17.

One would expect by studying the air movement in Figure 7.15, that placing the pipes beside ground beds would improve uniformity of distribution and reduce cold spots. However, it has been shown that, in fact, uneven heating of the soil occurs, which may be detrimental. Placing the heat pipes overhead helps to produce a more uniform air circulation pattern as shown in Figure 7.18.

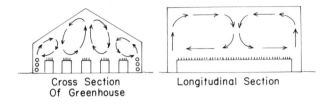

Cross Section
Of Greenhouse

Longitudinal Section

Figure 7.15   Air pattern in a greenhouse heated with perimeter pipe.

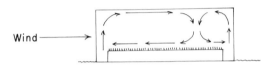

Wind

Figure 7.16   Effect of wind on air patterns. Note the shifting of the air pattern as compared to Fig. 7.15.

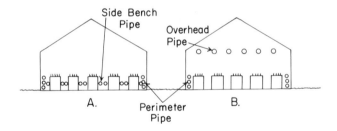

Side Bench
Pipe

Overhead
Pipe

A.

Perimeter
Pipe

B.

Figure 7.17   Radiant pipe (A) along the side of beds and (B) overhead.

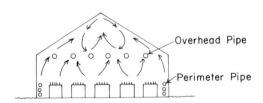

Overhead Pipe

Perimeter Pipe

Figure 7.18   Air currents affected by overhead radiant pipe. Note reduced dropping of cool air; compared with Fig. 7.15.

Calculations to determine the amount of radiant pipe. To calculate the amount of piping needed in a greenhouse we must know the heating requirement (H) at the design temperature. That figure from our example 35-foot by 75-foot greenhouse was, H = 485,604 Btu per hour. We need to put enough pipe in the greenhouse to radiate that amount of heat. It is not quite as simple as just finding how much radiation there is from a lineal foot of pipe, for the amount of Btu per hour per lineal foot of pipe is dependent on the air temperature, the source of energy (hot water or steam), and the stacking (Table 7.7).

Table 7.7.   Heat radiation in Btu/hr/lineal foot of pipe in a 60°F (15°C) greenhouse under different installation configurations.

Pipe and placement	2" pipe—180°F (82°C) hot water	1¼" pipe—steam
1 coil overhead	195	180
1 coil side	145	162
2 coils side—vertical stacking	275	312
3 coils side—vertical stacking	395	430
4 coils side—vertical stacking	505	545
5 coils side—vertical stacking	590	640
6 coils side—vertical stacking	645	702
1 fin coil side	790	1020
2 fin coils side — vertical stacking	1300	1800

Source: Hart, S. 1950. Studies of heating, cooling, and humidity control within greenhouses, Ph.D. thesis, Cornell University, Ithaca, NY.
Amer., Soc. Heating, Refrigeration, Air Conditioning Engineers Inc. 1977. Handbook and Product Directory: Fundamentals.

To solve our example we decide to use four overhead lines and the rest around the perimeter. The heating system is steam. The greenhouse has 220 feet of perimeter available, but some area must be left for doors, so for our example we will use 200 feet. From Table 7.7 it can be seen that eight 1¼" overhead pipes would radiate (8 × 75 feet × 180 Btu per lineal foot) 108,000 Btu per hour. This is subtracted from the total heat requirement, 485, 604 minus 108,000 equals 377, 604. There are 200 feet available to place the pipes so divide the Btu required by 200 or 1888 Btu per lineal foot. From Table 7.7 we see that 1¼ inch 2-fin side coil vertical stacking would solve the problem. The amount of pipe to order therefore would be 600 feet of 1¼ inch steam pipe for the overhead installation and 400 feet of finned 1¼ inch steam pipe for the perimeter installation.

Perimeter pipe styles. Perimeter pipe can be found in two styles, box type or trombone type, as shown in Figure 7.19. The trombone type gives more uniform heating to the length of the greenhouse because as the steam or hot water enters the pipe it goes the whole length of the greenhouse before it returns in the second pipe, and then the whole length before entering the third. The third pipe will be cooler than the first. In the box type, the steam or hot water enters uniformly on all three pipes together before going the length of the greenhouse, so that the entering end would be warmer than the exit end.

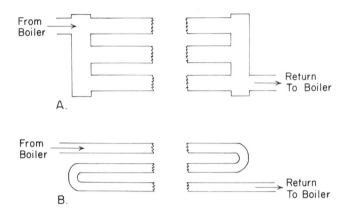

Figure 7.19   The (A) box and (B) trombone styles of perimeter piping.

HOT WATER VS. STEAM

The choice of steam or hot water is dependent on the particular situation. Generally a hot water system gives a more uniform greenhouse temperature, but steam is a more efficient way to move large quantities of Btu. Most large greenhouse ranges use steam systems.

Hot water systems require circulation pumps to move the water through the pipes as shown in Figure 7.20. There are still some hot water gravity fed systems, but these are slow to respond and inefficient (Fig. 7.21). The hot water rises and the cold settles. This action circulates the water.

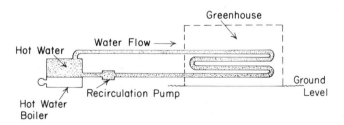

Figure 7.20   Pump-operated hot water system.

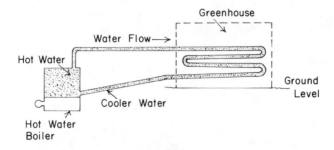

Figure 7.21   Gravity feed hot water system.

Hot Water Controls

The only control needed for the gravity feed hot water system is a means to turn the burner on and off. The hot water recirculating system needs an aquastat for the boiler and an on-off control for the pump. When the water temperature is less than desired the aquastat turns the burner on and heats the water. When higher temperatures are needed in the greenhouse, the pump is turned on which moves hot water from the boiler to the greenhouse and replaces it with cooler water from the greenhouse. This cools the boiler water and activates the aquastat which turns on the burner.

Steam Control

The control of the steam system is a little more complicated. An advantage of steam is that its own force or pressure moves it from the boiler to the greenhouse and it does not have to be pumped. Many systems are controlled by turning the burner on and off. The burner heats up the water which forms steam that passes through the pipes to the greenhouse. When the steam enters the radiation pipe in the greenhouse some of it condenses. Remember that 960 Btu are obtained for each pound of water condensed. To handle the condensate and separate it from the steam, there is a steam trap at the end of the pipe as it exits the greenhouse. Steam traps stop steam but allow water or condensate to pass through. The condensate will return to the boiler either by gravity or more commonly by condensate pumps (Fig. 7.22).

The steam system is controlled by two methods, control of the burner or steam valves in the pipe. When the temperature in the greenhouse gets low a controller turns the burner on and when the greenhouse temperature gets high the controller turns the burner off. The more efficient systems maintain a constant pressure of steam in the boiler all the time, for example 10 pounds. When there are 10 pounds of steam pressure in the boiler the burner is turned off. When the greenhouse needs heat, a valve in the pipe is opened and allows the steam to pass to the greenhouse, which in turn reduces the pressure in the boiler and turns on the burner which produces more steam.

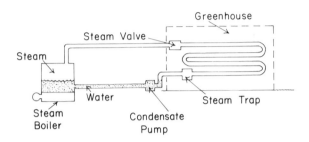

Figure 7.22   Steam heating system.

Infrared Heating

The Co-Ray-Vac infrared heating system used in greenhouses consists of a series of small gas (natural gas or propane) burners spaced about 20 feet a part in a 3 or 4 inch metal pipe. An aluminum reflecter placed over the pipe helps reflect the IR heat down to the plants. A large vacuum pump placed at the end of the pipe system draws out the burned gases. The system is very efficient and most of the heat from the burned gas stays in the greenhouse

The problem with this system appears to be getting uniform temperature control. If the greenhouse contains tall plants, the IR is absorbed by the plants before it reaches the soil and the result is cold soil. A supplementary soil heating system would be useful in this situation. The location of the thermostat is very critical. If the IR is able to radiate directly on the thermostat it will warm up quickly and turn the system off. If the thermostat is shielded (as would be the case with a conventional system), it would be on for a long time. The grower must try various locations and temperature settings to obtain the desired results.

INSULATION OF GREENHOUSES

The heat loss from a greenhouse is five to ten times greater than that of and average residential house. Glass houses have laps in the glass and other joints that allow exfiltration of air. Plastic houses, although tighter, allow long wave radiation to pass readily through the film, therefore, both types of structural covers allow large heat losses. There have been some recent studies to determine ways to insulate green houses at night to help reduce heat losses. There are three basic systems: (a) movable night curtains, (b) a plastic cover for the existing structure, and (c) permanent reflective insulation of the north wall and roof. Each of these systems can reduce the heat loss up to 50%.

Night Curtain

The night curtain serves as a blanket or shield over the crops in the greenhouse to reduce both radiation and convection losses (Figure 7.23). This energy conservation scheme is probably the most efficient method to reduce heat losses at night and not have a great reduction of sunlight during the day. Almost any material (polyethylene or black cloth) used as a thermal blanket at night will reduce heating costs by 50%. Most thermal blankets are suspended by wires and pulled back and forth with a pulley system

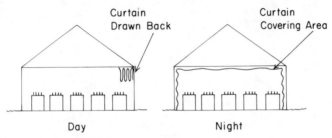

Curtain Drawn Back   Curtain Covering Area

Day   Night

Figure 7.23 Automatic night covering for insulation.

Cornell has developed a blanket system that rolls up the blanket, is sealed on the edges and is multi-layered. Its effectiveness in a commercial greenhouse situation was almost 90% during a mid-winter month. This system solves some of the major problems with the use of blankets. The rolling system is compact when unfurled and casts a very slight shadow during the day. Pulling the blanket back and forth is done via nylon straps in the edges, which means the cloth (blanket) is not stressed, nor folded, so its life will be greatly extended. Any debris or water that falls on top of the blanket is thrown off in the closing process and not collected in the accordian folds of the blanket system. Dripping from the underside of many blankets is very annoying to people and can cause disease problems with plants. Condensation is caused because the single layer blanket material is cold and the warm humid air under the blanket hits the surface and condenses water. With the multi-layered blanket, the bottom layer is not cold and there is no condensation. The major problem with the Cornell blanket is it is more costly than other systems. It appears to be a question of economics, i.e., savings in fuel vs cost of installation.

Other disadvantages of blankets in general are the difficulties of installation in older and/or small houses because of heating pipes, posts and other protrusions. Most new greenhouses are designed with an energy truss which allows for easy installation of a thermal blanket (Figure 7.25).

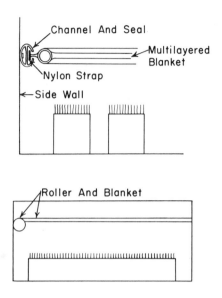

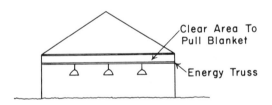

Figure 7.24.   Cornell's multi-layered thermal blanket system.

Figure 7.25.   Energy truss to allow for easy installation of a thermal blanket.

Extra Plastic Covering

The extra layer of plastic works well as an insulation on both plastic and glass houses, but for different reasons. The extra layer on a plastic house either in place or air-inflated (see Chapter 1) forms a thermopane effect between the two layers. The two layers should not be too far apart or air currents between the plastic sheets will short circuit the effect.

Thirty to 40% savings over a single layer house have been reported. A plastic sheet placed over a glass house has given a 50% reduction in heat loss. The plastic reduces the exfiltration of the air through the laps in the glass as well as providing a thermopane effect. The combination of plastic and glass seems to work well because the glass is not transparent to long wave radiation and the plastic resists exfiltration. The disadvantages of the plastic cover have been the loss of light during the dark months of the year.

A single layer of plastic over glass has resulted in heat savings about equal to double poly over glass, with the added advantage of more light. The single poly layer can be kept taut by installing a 12 to 18 inch layflat tube under the polyethylene sheet, the long way of the greenhouse, about half way down the roof. Inflating the tube with a small air pump (similar to the system used to inflate a double poly layer) worked satisfactorily (Figure 7.26).

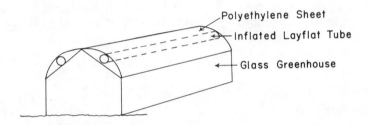

Figure 7.26. Single poly over a glass house with a layflat tube inflated to keep the sheet taut.

Polystyrene pellet insulation

Small polystyrene pellets (1/8 inch diameter) are blown between the layers of a double poly greenhouse at night and removed by suction in the morning. The insulation values are very high. The problems are static electricity (avoided by treating the pellets with glycol), a large volume of pellets to store during the day, the pellets must be kept dry and sizing the system for large-sized greenhouses.

Liquid foam insulation

A foaming material is added between the layers of a double poly greenhouse at night and the system is stopped during the day. The foam material increases in a ratio of 200 to 1, i.e., one gallon of the liquid will produce 200 gallons of foam. There have been problems with the foam especially in very cold temperatures, and leaks.

North Wall Insulation

Reflective insulation on the north wall and roof may show some potential. Engineers have shown on a bright day more light is lost through the north wall of a greenhouse than enters, so in effect the north wall is not serving the original purpose. Therefore, if the north wall were reflective, that is capable of reflecting the sunlight back in, and insulated to reduce heat loss, there should be a benefit. Measurements have shown support for this conjecture. In fact, on bright days a north bench will be brighter next to the north reflective insulated wall than next to a normal glass wall. North roof reflective insulation is being experimented with and preliminary results look interesting. During the winter on bright days it was brighter on the north half of an east-west oriented greenhouse, but on dark days it was darker. The savings in fuel were large, greater than 50% when the whole north roof was covered. The disadvantages are the danger of excessive snow loads due to the lack of melting of snow over the insulated portion. It may be too dark for growth under the north roof and the insulation material may have to be removed during the summer months to allow more light when the angle of the sun is increased.

8

WINTER VENTILATION

Winter ventilation of greenhouses is used to reduce interior temperature and relative humidity. The temperature must be reduced either because the heating system produced too much heat or the sun raised the temperature too high for plant growth. Exchanging the outside air with the inside air will lower the temperature. The cooler the outside air the faster the temperature change will be accomplished.

Many times during the late fall, winter, and early spring the greenhouse remains closed for several days, because outside conditions are dark and cold. Under these conditions the relative humidity in the greenhouse may get very high and remain high for days. This condition promotes disease and inhibits soil drying. It has been demonstrated by pathologists that many diseases require high relative humidities for their germination and growth. Perhaps the classic example is rose mildew a serious disease, that becomes a major problem during times of high relative humidity. The detrimental effects of lack of soil drying are less easy to demonstrate, but watering frequency is greatly reduced, which reduces the application of fertilizer. Introducing outside air reduces the relative humidity in the greenhouse as well as the temperature. This will be true whether it is raining or not as long as the outside temperature is cooler than the inside temperature.

Relative humidity is defined as the amount of water in a volume of air in relation to the amount of water that volume of air could hold at saturation at a given temperature. For example, if we use an outside air temperature of 40°F (4.5°C) and 100% relative humidity and bring this air into the greenhouse (obviously an equal volume of greenhouse air had to be removed) and heat it to a temperature of 70°F (21°C), the relative humidity of that volume of air would be reduced, since warm air holds more moisture than cool air. There will be mixing with the existing greenhouse air and overall there will be a reduction in the relative humidity, depending on the quantity of 40°F (4.5°C) air brought in. The end result would be the possibility for greater evaporation of free water from plant leaves, transpiration, or general drying of the greenhouse. This principle is used and has been used by rose growers to prevent mildew. It is still the most effective method to control this disease.

Heat Exchangers

Preliminary research is underway to investigate the feasibility of using heat exchangers economically in the greenhouse. Heat exchanges are used in large commercial buildings to reduce energy losses and still have exchange of outside air. The principle is simple. Outgoing (warm, humid) air is used to raise the temperature of the incoming (cold, dry) air. This is done by a number of clever schemes, but a system of passing the air flows by one another in a long duct separated by a metal sheet can be effective. If a system can be developed, then the high relative humidity problems in winter greenhouses can be solved, without resorting to the present system of ventilating warm air out and taking cold air in. The energy saving can be significant.

TYPES OF VENTILATION

There are three types of winter ventilation: natural ventilation, tube ventilation, and fan-jet ventilation.

Natural Ventilation

Most greenhouses are constructed with top and side ventilators (Fig. 8.1). When the top ventilators are open air will leave and if it is the only opening (that is no side vents open) cold air will also enter. The quantity of air exchanged (ventilation) with only the top open depends on the temperature differential between the inside and outside, the wind, the area of opening, the distance between the inlet and outlet, and other variables. It is a difficult computation to make and in most cases is determined by experience, i.e. knowing what happens in each greenhouse. The major disadvantage of this system is that a relatively small opening of the ventilator is really a rather large area (for example, a one inch opening in a 75-foot long ventilator is 6.25 square feet) and if the outside conditions are very cold, the temperature change can be very rapid.

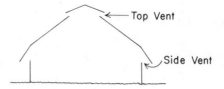

Figure 8.1   Top and side ventilators in a greenhouse.

Ventilators can be opened and closed by electric motors and combined with a temperature sensor. The hand control of a greenhouse for proper temperature to avoid overheating or overcooling is a difficult art and comes only with experience. A grower must be constantly vigilant to observe the weather and make adjustments accordingly. It is almost impossible to achieve uniform temperatures in small greenhouses with natural ventilation. Automatic control of ventilation is a great improvement over hand operations because the temperature controller (see Chapter 10) ensures a constant greenhouse temperature.

Tube Ventilation

Ideally, the outside air and inside air should be exchanged and mixed quickly and uniformly. This is accomplished rather efficiently with the tube ventilation system, which is simple and inexpensive. It includes a flexible plastic tube with numerous 1- to 2-inch holes and an exhaust fan capable of removing about a tenth of the cubic volume of the air in the greenhouse per minute. The fan can be one used for summer ventilation or a special exhaust fan installed in any outside wall of the greenhouse. The tube is placed in the upper area of the greenhouse as shown in Figure 8.2.

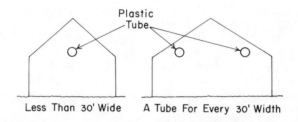

Figure 8.2   The placement of plastic ventilation tubes.

The tube will run the length of the greenhouse with one end open to the outside and the other closed. When the exhaust fan is on it creates a negative pressure inside the greenhouse. Since the tube is open to the outside, where the pressure is greater, air will rush in the opening and inflate the tube. The holes in the tube will allow the air to escape into the greenhouse (Figure. 8.3). As air comes out of the holes it mixes with the air inside the greenhouse within 20 diameters of the hole size from each hole. Therefore, using two-inch holes in the tube, the outside air is thoroughly mixed with the inside greenhouse air 40 inches from the holes. (Fig. 8.4).

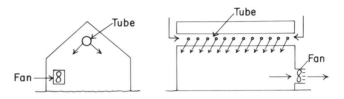

Figure 8.3   The path of outside air into the greenhouse when ventilated by the tube system.

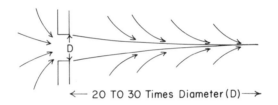

Figure 8.4   Air pattern through round hole.

To compute the tube diameter and the number of holes in it the following information is necessary. It has been shown that for an average glass house (not true for plastic) it is possible to admit through the laps and joints of the glass approximately 2 cubic feet of air per minute per square foot of floor area. For our example greenhouse this would be (35 × 75 × 2 = 2625 × 2) 5250 cfm. To calculate the ventilation rate

$$Q = \frac{K}{(t_i - t_o)}$$

where Q = cfm/square foot of floor area, K is given an empirical value of 50 for °F and 27.7 for °C, and $t_i - t_o$ is the difference between the desired inside and actual outside temperatures. The value of Q will vary according to the solar input. Table 8.1 shows a few values for a bright sunny day.

Table 8.1.   Cfm/sq ft of floor area (Q) needed to maintain inside temperatures on a bright sunny day with various outside temperatures.

Outside (t_o) in ° F (° C)	Inside (t_i) in ° F (° C)	Difference (t_i-t_o) in ° F (° C)	Q
15 (–9.5)	65 (18)	50 (27.5)	1.0
32 (0)	65 (18)	33 (18)	1.5
40 (4.5)	65 (18)	25 (13.5)	2.0
49 (9.5)	65 (18)	16 (8.5)	3.0
52 (11)	65 (18)	13 (7)	4.0
55 (13)	65 (18)	10 (5)	5.0
57 (14)	65 (18)	8 (4)	6.0
58 (14.5)	65 (18)	7 (3.5)	7.0

From Table 8.1 it can be seen that tube ventilation has a practical limit at about an outside temperature of 50°F (10°C). Above this temperature side vents or other means of allowing outside air to enter will have to be used. We can, therefore, design a system using 4 cfm per square foot for floor area. For our example greenhouse this would be 4 × 35 × 75 = 10,500 cfm. An ideal design would be 2 5000-cfm exhaust fans. One fan is used when outside air temperature is below 40°F (4.5°C) and both fans for above 40°F (4.5°C). Tube length should be no more than 100 feet with just one end open to the outside. It is possible to have both ends exposed to the outside and then a 200-foot length could be used (Fig. 8.5).

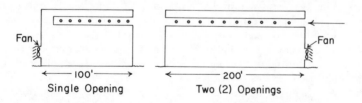

Single Opening   Two (2) Openings

Figure 8.5 The length of tubes.

Four-mil plastic tubing is recommended and can be obtained in various widths which inflate to different diameters as seen in Table 8.2.

Table 8.2.   The flat width and inflated diameter of various plastic tubing.

Flat width in inches	Inflated width in inches	Inflated cross sections in sq ft
20	12.5	.85
30	19.2	2.0
36	22.6	2.8
40	25.0	3.4
48	30.0	4.9

Two-inch holes are generally punched in the plastic tubing in the four and eight o'clock positions of the inflated tube. The area of the holes should not be more than 130% of the area of the inlet diameter. In our example greenhouse, we designed for 4 cfm/sq.ft. of floor area for a total of 10,500 cfm. An inlet velocity of 2200 feet per minute per square foot has proven to be satisfactory, therefore, we need (10,500 ÷ 2200) 4.8 sq.ft. of inlet. This can be achieved with one 48-inch flat width tube. There are 3.14 square inches in a 2-inch diameter hole, therefore, (1.30 × 4.9 × 144 ÷ 3.14) 292 holes in the tubing. The holes can be spaced a uniform distance, in this 75 foot greenhouse the holes would be 292 ÷ 2 = 146 pairs; and 75 ÷ 146 = 6.2 inches apart, or the holes can be spaced closer in the cooler areas and further apart in the warmer end of the greenhouse. Tubing may also be purchased with pre-punched holes.

A temperature controller (thermostat) turns the exhaust fan on and off as the temperature fluctuates. When the fan is on the outside air enters the tube at the wall and exists via the holes in the tube. It mixes with the warmer inside air within 3.5 feet. At the same time an equal amount of inside air is being exhausted by the fan. As soon as the temperature controller senses that the air temperature has been lowered to the desired temperature it turns off the fan.

Fan-jet Ventilation

The tube ventilation system has been improved not only to allow for uniform ingress of cool air but also to maintain a steady stirring of the air which reduces stratification. The same basic system is used except the tube is disconnected from the outside wall, a motorized louver is placed on the outside wall inlet, and a fan is placed a few feet from the inlet louver and attached to the tube. The fan is capable of blowing the air through the tube and out the holes. When the temperature or humidity in the greenhouse is as desired the fan is on and recirculating the air in the greenhouse through the tube holes (Fig. 8.6). When the temperature or humidity is not as desired, the exhaust fan starts to remove inside air and the inlet louver opens to let in outside air. The outside air is drawn into the fan and tube for distribution (Fig. 8.7).

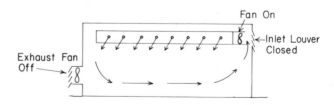

Figure 8.6   The air pattern of fan-jet system recirculating inside air.

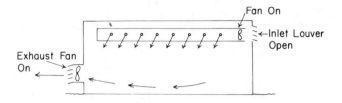

Figure 8.7   The air pattern of fan-jet system recirculating outside air.

Horizontal Convection System

The slow movement of air in a horizontal direction around the greenhouse, using small fans, was first advocated by J. Koths of the University of Connecticut, to improve uniformity of temperature. For small houses, less than 60 feet, just two fans are necessary to circulate the air. Large houses require more fans in series (Figure 8.8). The 18-inch fans run by 1/4 hp motors, are hung 5 or 6 feet above the ground and pointed approximately 15° toward the center. As a general rule of thumb to determine the size of the fans; the total CFM of the fans should equal about 1/4 of the volume of the greenhouse. In our example 35 × 75 foot greenhouse, the volume is 30,187 cubic feet. Therefore, the 4 fans should have a total CFM (free air) of 7546 CFM or 1886 CFM each.

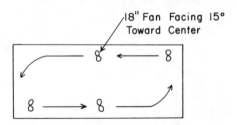

Figure 8.8   Horizontal convection system showing the placement of the fans.

Turbulators

Turbulators are specially designed fans for greenhouse use, that are hung from the greenhouse roof to move and mix large quantities of air. The placement of the fans is in the center of a 2500 square foot area (Figure 8.9). The fan (1/6 hp) will move almost 15,000 CFM. Large turbulators are available. The results have not been positive for all crops and temperature and air flow measurements have shown uneven distribution.

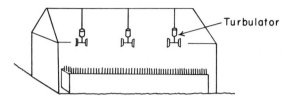

Figure 8.9   Turbulators suspended from the roof of the greenhouse.

9

SUMMER COOLING

The greenhouse structure has been designed and positioned to collect the maximum amount of sunlight, which is necessary for maximum plant growth. This orientation causes serious heating problems in the summer when the outside air is warm and the light intensity is maximum. It has been estimated the sun radiates between 200 and 285 Btu per square foot on the earth's surface per hour, depending on the location. Areas near cities or the coast where there are dust or moisture particles in the air will have a lower heat load. Figure 9.1 shows the relationship of intensity to Btu.

The most common methods of summer cooling are shading, natural ventilation, and fan ventilation. Evaporation cooling is also effective but can be expensive to install and more difficult to maintain than the other methods.

SHADE

If the irradiance from the sun can be reduced, the heat load will be reduced. Shading the greenhouse reduces the air temperature (Table 9.1). Light is necessary for plant growth so there is a limit to the amount of shading desirable. Table 9.2 shows the effect of shade on air temperature, light intensity, and leaf temperature. When the weather turns rainy or cloudy for a few days shading becomes a problem, but shading is still the most common means of controlling summer heat.

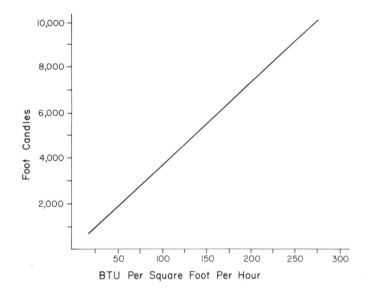

Figure 9.1   The relationship of solar irradiation (ft-c) to heat load (Btu/sq ft).

Table 9.1.   Air temperature in °F (°C) in a shaded and an unshaded greenhouse.

Outside	Unshaded greenhouse	Shaded (60%) greenhouse
82.8 (28.2)	99.2 (37.3)	92.8 (33.7)

Source: Gray, H. 1948. A study of the problems of heating, ventilation and air conditioning greenhouses. Ph.D. thesis Cornell University, Ithaca, N.Y.

Table 9.2.   The effect of 50% shade on the greenhouse air temperature, light intensity, and leaf temperature.

	Air temp. in °F (°C)	Light intensity in ft-c (lux)	leaf temp. in °F (°C)
Unshaded	97 (36)	6500 (70200)	104.6 (40.3)
Shaded	90 (32)	2500 (27000)	89.0 (31.6)

Source: Gray, H. 1948.

Paint

There are special shade paints, such as that produced by the Garland Paint Company, that stick well to glass yet can be readily removed with water and a scrub brush. Color does not apear to be important and most shade paint is white although a green tint is sometimes added. There are many home concotions used for shade paint. Among them are mud, linseed oil and lime, and white lead and gasoline. The prerequisites for a shade paint material are that it should be easy to apply, preferably with a sprayer, should not come off easily with rain, yet should be easy to remove in the fall when temperatures are cooler and light intensities are decreasing. To remove the various shade paints, the following mixture has been reported to do a satisfactory job. Mix in one gallon of hot water, four and a half pounds of sal soda, and one pound of tri soda, stirring until the powders dissolve. Add one gallon of commercial hydrofluoric acid (52%). Mix this into 23 gallons of cold water. It is ready for immediate use. To clean, the compound should be applied with a large brush or sprayed on and then rinsed off with water. No scrubbing is required and the compound is harmless to everything except silk.

Lath

Aluminum or wooden lath can be used as a shade. These are laid on the greenhouse structure or a more elaborate design can be rolled up and down the roof. This method of shading can be adjusted if necessary. It is more expensive than other methods and is difficult to control for a large (more than one acre) range.

Cloth

There are a number of materials that can be used for example, tobacco cloth, aster cloth, or saran cloth. Saran cloth is probably the most common and comes in various densities to give certain percentages of shade. The cloth is applied to the inside of the greenhouse to avoid wind and rain problems. This is usually a semipermanent installation that cannot be easily adjusted for varying weather conditions.

NATURAL VENTILATION

During the summer, the sun heats the air in the greenhouse and unless the hot air is removed the air temperature will climb to 130° F (54° C) or more. Most plants will be damaged at an air temperature over 110° F (43° C). A relatively simple way to avoid this problem is to remove the hot air. Most greenhouses are constructed with top and side vents as shown in Figure 9.2 to allow the air to enter and to leave.

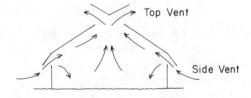

Figure 9.2   Air patterns into and out of a greenhouse ventilating system.

Since warm air rises, it will be at the top and when the top vent is open the air will stream out. To speed this flow the side vents can be opened. In some parts of the country greenhouses are designed so the sides can be completely removed, which allows even more airflow.

In natural ventilation, we must consider two forces: temperature differential between the inside and outside, and the wind. Both forces are usually acting together so it is difficult to get exact measurements. Under conditions of no wind all vents should be opened to their widest to get maximum airflow. The greater the difference between the inside and outside temperature the greater the airflow. When the wind blows more than seven miles per hour the side vents and leeward top vent should be opened to the widest position and the top vent on the windward side should be closed. This causes a slight lowering of the pressure right above the leeward vent which increases airflow (Fig. 9.3).

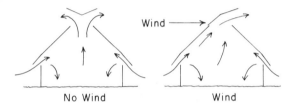

No Wind   Wind

Figure 9.3   Vent positions with and without wind.

Computation of Ventilation Rates

The number of cubic feet of air flowing through the ventilators per minute (Q) is equal to the area of the opening (A) times the average velocity in feet per minute (V). Therefore, $Q = A \times V$. Unfortunately, physical measurements of V are difficult and it is believed there is not a straight-line relationship between V and temperature. V can be expressed as: $V = K(t_i - t_o)^m$, where K is a constant for each house dependent on the ventilation distance between the top and side vents and m is the slope of the actual air velocity at various inside and outside temperatures. Let us use our example 35-foot by 75-foot greenhouse with continuous side and top vents that open to a width of 12 inches. Velocity measurements on an actual 35-foot by 75-foot greenhouse recorded a K of 62.5 and a slope of m of .344., V, therefore, becomes $62.5 (t_i - t_o)^{.344}$. Assuming there is no wind and a 10°F differential between inside and outside $(t_i - t_o)$ then V = 138 feet per minute. Our example greenhouse has an outlet area (top vents) of (75 ft × 1 ft. × 2) 150 sq ft., therefore, A equals 150. There is (150 × 138) 20,700 cfm of air moving through the greenhouse.

Table 9.3.   Airflow (cfm) in the example greenhouse, t_i-t_o = 10°, V = 138 ft/min.

Opening of vent in inches	Total vent area (sq ft) (A)	Total cfm (Q) (A × V)
3	37.5	5,175
6	75.0	10,350
9	112.5	15,525
12	150.0	20,700

Table 9.4.   Airflow (cfm) as the temperature differential (t_i-t_o) varied in the example greenhouse with the vents wide open, A = 150.

Temperature differential (t_i-t_o) in °F	Velocity of air (fpm) (V)	Total cfm (Q) (A × V)
2	80	12,000
5	110	16,500
7	122	18,300
10	138	20,700

The effect of ventilator opening and temperature differential on the airflow through our example greenhouse can be seen in Tables 9.3 and 9.4. It is clear the opening of the ventilators is extremely important in controlling the airflow through the greenhouse. It is also interesting to compute the amount of Btu that are being removed by this airflow. Heating and cooling engineers use the figure 0.24 Btu to raise one pound of air 1°F. One pound of air has a volume of 13.7 cubic feet, therefore it follows that one cubic foot of air gains 0.0175 Btu when heated 1°F. To determine the amount of Btu removed each minute the following formula is used: H = Q × 0.0175 (t_i-t_o), where H is the Btu removed per minute, Q is the cfm of ventilated air, t_i-t_o is the temperature differential between inside and outside. Thus to solve for our example greenhouse with wide open vents and a 10°F temperature differential H = 20,700 × 0.0175 (10) = 3622 Btu/minute. Therefore, in one hour (60 × 3622) 217, 320 Btu would be removed. This may seem like a large amount of heat removed, however if we assume a solar radiation of 200 Btu per square foot per hour, then this example greenhouse would have an incoming heat load of (200 × 2625) 525,000 Btu per hour. The above ventilation rate would only account for half of the heat load. The rest of the energy would be absorbed by the objects in the greenhouse, plants, benches, floors and so forth. Some energy would be used in transpiration of water from the plants and some would be reradiated.

FANS

To improve the removal of heat from the greenhouse it is possible to use exhaust fans. These have the advantage of moving more air than natural ventilation can at normal temperatures, and using a proper design actually exhaust approximately 25% less of the greenhouse volume. Exhaust fans used in the greenhouse are generally the propellor type. There are innumerable styles on the market. The fan should be designed for continuous operation and the electric motor should be enclosed to prevent damage and premature wear from moisture and dust. The fan should be rated in cfm at a static pressure of at least .1 inches, because when the fan is operating there is a static pressure or negative pressure in the greenhouse. The cfm rating should be certified by the Air Moving and Conditioning Association Inc. (AMCA).

The exhaust fan is placed on one side wall of the greenhouse and the air inlet is on the opposite sidewall. Since there is a slight negative pressure and the airflow is across the greenhouse, the volume of air above the eave will be undisturbed. The undisturbed air is about 39% of the total volume of our 35-foot by 75-foot greenhouse (Fig. 9.4).

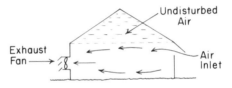

Figure. 9.4   The air pattern in a fan-ventilated greenhouse.

Computation of Ventilation Rates

To calculate the volume of a greenhouse to determine fan ventilation rates it is not necessary to calculate the volume above the eave. Therefore a general rule is to multiply the square footage of the greenhouse by 8 to obtain the volume of air to be changed. Using our example greenhouse there is (2625 × 8) 21,000 cubic feet. The general rule is to remove this amount of air in one minute, therefore a fan capacity close to 21,000 cfm is needed. To obtain uniform air movement, normally a few fans are used. Fan spacing should not be more than 25 feet apart. The velocity of air into and out of a fan is vastly different. Since these are exhaust fans the air is flowing out of the greenhouse and it is the inlet air flow that is important. The flow into a fan is rather uniform and the velocity not very great as shown by the arrows in Figure 9.5. The velocity 3 or 4 feet from the inlet is just 12% of what it is on the outlet side, which can be demonstrated by standing on either sides of a greenhouse exhaust fan.

Whether the fans should be placed on the long or the short wall of the greenhouse will depend on each greenhouse situation. Ideally the opposite wall should be clear. Drawing the air the long way (placing fans on the short wall) would be best, however this is not always possible. The advantage of the free-standing greenhouse situation with the short wall available is that just two fans (10,500 cfm each) would be needed. In the case of the corridor-connected greenhouse, where only the long wall is available, at least three fans would have to be used, i.e. fans spaced every 25 linear feet (Fig. 9.6).

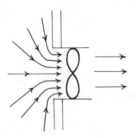

Figure 9.5   The air flow pattern through an exhaust fan.

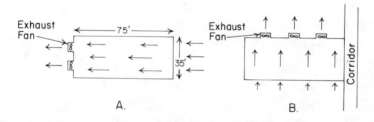

Figure 9.6   The fan placement and air pattern for (A) free standing greenhouse and (B) corridor-connected greenhouse.

The fans should also be placed on the side opposite the normal direction of wind and the fans in adjacent greenhouses should not be opposite one another.

The requirement of one air change per minute or 21,000 cfms for our example greenhouse is the same order of magnitude as that obtained with natural ventilation. Interestingly, if the temperature differential becomes greater than 10°F (5.5°C), natural ventilation will move more air.

There are two alternatives for improving heat removal, and these can be seen from the determination of Btu removed, the formula $H = Q \times .0175 (t_i - t_o)$. Increasing Q (cfm) or reducing the outside temperature

(t_o) will remove more Btu. Table 9.5 shows the results of increasing (Q) by increasing the fan capacity (cfm).

Table 9.5. The effect of increasing the capacity (cfm) of the exhaust fan on heat removal from our example greenhouse, assuming a 10°F differential (t_i-t_o).

Exhaust fan rating cfm (Q)	Air exchanges per minute	/H	Btu removal per hour
10,500	0.5	1838	110,250
21,000	1	3675	220,500
31,500	1.5	5513	330,750
42,000	2	7350	441,000
52,500	3	9188	551,250

There are limitations to the amount of air that can economically and feasibly be drawn through a greenhouse. It has been shown that three air changes per minute is about maximum. A higher rate causes excessive air and leaf movement, plus the costs of installtion and electricity will be high. In our example greenhouse, using one air change per minute would require almost one horsepower of energy and three changes would require three horsepower.

The other alternative, decreasing the outside temperature (t_o) of the in coming air can be accomplished by evaporative cooling.

EVAPORATIVE COOLING

If we cool the incoming air, therby increasing the differential [t_i-t_o in our formula H = Q × .0175 (t_i-t_o)], heat removal from the greenhouse is increased. Table 9.6 shows the results of decreasing the outside air temperature (t_o). Two methods have been tried to cool the incoming air, mechanical refrigeration and evaporation of water.

Table 9.6. The effect of decreasing the outside air temperature (t_o) on the heat removal with 1 air exchange per minute and a constant inside temperature (t_i).

Temperature Differential (t_i-t_o) (°F)	H	Btu removal/hr
10	3150	189,000
15	4725	283,500
20	6300	378,000
25	7875	472,500

Mechanical refrigeration to cool the incoming air is extremely expensive because of the size of the equipment needed to remove such large heat loads. Consequently, there are only a few installations of mechanical refrigeration equipment, usually in special research green-houses.

Evaporative cooling has been used very successfully to cool green-houses. The pad and fan system has been the most popular. The exhaust fans used for winter tube ventilation (Chapter 8) are used as part of the system. The pad is placed on the sidewall opposite the fan and serves as a wetted area where evaporation and cooling of the incoming air occurs, as it enters the greenhouse through the pad.

As water evaporates it requires heat energy (960 Btu to evaporate 1 pound of water). This heat is called latent heat. The rate and amount of water that can be evaporated is dependent upon the temperature of the air and the amount of water vapor the air already contains. The drier the air the lower the temperature to which that volume of air can be cooled.

Cooling engineers measure relative humidity with a psychrometer, an instrument with two thermometers. The dry bulb thermometer measures the temperature of the air, sometimes called the sensible heat because it is the temperature we feel. The wet bulb thermometer has a thin, moist muslin cloth around the base of the bulb. Air moving across the thermo-meter at a speed greater than nine feet per second causes the water on the cloth to evaporate (remember evaporation requires heat) and heat is removed from the thermometer bulb. (A sling psychrometer is whirled by hand. A motorized psychrometer has a fan.) The wet bulb thermo-meter will be cooler than the dry bulb thermometer. When the tempera-ture of the wet bulb stops falling (after a few minutes), it has come into equilibrium with the air, i.e. the rate of water loss (evaporation) is steady. The wet bulb thermometer will be some degrees cooler than the dry bulb, and this difference is called the wet bulb depression. The amount of cooling or wet bulb depression will be related to the amount of water in the air (relative humidity) which can now be determined by referring to the psychrometric chart (Fig. 9.7). If the air is saturated there would be no evaporation because the air could not hold any more water and con-sequently there would be no depression of the temperature. If the air were very dry (low RH) there would be a large depression. For example a volume of air at 80°F (27°C) with an RH of 30% would have a wet bulb reading of 60°F (15.5°C) or a wet bulb depression of 20°F (11°C), air at 100°F (37.7°C) and an RH of 30% would have a wet bulb temperature of 75°F (24°C) or a wet bulb depression of 25°F (14°C). This information is shown on the psychrometric chart (Fig. 9.7).

To determine relative humidity from the chart. First measure the dry bulb and wet bulb temperatures. Locate the dry bulb and wet bulb temp-eratures on the chart. Draw a line straight up from the dry bulb tempera-ture. From the wet bulb temperature, draw a line parallel to the dashed line. Where the two cross is the relative humidity. Interpret from the curved series of relative humidity lines.

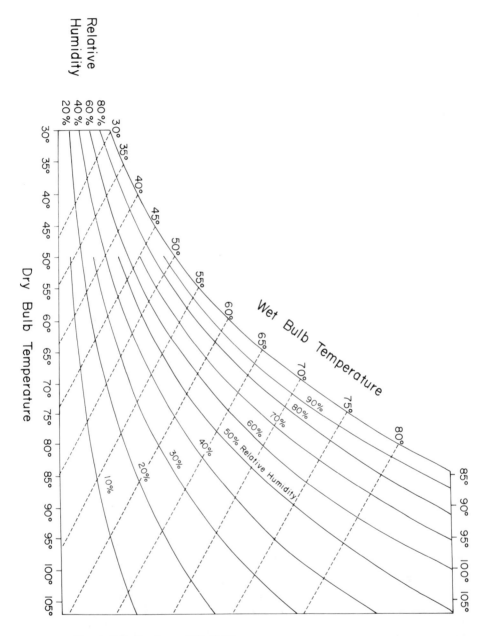

Figure. 9.7 Psychrometric chart.

Efficiency of the Cooling System

The efficiency of the pad and fan system is dependent on a number of factors: type of pad material, thickness and density of the pad, velocity of the air through the pad, resistance of the pad to air flow, degree of wetness of the pad, water distribution, pressure characteristics of the fans, position of the pads and fans, tightness of the greenhouse, outdoor dry bulb temperature and wet bulb temperature, and force and direction of wind. As a general rule of thumb one can figure on 80% efficiency although a well-designed and well-maintained system can achieve 90%. The efficiency of a pad and fan system is calculated by:

$$E = \frac{tdb_o - tdb_i}{tdb_o - twb_o}$$

where E is the efficiency in %, tdb_o is the dry bulb temperature outside, tdb_i is the dry bulb temperature inside, and twb_o is the wet bulb temperature outside. The wet and dry bulb temperatures are measured outside and the inside dry bulb temperature is measured a few inches from the wet pad. For example if the outside wet and dry bulb temperatures were 75°F (24°C) and 100°F (37.7°C), and the dry bulb inside the greenhouse by the pad was 80°F (27°C) then

$$E = \frac{100 - 80}{100 - 75} = \frac{20}{25} = 80\%.$$

It must be noted that the inside dry bulb temperature is measured near the wet evaporative pad and not in the middle of the greenhouse or by the exhaust fans. As the cooled air moves across the greenhouse it begins to pick up heat and in most systems will be 7°F (4°C) to 10°F (5.5°C) higher at the fan than when it entered.

Cooling Design Calculations

We have discussed fan installation in the previous section (Fans). The same principles are used for the evaporative cooling system, except a few added factors must be considered such as location of the greenhouse with reference to distance above sea level, light intensity, allowable temperature rise, and size of the greenhouse, which affects air velocity.

The basic design considerations to determine the fan size (cfm) for a greenhouse use a base of sea level to 1000 feet, shading of the greenhouse to allow a maximum of 5000 ft-c (54000 lux) of light, and an allowable increase in temperature from pad to fan of 7°F (4°C). If our 35-foot by 75-foot greenhouse has the above standards then the fan capacity in cfm will be 8 times the square feet of the greenhouse (8 × 2625) = 21,000 cfm.

Altitude. The higher the greenhouse is located above sea level the lower the efficiency of cooling, because the air is less dense. Therefore, to compensate for the lost weight of air the capacity of the fan must be increased. The local standard barometric pressure is a good measure of elevation and shows the relationship to the standard sea level barometric pressure. For example, if the local barometer reading were 28.92, the relationship to the standard sea level pressure, 29.92, is (29.92 ÷ 28.92) = 1.03. Table 9.7 gives the elevation factor (F_e) for various altitudes.

Table 9.7.   The calculated elevation factor (F_e).

	Elevation above sea level in feet								
	< 1000	1000	2000	3000	4000	5000	6000	7000	8000
Factor for evaluation (F_e)	1.00	1.04	1.08	1.12	1.16	1.20	1.25	1.30	1.36

Light intensity. The higher the light intensity in the greenhouse the greater the solar input or heat load. To obtain greater cooling capacity more fans are needed. Light intensity and heat input show a straight line relationship as shown in Figure 9.1. The factor for adjustment to compensate for changes in light intensity is maximum desired ft-c divided by 5000 ft-c. Remember 5000 ft-c (54,000 lux) was the standard level. Calculations for various intensities (F_l) are shown in Table 9.8.

Table 9.8.   The calculated factors for light (F_l).

	Maximum intensity in foot-candles (lux)								
	4000 (43200)	4500 (48600)	5000 (54000)	5500 (59400)	6000 (64800)	6500 (70200)	7000 (75600)	7500 (81000)	8000 (86400)
Factor for light intensity (F_l)	.8	.9	1.0	1.1	1.2	1.3	1.4	1.5	1.6

Temperature rise. The standard allowable temperature rise from pad to fan was 7°F (4°C). If more or less is desired or allowable, a factor should be computed. To reduce the temperature rise more fan capacity is needed and if a higher rise is allowable then less fan capacity is required. The factor for adjustment in the cfm requirement to compensate for a change in the temperature rise from the pad to the fan (F_t) is 7.0 divided by the temperature rise. Table 9.9 shows the relationship of various temperature rises.

Table 9.9.   The calculated factor (F_t) for the temperature changes between the pad and the fan.

	Pad to fan temperature rise in °F (°C)						
	10(5.5)	9(5)	8(4.5)	7(4)	6(3)	5(2.5)	4(2)
Factor for temperature rise (F_t)	.7	.78	.98	1.0	1.17	1.4	1.75

Velocity. The pad and fan system is designed to have 100 feet between the pad and fans. There are situations where this is not possible. Distances shorter than 100 feet reduce the velocity of the air through the greenhouse and, therefore, its effective cooling. To compensate, more air must be moved. This increment can be determined by the factor for velocity (F_v) which is 10 divided by the square root of the distance between pad and fan. The calculated F_v for various fan to pad distances are shown in Table 9.10.

Table 9.10.   The calculated factor (F_v) for reduced velocities caused by reduced distance between the pad and fan.

		Pad to fan distance (ft)							
		20	25	30	35	40	45	50	55
Factor for velocity (F_v)		2.24	2.00	1.83	1.69	1.58	1.48	1.41	1.35
	60	65	70	75	80	85	90	95	100
Factor for velocity (F_v)	1.29	1.24	1.20	1.16	1.12	1.08	1.05	1.02	1.00

Example. Let us use our example 35-foot by 75-foot greenhouse located at an elevation of 5000 feet, with a maximum of 7500 ft-c (81000 lux) of light, a desired 5°F (2.5°C) temperature rise across the greenhouse and a pad-to-fan distance of 35 feet. To determine the fan capacity: Cfm required = $F_1 \times F_v \times F_e \times F_t \times 8 \times 35 \times 75$ = 1.4 × 1.69 × 1.2 × 1.4 × 8 × 35 × 75 = 83,472 cfm. If we had not added the factors for elevation, temperature, velocity, and light to our determination the calculation would be only 21,000 cfm. The system would obviously not have been very effective under the conditions given above.

Pad Size Computations

It has been found that an air velocity of about 150 feet per minute through a 2-inch aspen pad gives a good evaporative efficiency. Higher flow rates reduce the efficiency and lower flow rates usually do not make major changes. Therefore, to compute the square feet of pad area required, the fan capacity (cfm) is divided by 150.

If we used our example greenhouse and conventional conditions the formula would then read 21,000 ÷ 150 = 140 sq ft of pad area. It is important to point out that the length of pad area should be the whole side of the greenhouse. Therefore, in this example the pad dimensions would be 4 feet by 35 feet if the air were drawn the long way or 1.8 feet by 75 feet if the air were drawn the short way (Fig. 9.8). In actual practice the 1.8-foot by 75-foot pad would be 2 feet by 75 feet as 2-foot pads are the narrowest manufactured. Extra pad size does not do any harm.

It is important that the pad be continuous or cooling problems will occur. For example if there is a door in the middle of the pad there would be an uncooled area 6 to 8 times the width of the door (Fig. 9.9).

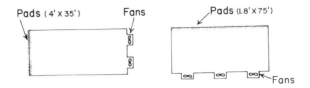

Figure 9.8 The pad size for two greenhouse configurations.

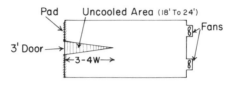

Figure 9.9 Area affected by obstruction in pad.

Pad Maintenance

The pad is critical for obtaining maximum efficiency of the cooling system. The most common pad material is aspen wood shavings. This material is relatively inexpensive and lightweight, it wets easily and holds moisture. The aspen is placed in plastic netting which in turn is placed in a wire frame generally 34 inches wide and 2 inches thick with heights varying from 24 inches to 120 inches. If the pads are too thick or too dense they will inhibit air flow and reduce the cooling efficiency. Conversely if the pads are thin and uneven, partially wet or with holes, air will stream through the path of least resistance and the efficiency will be greatly reduced. Maintenance of the aspen pad is a continuous problem and it must have regular inspections. The aspen pad material is replaced each year. There are newer pad materials available with much longer life, but their costs are also greater. The newer pads, made of special cellulose materials, are treated to resist rot and better designed than aspen. As a result, 40% less pad area is necessary for the average installation.

Water quality. There are 2 major problems in the recirculating water system for the pads, i.e. a buildup of soluble salts and algae. To avoid the algae an algaecide can be added. Any algaecide used in swimming pools will be satisfactory. Algae problems are greatest when the cooling water is obtained from ponds or steams without any chemical treatments.

Water is evaporated from the pads and make-up water is added to replace that lost by evaporation. However, in the evaporation process the dissolved salts in the water stay behind and become more and more concentrated. In areas where the water is naturally high in salts, a bleed-off valve should be added to remove a small percentage of the water. If the salts are allowed to accumulate, they will reduce the evaporative efficiency (Fig. 9.10).

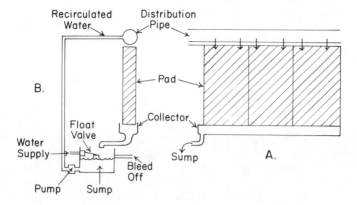

Figure 9.10 Front (A) and side (B) view of the pad system of evaporative cooling.

One advantage of the pad and fan system is that the air is filtered; dust, weed seeds, and even some insects are removed. Many operators add insecticides to the pad water to control incoming insects. It has been especially effective for thrips.

Water quantity. The quantity of water used will vary from day to day and depend on the evaporative rate. Under ideal or maximum evaporative rates as much as one gallon per minute is lost for every 100 sq ft of pad area. The pump should recirculate approximately one-third of a gallon per minute per lineal foot of pad. For our example greenhouse using a 75-foot pad, the pump should recirculate 25 gallons per minute.

Packaged Evaporative Coolers

Packaged evaporative coolers are completely contained units. Electricity and water must be hooked up; then they are ready to operate (Fig. 9.11).

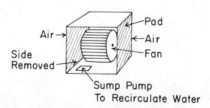

Figure 9.11 Cutaway view of a packaged evaporative cooler.

Three sides of the unit cooler are wet pads to serve as the evaporative surface and the fan inside the unit pulls the air through the pads and blows the cooled air into the greenhouse (Fig. 9.12).

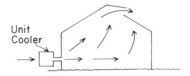

Figure 9.12   The air patterns caused by the packaged evaporative coolers.

These units work well for greenhouses under 20 feet. The principle is the same as for the pad and fan system. One disadvantage of these units is that the cool air is not distributed evenly in the greenhouse because it is blown into the greenhouse through a small opening, unlike the pad and fan system which draws air in through a large opening (Fig. 9.13). A second disadvantage is that the greenhouse is under a slight positive pressure, whereas with the pad and fan system it is under negative pressure. Therefore, the whole house must be cooled and the area above the eaves must be calculated when computing the volume of the greenhouse. Calculations of volume for the pad and fan system use only the area below the eaves. The computations for the number of units would be the same as that for computing the fan capacity of the pad and fan cooling system. (Fig. 9.14).

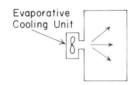

Evaporative
Cooling Unit

Figure 9.13   The air flow from a packaged evaporative cooler.

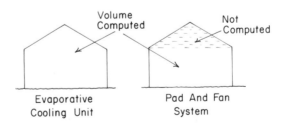

Volume
Computed

Not
Computed

Evaporative
Cooling Unit

Pad And Fan
System

Figure 9.14   The calculated volume for packaged evaporative coolers and pad and fan system.

10

TEMPERATURE CONTROLLERS

The method and accuracy of temperature control in a greenhouse affects the quality and the timing of the crops. No matter how well the basic heating and ventilation equipment is designed, the limitation will be the controller. Most greenhouses do not have good temperature control systems and the maintenance is usually poor. It is rather common to find heating systems that costs thousands of dollars to purchase and burn thousands of dollars of fuel controlled by a twenty-five dollar thermostat that was never calibrated.

THERMOSTATS

A thermostat is a device that is adjustable, senses temperature changes quickly, and sends a signal to activate or deactivate a part of the system (fan, vent, burner, valve). The temperature sensing element operates on the principle of the expansion and contraction of metal, air, or liquid (Fig. 10.1(A)).

The metal sensor is made of two strips of metals that expand and contract at different rates. The air sensor works by the expansion and contraction of air enclosed in a bellows. The air increases in volume as the temperature rises, thereby stretching the bellows. The bellows contracts when the temperature falls and the air volume decreases (Fig. 10.1(B)). The liquid sensor works when expanding liquid in the sensing element lifts a plunger during a rise in temperature. A decrease in temperature causes the liquid to contract, thus lowering the plunger (Fig. 10.1 (C)).

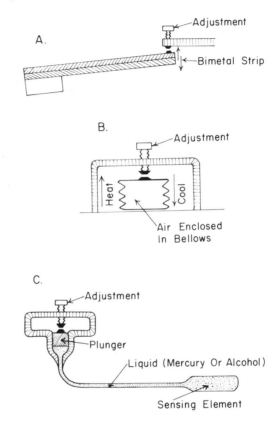

Figure 10.1 Temperature sensing elements: (A) metal sensor (B) air sensor (C) liquid sensor.

The accuracy of these systems depends on how well they are made. The metal and air sensor thermostats are compact and react to the temperature right at that site, whereas the liquid sensor element can be remote from the thermostat. It is commonly found on refrigeration units where the sensing bulb is inside the refrigerator and the adjustment mechanism (thermostat) is outside. All of these systems, since they are mechanical, have lag times, must overcome friction, and have hysteresis effect (i.e. do not return to the same position after a change).

The signal sent by the thermostat can be electrical or pneumatic. The electric thermostat is the most common (Fig. 10.2). As the air temperature cools the bimetallic strip bends upward until contact is made which completes the circuit and starts the burner. As the air heats up, the bimetallic strip straightens out and contact is broken, thereby stopping the heating cycle. The adjustment screw allows the thermostat to be functional over a wide range, commonly 50 to 90°F. This type of thermostat is rarely more accurate than ± 3° F (1.5° C). The limitations are that it generally has just one function, e.g. turning the fans on at 70° F (21° C) and off at 69° F (20.5° C). When there are a series of functions in a system that must be turned on or off at different temperatures, separate thermostats are needed for each function. This causes problems with adjustment and dissimilarity of reaction to a temperature change.

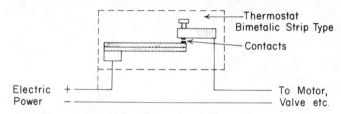

Figure 10.2 Bimetallic electric thermostat.

It is possible to get electric thermostats with multiple operations. The Team I & II controllers of the Acme Engineering and Manufacturing Corporation are examples. For most existing greenhouses electric thermostats are easier to install and maintain. For new installations, pneumatic controls should be considered.

The pneumatic system has the advantage that one thermostat controls all the events in a system, i.e. heating, ventilation, and cooling. The pneumatic is used by larger operations, it is complex and requires special equipment such as a separate air system. A bimetallic strip is adjusted so it is close to an orifice through which some air leaks out (Fig. 10.3). Because of the air leak the air pressure in the line is about 7 pounds, or approximately half, assuming that 15 pounds is full pressure. As the air in the greenhouse heats up the strip expands away from the orifice and more air leaks out, thereby reducing the pressure on the line. The opposite occurs as greenhouse air cools. The air pressure in the whole system will be uniform and, therefore, controlled by the thermostat. The advantage of this system is that different functions can be started and stopped at different pressures or in reality at different temperatures. Special equipment is needed to start electric motors and to open and close valves.

A transducer is a pneumatic controller that starts and stops an electric motor (Fig. 10.4). It is activated by the air pressure in the control line. As the pressure in the line is lessened, a bellows contracts until, the electric contacts meet, thereby completing the electric circuit. As the greenhouse temperature gets warmer the thermostat reduces the amount of air leaving the control line. The pressure in the control line increases, expanding the bellows and breaking the electric contact, and thereby stopping the motor.

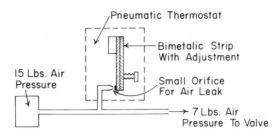

Figure 10.3   Schematic of the pneumatic thermostat.

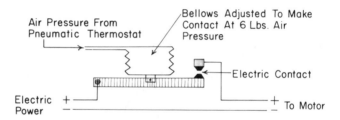

Figure 10.4   Transducer for converting air control to electric power.

A pneumatic valve works on a slightly different principle (Fig. 10.5). The valve plunger in the valve is the same as that for an electric or hand valve. The airtight globe on top is divided in the middle by a rubber diaphram. At 7 pounds of air plus the pressure of the spring (8 lb rated) in the upper half, the valve is closed as there is equal force, i.e. 15 pounds on the bottom. As the pressure on the line is reduced, say to 6 pounds, the pressure on the lower chamber is greater and the valve begins to open. Depending on the valve and other adjustments full opening could occur at 3 pounds of air pressure. The closing process follows the reverse path.

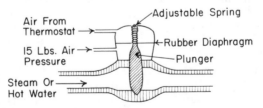

Figure 10.5   Pneumatic steam or water valve.

Heating engineers like the pneumatic system for there is an infinite valve opening to let steam through, whereas an electrical system is either fully open or closed — or at best one-quarter, one-half, three-quarters, and full — which causes overreaction to a temperature change. The pneumatic system allows one thermostat to control temperature over a wide range, and operate the cooling as well as the heating systems.

LOCATION OF THERMOSTAT

There are a number of factors that should be considered in placing a thermostat in the greenhouse. It is most important that the thermostat be in a position to register the average temperature of the whole greenhouse; it should not be too sensitive, which might cause overcontrol, not so damped that it responds too slowly to temperature changes. Most thermostats are placed in the center of the greenhouse at eye level, which may not be the best position. A review of the air currents in a greenhouse in Chapter 7 shows that currents of cool air were settling in the middle of the greenhouse. Many thermostats also face south and are exposed to the bright, hot sun during the day.

The ideal position is difficult to determine and in actual fact, will vary according to the wind, temperature differential, and size of the crops. To help avoid some of the problems caused by these variations, an aspirated insulated box should be used to house the temperature sensing, temperature measuring, and alarm systems (Fig. 10.6). The aspirated box will protect the thermostat from radiation and even from differential wind currents or temperature stratification. If the thermostat is housed in an aspirated box, these factors are less critical and convenience of inspection, for instance, becomes more important in choosing the location.

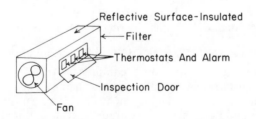

Figure 10.6   Aspirated thermostat box.

CALIBRATION OF THERMOSTATS

A thermostat has a dial or adjustment that is marked in degrees. It must be calibrated to ensure accuracy.

A mercury therometer, or preferably two, should be calibrated. The thermometers are placed in a slurry of ice and water. Both thermometers should read 32°F (0°C), if not, obtain more thermometers. For greater accuracy, put distilled water and ice in a vacuum bottle. Place the thermometers in a cork in the thermos top (Fig. 10.7). If both thermometers read 32°, replace the slurry with warm water, between 60° to 70°. The thermometers should both read the same temperature. The two thermometers can then be ideally placed in a motorized psychrometer (Chapter 9). As the fan blows across the two thermometers, they should give a fairly accurate measurement of the air temperature.

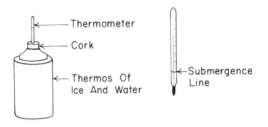

Figure 10.7   Thermos to calibrate thermometer.

Checking thermostats during the day is very difficult because of the rapidly changing conditions. Therefore, calibrate the thermostat at night. Place a test light across the electric leads of the thermostat so the light will be on when contact is made. Set the thermostat at the desired setting, turn on the motorized psychrometer, and note the temperature. Wait until the thermostat is activated or deactivated and note the temperatures on the two thermometers in the psychrometer. Record a few heating and cooling cycles. These readings will indicate the accuracy of the thermostat and will give the range over which the thermostat is operating.

MEASURING AND RECORDING TEMPERATURES

All measuring and recording equipment (thermometers, thermographs, thermisters, and thermocouples) can and should be calibrated as described above. The sensing element of the measuring or recording equipment should be inside the aspirated thermostat box. If the sensing equipment is outside the aspirated box and not shielded, during the day the temperature will record higher than the actual air temperature owing to radiation and at night it may be lower because of radiation losses.

A continuous recording of greenhouse temperature is valuable for indicating temperature adjustment problems and pinpointing when they began. Electronic temperature measuring equipment such as thermisters or thermocouples are excellent. They allow for remote sensing of a series of greenhouses and can be inspected at one location, but are expensive.

Thermographs are relatively cheaper, but are not remote and are not as accurate. They do show trends and can pinpoint times of equipment breakdown or other problems.

The thermometer is still the single most common recorder of temperature in a greenhouse. The thermometer should be calibrated at least once a year and kept in an aspirated box for an accurate indication of temperature.

The measurement of greenhouse temperatures is very difficult because of rapid fluctuations in temperature and radiation gains and losses. The more accurate the temperature measuring equipment, the more variation will be measured. It is not uncommon to observe variations of 15 to 20 degrees F (8 to 11 degrees C) when measuring with thermocouples.

Good judgment must, therefore, be used when making temperature measurements. Accurate temperature controllers enable the manager to regulate crop timing and heating costs.

COMPUTERS

The computer is rapidly replacing the thermostat in European greenhouses. Computers have a number of advantages that insure they will also replace the thermostats in the United States. The advantages include: temperature setting can be made easily and the temperatures set will be the control temperatures, the response time to temperature change is rapid and without hysteresis, the temperature sensor is stable over long periods of time and does not require frequent calibration, and the system is flexible. The disadvantages are: the initial cost of replacing the existing thermostats is high and unfamiliarity with computers.

There are three basic temperature functions the computer can control in a greenhouse; monitoring, alarming, and controlling.

How Do Computers Work

A general review of the functions of the various parts of the computer system will help with the system design. The sensor can be a thermocouple, thermistor, or transistor. The thermocouple is basically two dissimilar metals welded together that generate an emf, which is dependent on temperature. The thermistor and transistor work about the same. A current is passed through these sensors and the resistance or amount which passes through is dependent on temperature. The sensors are wired to an Analog to Digital board (A/D board). This electronic equipment converts the analog current or emf into a digit. The computer can be programmed, i.e., given a set of instructions. Programs are written in special languages and exact procedures are followed. The digit the A/D board read is shown to the program. The program has been told when the digit is, for example, below a certain number (greenhouse set temperature) it gives some command. The computer will activate a relay, which in turn will activate the steam valve in the greenhouse. The valve will stay open until the digits from the A/D board are raised above the programmed set temperature or until the program tells it to close. One of the advantages of a program is it can be made to anticipate. It will anticipate a change in temperature and will open and close valves before the actual set temperature is achieved. This system avoids overriding temperatures.

Another common part of a computer is the cathode ray tube (CRT) or TV-like tube that can be programmed to show the temperature in the greenhouse. A "floppy disc" is used with most small computers. The disc contains the special program and is also used to store information in a permanent form. The disc is placed in the disc drive (like a record player). The program can also be held on chips in the computer. A typewriter or keyboard are also present and that is how you communicate with the computer. There are RAM and ROM, but these have to do with the power of the computer. A computer friendly program is very easy to use as it asks simple questions that many times require only a yes or no answer.

As of this date, only Oglevee Associates of Connellsville, Pennsylvania have a computer system for greenhouse use in the United States. There are numerous systems in Europe.

The experience at Cornell using the computer for monitoring, alarming and control have been very positive. The monitoring system constantly averages the temperatures in a series of greenhouses (30) and writes this average on the floppy disc every 10 minutes. At any time the current temperature is shown on the CRT. Key a code number and the average temperature for last night will appear for each greenhouse, key another code and the highest and lowest recorded temperatures for last night in each greenhouse will appear. The same can be done for day temperature. This information is permanently held on the floppy disc and can be hard-copied, i.e., printed on paper.

The alarm system is simple. The high and low temperatures we wish to tolerate are put into the program (They can be easily changed). If the temperature in any greenhouse reaches these limits, the computer is programmed to ring an alarm.

Control is really the most important function for the computer. It will give more accurate temperatures than can be obtained with thermostats and at the same time save energy. The computer can be programmed to anticipate changes that occur moment to moment, hour to hour, or season to season.

Let us use a steam heating example in a greenhouse with perimeter heat pipes and describe the operation of a good thermostat and a computer. The temperature in the greenhouse is falling and the thermostat reads 70° F (set point), closes its contacts and passes a current to the steam valve which opens and steam enters the pipes. The temperature in the greenhouse continues to fall. We have measured temperatures falls of 8° to 10° before the warm air reaches the thermostat in the middle of the greenhouse. The temperature begins to rise, but remember the steam valve is still open and will shut off when the temperature reaches 70°. Now the pipes are full of steam and the temperature continues to rise. We have measured large temperature overrides of 8° to 10°. If there is another thermostat for cooling, it may turn on and vent some of the warm air. The computer would be programmed to avoid this problem. When the temperature is decreasing and reaches 70°, it will activate the steam valve and remembers how long it was on the last time in the heating mode. It will half that time and continue to half the on time until it is not on long enough to bring the temperature back to 70°F. At that point it will double the previous time. Using this procedure, excess steam is not added to the greenhouse, which has a potential of energy savings.

The computer can also control the ventilation, cooling, watering, CO_2 enrichment, RH, photosynthetic lighting, photoperiod lighting, shade cloth and thermal blankets.

11

CARBON DIOXIDE
ENRICHMENT

Carbon dioxide (CO_2) is necessary for photosynthesis, the sugar-manufacturing process of plants. It is relatively easy and inexpensive to add CO_2 to the greenhouse environment. There are a number of studies that demonstrate the benefits of higher than ambient levels. According to some studies, when the natural CO_2 levels are lower than ambient, photosynthesis stops or is greatly retarded.

Under average conditions it is assumed that ambient CO_2 levels are approximately 300 parts per million (ppm). This level will vary with location. In industrial areas it run over 400 ppm, whereas in rural areas it may be less than 300 ppm.

There are three basic ways to obtain CO_2: 1) from aerobic breakdown of organic matter, 2) as pure CO_2 in solid or liquid form, and 3) from the burning of fossil fuels, especially natural or propane gas. It has been shown that one of the benefits of mulching, especially of crops such as roses, is the additional CO_2 produced as the mulch decomposes. This is not considered a reliable method, so it is not recommended but should be acknowledged as a source. Pure CO_2 is available in most locations as a liquid or solid. Dry ice is placed in a cylinder and the CO_2 is released under pressure as the dry ice sublimates (a system not used much because of the inconvenience); or liquid CO_2 kept in refrigerated tanks is released under pressure as needed. The CO_2 in both cases is regulated with pressure regulator valves and/or gas flow meters to obtain the desired amount.

The combustion products of natural gas or propane are CO_2, water, and about 100,000 Btu per 100 cubic feet of gas. Therefore, if gas is burned in the greenhouse, the level of CO_2 will be increased. The CO_2 level is controlled by regulating the amount of gas burned (Fig. 11.1).

For accurate application, the CO_2 level should be measured and the equipment regularly adjusted. The CO_2 level can be measured precisely with a Beckman IR Gas Analyzer, but this equipment costs a few thousand dollars.

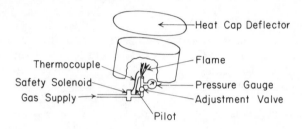

Figure 11.1 Carbon dioxide burner.

A few general assumptions will simplify the calculation of the amount of CO_2 and gas needed. It is difficult in a practical sense to be very accurate because the exfiltration rate of the CO_2 from the greenhouse is unknown. The rate of exfiltration will depend on the concentration of the CO_2, the temperature difference between the inside and the outside, the area of cracks, and so forth. For calculation and design purposes an exchange rate of once per hour will be used, the exfiltration rate will be ignored, and the 300 ppm CO_2 normally in the greenhouse will not be taken into account.

One cubic foot of gas (natural or propane) when burned will produce approximately 0.1 pound CO_2. 0.1 pound of CO_2 per 13,700 cubic feet (air weighs 1 lb/13.7 cu ft) will increase the CO_2 level 100 ppm. If we add 1 pound of CO_2 to 13,700 cubic feet of air, the level of CO_2 will be 1000 ppm.

Let us use our example 35-foot by 75-foot greenhouse with a volume of 30,187 cubic feet. (See Chapter 19 for computation of greenhouse volume). If we wish a CO_2 level of 1000 ppm then we must add 2.2 pounds of CO_2 per hour or burn 22 cubic feet of natural gas per hour. This is assuming 1 complete air change per hour. As soon as ventilation of the greenhouse starts, either by fans or natural ventilation, the air exchange rate may go from one exchange per hour to 60 times per hour, so it would be wasteful to continue with the CO_2 application. Many installations are designed to turn off the CO_2 equipment as soon as the ventilation equipment starts.

There is equipment available that will give a quick test. The equipment includes a gas sampler that draws an accurate sample of air through a glass tube filled with a chemical that changes color when in contact with CO_2. CO_2 reacts with hydrazine to form carbonic acid monohydrazide which in turn discolors a redox indicator, usually crystal violet. The more CO_2, the more chemical that changes color. The length of the color in the tube is compared to a chart that has been calibrated with known CO_2 concentrations. The accuracy is not good, but it does indicate relative ranges ($\pm$ 100 ppm) and is a useful instrument for anyone using CO_2 enrichment.

Other Sources of CO_2

Many greenhouses are heated with natural gas so it would appear that the stack gas would be a CO_2 source. This is not possible without careful controls. Stack contains CO_2 and also toxic gases such as ethylene, from incomplete combustion, and nitric oxide. The nitric oxide is formed by the high flame temperature in the boiler converting the nitrogen in the air to nitric oxide. This gas will cause phytoxicity.

12

PHOTOPERIODIC CONTROL

It was demonstrated in the early 1930s that a number of floricultural crops would respond to low levels of light during the night. The first responses recorded were differences between the flowering activity of plants grown in natural light and that of plants exposed to light at night. The phenomena was called photoperiodism, a misleading term; further investigation showed it was the dark (night) period that was critical rather than the length of the light (day) period. Today, there is a great deal of literature describing the effects of daylength on reproductivity, size, morphology, pigmentation, and so forth. Most greenhouse operators using the principle of photoperiod are interested in making plants flower or stay vegetative. Since natural daylength conditions are not constant, the daylight must be altered artificially to produce long or short days.

LONG DAY

It has been shown that providing light at night (about four hours in the middle of the night) will cause many plants to respond as though they were growing under long days. The long day phenomena is apparently most responsive to red light. It so happens the incandescent lamp is the most efficient producer of red light. It is also inexpensive and easy to install.

The life of the incandescent lamp is relatively short, approximately 1000 hours (fluorescent lamps have a 10,000 hour life). There are lamps sold as "extended life", which last longer. Also, growers have found that lamps rated for 230 volts used in 110-volt systems have a longer life, but the output is reduced and the light quality altered. This method of prolonging the life of the lamps may not produce the desired effect on the plants.

The actual amount of light needed to cause the photoperiodic response is relatively low. Some crops have been reported to respond to as low as 0.3 ft-c (30 lux). Most systems are designed for 10 ft-c (100 lux) and it is assumed the level will fall off to 5 ft-c (50 lux) on the edge of the bench. The height above the plant and the lamp wattage used to achieve 10 ft-c (100 lux) of light for various bench widths are shown in Table 12.1. The light levels should be measured, which can be done with a hand-held light meter (such as a General Electric model 214). Another way of determining the effectiveness of the light level is to watch the plants grow. If the outside rows are shorter and quicker to flower than the inside ones, the light levels are probably too low.

Table 12.1.   Lamp height and wattage for 10 ft-c ($\pm$ 5) or 108 lux ($\pm$ 50)

Bench width (ft)	Height from bench to bottom of reflector (ft)	Spacing (ft)	Lamp wattage
3	2.0	3	25
4	2.6	4	40
5	3.3	5	50
6	4.0	6	75

Most installations use two plastic-coated, No. 14- or No. 16-gauge wires strung the long way over the bench or crop to be lighted. The lamp holders shown in Figure 12.1 are screwed into the electric wires. Reflectors help direct the light to the crops. Probably the most common reflectors are aluminum pie plates. They are inexpensive and do a fair job of reflection. It is also possible to purchase lamps with built-in reflectors, but they are more costly (Fig. 12.2).

Care must be taken not to overload the electrical system. Remember that watts equals amps times volts. Most photoperiodic systems, if they are flexible, should use a 110-volt service (220-volt would be too dangerous especially under greenhouse conditions). Most circuits are fused for 20 amps, which means that each circuit will produce (20 × 110) 2200 watts; more wattage than this might blow the fuse or worse, heat the wires enough to start a fire. Therefore, 21 100-watt lamps or 35 60-watt lamps can be lit on this circuit.

Since the lighting period is at night, usually four hours long, a 24-hour time clock is installed to activate the system (Fig. 12.3).

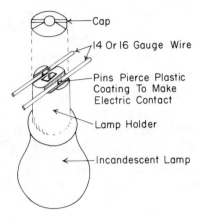

Figure 12.1 Lamp holders for incandescent lamps.

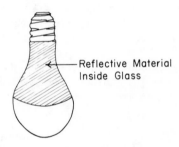

Figure 12.2 Reflective incandescent lamp.

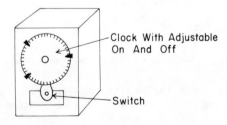

Figure 12.3 24-hour timeclock.

If the system is very large the timer is used to activate a motor starter (equipment that is capable of switching very large amperages). For example if a one-acre plot were to be lit to 10 ft-c, it would require approximately 400 100-watt lamps for an electric power of about 360 amps.

It has been shown that the light period is actually needed for short but frequent times during the photoperiod. For example ten second flashes of light every minute or three minutes of light out of every ten minutes will cause the same photoperiodic response as continuous light. This practice can save a great deal of electricity, for the lamps are on only 10 to 30% of the time. It does not shorten or in any way harm the life of the incandescent lamps; in fact it lengthens their effective lives. Flashing light requires special equipment to turn the system on and off, which does have a large initial cost and wear factor. Consequently, flashing light is not commonly used.

SHORT DAYS

There are times of the year when the natural days are too long for the desired short-day response. To cause a short day, plants are covered with an opaque black cloth. A black sateen-type cloth with a very close weave has proven satisfactory. Lengths of the black cloth are sewn into the desired sizes.

For covering a single bench, a frame is built on the bench to hold up the black cloth (Fig. 12.4). It is usually made by stringing wire between braces made of pipes.

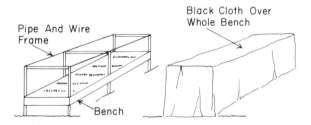

Figure 12.4 Pipe and wire frame to hold black cloth.

The cloth is pulled open the first thing in the morning and closed the last thing in the evening, by hand. Sometimes two or more benches can be covered at one time. The weight of the black cloth is the limiting factor on the size of the area that can be covered. A fifty-foot length is about as long as can be covered with one cloth.

There are commercial systems (Simtrac) that will automatically pull curtains of black cloth over a whole greenhouse (Fig. 12.5).

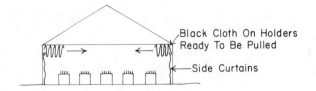

Figure 12.5 An automatic black cloth system.

This system saves a great deal of labor but it is expensive and difficult to install on older houses with pipes, posts, and other protuberances. With fuel prices soaring, there are a number of growers looking at these systems for night insulation in the winter and photoperiod control in the summer.

13

SUPPLEMENTARY GREENHOUSE LIGHTING

Low light intensity during the winter months is the limiting factor for plant growth, especially in the northern areas where the light intensities may be less than 1000 ft-c (10800 lux) in the greenhouse during the brightest period of the day. In addition, the duration of natural light is short. It has been shown that supplemental lighting in the greenhouse to increase the light level by 500 to 1000 ft-c (5400 to 10800 lux) greatly increases productivity during this important flower-marketing period.

Measuring Light

It is very difficult to get a meaningful measure of light, therefore, always interpret light readings with skepticism. The common term of measure in the floriculture industry is the foot-candle, which is unfortunate because it is the poorest of the three basic methods. The three methods are: photometric, radiometric and quantum. Photometric is used especially by lighting engineers, because this system closely parallels the human eye in sensitivity, i.e., it peaks in sensitivity in the yellow green. The terms used to measure in photometrics are foot-candle (ft-c), lux and lumens (lm) (Table 12.1).

Radiometrics take into account the whole spectrum of energy from the short (280 mm) to the long (2800 cm) wave lengths. The engineer commonly uses this measurement because it gives total energy. The terms used to measure radiometrics are watts (W), joules (J), ergs, langleys, calories and Btu (Table 12.1).

Quantum measurements are primarily for measuring the light used by plants, i.e., the visible spectrum between approximately 400 and 700 nanometers (nm). The terms used to measure quantum are einsteins (E) and moles (mol) (Table 12.1).

All sources of light including the sun are not the same, so it is very difficult to interpret the value of a light source for plant growth if it is measured in foot-candles or watts. A measurement in micromoles (μmol) actually describes the amount of usable light energy (quanta or photons) that a plant would receive for plant growth.

The greenhouse manager is more comfortable with the foot-candle because he has a feeling for how "bright", a similar problem occurs with Fahrenheit and Celsius.

Table 12.1.   Conversion factors for various radiation readings.*

Type of measurement	Instantaneous measurements	Full Sun
Photometrics	1 lux = 1 lm/m² = 0.0929 ft-c	illuminance $\approx$ 100 K lux
Radiometrics	1 W/m² = 1.443 × 10^{-3} cal/cm²/min = 1.443 × 10^{-3} langleys/min = 1.0 J/s/m² = 1000 erg/s/cm² = 0.317 Btu/ft²/hr	total irradiance $\approx$ 1000 W/m² photosynthetic irradiance $\approx$ 500 W/m² near IR
Quantum	1 μmol/s/m² = 1 μE/s/m² = 6.022 × 10^{17} photons/s/m² = 6.022 × 10^{17} quanta/s/m²	PPFD $\approx$ 2000 μmol/s/m²

Source: Radiation Measurements and Instrumentation, 1982. Publication 8208-LM, Li-Cor, Lincoln, NE.

TYPES OF LAMPS

Lamp manufacturers have made great strides in improving lamp output or efficiency. An incandescent lamp converts 8 to 10% of the electrical input into visible light, a fluorescent lamp converts about 20%, and a high intensity discharge (HID) lamp convert 30%. The use of HID lamps for supplemental lighting of greenhouses has been shown to be economical for some floricultural crops. Fluorescent lamps do not have the light output or lamp life of the HID lamp, and the installation costs are generally higher. A more thorough review of fluorescent lamps is given in Chapter 6.

There are two types of HID lamps used for supplemental greenhouse lighting: metal halide and high pressure sodium. These lamps are similar in basic construction; both have a gaseous discharge arc tube. In the metal halide lamps, the arc tube contains halides (usually iodides). The arc tube of the high pressure sodium lamp contains sodium. The discharge of electricity through the arc tube heats up and evaporates these materials, which in turn cause the radiation of light (Fig. 13.1). Each HID lamp must have a current-limiting device (ballast) to control the electrical input into the lamp.

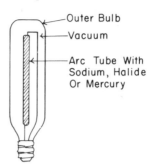

Figure 13.1 HID lamp.

The high pressure sodium lamp is the most efficient type of lamp. An incandescent lamp produces 35 lumens per input watt, whereas the high pressure sodium lamp produces over 100 lumens.

HID lamps are produced in a number of sizes but for supplemental lighting 400-watt or 1000-watt lamps are generally used. The higher the wattage, the greater the efficiency of lumen output. The HID lamps have a rated life of 20,000 to 25,000 hours. This compares to fluorescent lamps with a rated life of 10,000 hours and incandescent lamps with a rated life of 1000 hours. Lamp life is rated on the basis of 10-hour burn, or on, periods. The hours are calculated when 50% of the test series of lamps have burned out. The life of an HID lamp almost doubles if it is burned continuously. The lumen output of the HID lamps over time is also very good. After 15,000 to 20,000 hours of burning there is less than a 25% decrease in lumen output. The cost of each lamp and ballast is expensive and, therefore, a properly designed reflector should be used to insure maximum efficiency. Manufacturers have designed special reflectors for each type of HID lamp.

INSTALLATION

The installation of supplemental lighting will depend on cost-effectiveness, the desired light level, uniformity of intensity in the greenhouse, and house size and shape.

The economic analysis will be discussed in Section IV. The desired light level is to some extent also an economic question, for the higher the level the higher the cost. As a general rule of thumb, 2000 ft-c (21600 lux) of light produces good plant growth. The three months of December, January, and February will average 1000 to 1500 ft-c (10800 to 16200 lux) of natural light. Therefore, 500 to 1000 ft-c (5400 to 10800 lux) should be added, depending on the area. Seattle, Washington, and central New York have a very low light intensity, less than 1000 ft-c (10800 lux) during the 3 dark winter months whereas less cloudy areas will be brighter.

A completely uniform lighting pattern in the greenhouse is very difficult to achieve. The center section of a greenhouse can easily be uniformly lit (Fig. 13.2). The sloping roof makes hanging the lamps on the sides impractical and, therefore, the outside benches are not as well lit (Fig. 13.3).

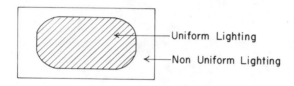

Figure 13.2 Area of uniform lighting in a greenhouse.

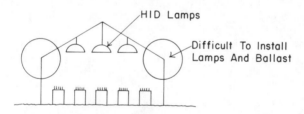

Figure 13.3 The difficult area to hang HID lights.

It is generally not recommended to try to light the outside benches of a greenhouse. The lighting manufacturers have computer programs that can be used to show proper spacing to obtain the most uniform light.

The electrical output of 400-watt HID lamps varys between 20 and 40 watts per square foot. This means a 400-watt HID lamp will light approximately 20 to 40 square feet of ground area. For example, if we wished to supplement the light in our example 35-foot by 75-foot greenhouse by 500 ft-c and concerned ourselves only with the center area, we would have 1875 sq ft of area to be lighted. Assuming that a 400-watt HID lamp would increase the light by 500 ft-c (5400 lux) and would light 40 sq ft, we would need (1875 ÷ 40) 47 lamps (Fig. 13.4). Each 400-watt lamp plus the ballast requires 475 watts to operate. To light this greenhouse (47 × 475) 22,325 watts are needed. The lamps would use 230 volts, therefore a (22,325 ÷ 230) 97-amp, 230-volt service would be required.

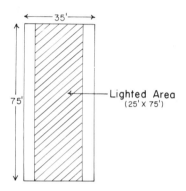

Figure 13.4   Area to be lighted in a 35' × 75' greenhouse.

HEAT ADDED

It should be noted that most of the electrical output will be converted into heat, which will be useful to the greenhouse during the winter. Supplemental lighting will reduce the heat required from the heating system. When the lights are on they use 22KW of electricity per hour and a kilowatt-hour produces 3,413 Btu per hour. Therefore, in our example greenhouse the lights will add 75,086 Btu/per hour. The average hourly heat required for the month of January for our example greenhouse was 208,116 BTU (see Chapter 7). The lights would produce about 36% of the heat requirement.

REFERENCES

ASHRAE. 1977. *Handbook and Product Directory-Fundamentals.* Amer. Soc. Heating, Refrigeration, Air-Conditioning Engineers, Inc. N.Y. NY.

Ashley, G. C. 1979. Heating greenhouses in northern climates with power plant reject heat. *HortSci.* 14(2):155-160.

Augsberger, N., H. Bohanon, and J. Calhoun. 1977. *The greenhouse climate control handbook.* Acme Engineering and Manufacturing Corp. Muskogee, OK.

Bishop, H., D. Crouch, and M. Eisentraut. 1981. The Celanese greenhouse study. Alberta Research Council, Alberta, Canada.

Burns, E., R. Pile, C. Madewell, J. Martin and J. Carter. 1976. Using power plant discharge water in controlled environment greenhouses. Tennessee Valley Authority, Muscle Shoals, AL.

Carpenter, W. and D. Bork. 1967. *Temperature patterns in greenhouse heating.* Florists' Review Reprints. Chicago, IL.

Carpenter, W., R. Mecklenburg, and W. Carlson. 1970. Greenhouse heating with horizontal discharge unit heaters. *Florists Review* 146 (3784):23-25, 54-55.

Carpenter, W. and W. Willis. 1959. Comparisons of evaporative fan-and-pad and high pressure mist systems for greenhouse cooling. *J. Amer. Soc. Hort. Sci.* 74:711-718.

Carpenter, W. and W. Willis. 1959. Comparisons of low pressure mist, atomized fog, and evaporative fan-and-pad systems for greenhouse cooling and plant response. *J. Amer. Soc. Hort. Sci.* 70:490-500.

Cleaver Brooks Co. 1970. *Boiler care handbook.* Lebanon, PA.

General Electric Co. 1971. High intensity discharge lamps. General Electric Bul. TP-109. Nela Park, OH.

Duncan, G. and J. Walker. 1973. Poly-tube heating-ventilation systems and equipment. University of Kentucky Extension AEN-7, University of Kentucky, Lexington, KY.

Friday, R. 1982. A look at compressor stations as sources of reject heat. Florists' Review. June 3, 1982.

Gray, H. 1956. Greenhouse heating and construction. Florists Publishing Co. Chicago, IL.

Gray, H. 1954. Greenhouse heating. *Cornell Bulletin 906.* Cornell University. Ithaca, NY.

Gray, H. 1948. A study of the problems of heating, ventilation, and air conditioning greenhouses. Ph.D. thesis, Cornell University, Ithaca, NY.

Hart, S. 1950. Studies of heating, cooling, and humidity control within greenhouses. Ph.D. thesis, Cornell University, Ithaca, NY.

Hurd, R. and G. Sheard. 1981. Fuel savings in greenhouses. Grower Guide No. 20. Grower Books, London.

Koths, J. 1964. Fan and tube greenhouse ventilation. *Extension Report #69.* University of Connecticut, Storrs, CT.

Koths, J. 1967. Air movement within greenhouses. Proc. Greenhouse Construction and Environmental Control Seminar, University of Massachusetts, Amherst, MA.

Leach, A. 1959. A study of greenhouse cooling. Ph.D. thesis, Cornell University, Ithaca, NY.

Maginnes, E. and G. Green. 1978. Greenhouse heating with exhaust gases. Acta Horticulturae. 115:343-349.

Ministry of Agriculture, Fisheries and Food. 1971. Boilers for nursery use. *National Agricultural Advisory Service Leaflet No. 2.* London, England.
Modine Manufacturing Co., 1976. *Engineering manual-greenhouse heating with unit heaters.* Modine Bul. 10-203. Racine, WI.

National Greenhouse Manufacture's Assoc. 1962. Standards for ventilating and cooling greenhouses. *Florists Exchange,* N.Y., NY.
Porter, L. 1937. Stimulating plant growth with artificial light. *General Electric Bul.* 1-31., Nela Park, OH.
Roberts, W. 1969. Heating and ventilating greenhouses. *Rutgers Extension Report, August 1969.* New Brunswick, NJ.
Stipanuk, D., R. Friday, R. Langhans and G. White. 1981. Waste heat greenhouse research. Cornell University, Ithaca, NY.

The Electricity Council. 1970. *Electric growing.* London, England.
U.S.D.A. 1950. Your farmhouse heating. *U.S.D.A. Misc. Publication 689:*1-24, Washington, DC.
Walker, J. and G. Duncan. 1074. Greenhouse ventilation systems. *University of Kentucky Extension Report AEN-30-* University of Kentucky, Lexington, KY.

Walker, J. and G. Duncan. 1973. Estimating greenhouse ventilation requirements. University of Kentucky Extension AEN-9, University of Kentucky, Lexington, KY.
_____. 1973. Air circulation in greenhouses. University of Kentucky Extension AEN-18, University of Kentucky, Lexington, KY.
_____. 1974. Greenhouse ventilation systems. University of Kentucky Extension AEN-30, University of Kentucky, Lexington, KY.
Wright, W. 1949. *Greenhouses, their construction and equipment.* Orange-Judd, NY.

SECTION III

Materials Handling

14

SOILS HANDLING

The amount of soil or media handled in a greenhouse depends on the type of operation. Bedding plant operations handle a large quantity of material in a relatively short period of time; pot plant operations handle a large quantity of medium on a year-round basis, cut flower operations may use a relatively small amount of medium. For all operations, soil handling is labor intensive and a great deal of material, both in volume and weight, must be moved. This process requires energy and the right equipment. Planning will eliminate some of the physical labor.

Dump trucks, front-end loaders on tractors, and fork lift trucks are designed to move great quantities of loose soil, bales of peat moss, and bags of perlite, vermiculite, and fertilizer. The storage area should be designed so that trucks and tractors can go right to the pile and load without hand labor.

SOIL MIXERS

There are a number of soil mixers on the market. The most successful is a modified cement mixer. This equipment can handle the weight of the soil and water and comes in a variety of sizes, holding up to 10 or more cubic yards of material. Used mixers are widely available because the cement mixing business is constantly upgrading to new and larger mixers.

The mixers are purchased either on or off the truck. The advantages of each system must be weighed for the particular operation. A fixed mixer has the advantage of being permanent for placement of conveyors, water, electricity and shelter, whereas the portable mixer mounted on a truck can go close to the area that needs the mix.

The various media ingredients such as peat moss and vermiculite are put in the mixer as well as water to reduce the dust, lime, and superphosphate and slow release fertilizers. If peat moss is used a surfactant is generally added to improve the wetting of the peat during the mixing operation.

Two common dangers of the mixing operation are overmixing and over wetting. Overmixing causes the ingredients to break down, i.e. become too fine, and overwetting causes the material to form into balls. Experience with a particular mix will determine the right mixing time and the right amount of water.

When unloading the mixer the medium should go directly onto a truck or conveyor to avoid excessive handling. The medium can be put into bins or hoppers that in turn can feed into pot- or flat-filling equipment.

POT AND FLAT FILLERS

Pot or flat fillers are designed to place a measured amount of medium into a container. The container is then conveyed away to be planted and placed in the greenhouse. Figure 14.1 shows a schematic of a complete mixing operation.

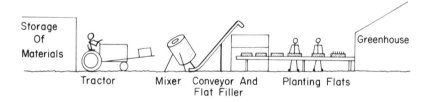

Figure 14.1 Schematic of a mixing operation.

INGREDIENTS

The most common materials used in mixes are soil, sand, wood shavings, peat moss, perlite, and vermiculite.

Soil is a complex material, and can vary from a muck to a sand. The disadvantages of soil are: the source may not be consistent from year to year; the soil must be sterilized; it may contain toxic materials (such as the weed killer Atrozene, commonly used for controlling weeds in corn fields); and it is heavy (50 lbs per cubic foot). The advantages are that the soil will be inexpensive if you own a large tract of land, and that it usually contains the minor elements. More and more growers, especially pot plant and bedding plant growers who use large quantities of medium are finding it hard to obtain good soil.

Sand is a relatively inert material that neither contains nor holds nutrients. If sand is added to a mix to improve aeration, more than 50% by volume must be added to obtain results. Sand is commonly used to add weight in artificial mixes (i.e. mixes that contain little or no soil). The source of the sand should be known or else the sand will have to be sterilized to avoid contamination with soil pathogens.

In some areas of the country wood shavings, chips, and sawdust are plentiful and inexpensive. The most noted problem with wood shavings is a lack of nitrogen. Microorganisms in the soil remove nitrogen from the soil in the breakdown process, thereby depriving the plants of the nitrogen. When wood shavings are used, an extra supply of nitrogen must be added. Experience has shown that an addition of nitrogen at the rate of 1 to 2% of the weight of the wood shavings will generally compensate. The type of wood, i.e. whether it decays slowly or rapidly, indicates whether 1 or 2% of nitrogen should be used. For example oak, hickory, poplar, and other hard woods decay faster than red wood, cypress, fir, and other soft woods. Wood products from walnut or cedar should be avoided as they have been reported to cause phytotoxicity.

Peat moss is generally packed in bales (6 to 7½ cubic feet) that fluff up to a volume of 9 to 17 cubic feet. When peat moss is dry it is difficult to wet and a surfactant such as Aqua-gro or Triton B-1956 should be added at the rate of 3 fl. oz per cu yd.

There are three kinds of peat moss, sphagnum, sedge, and reed. The sphagnum type is most desirable because it lasts longest. Peat moss comes from Canada, Germany, Ireland, Norway, and other countries. Because each lot may be coming from a different bog or different layers in a bog, a broad statement is difficult to make about their merits. Price is probably the biggest factor in selecting a source.

Perlite is a volcanic rock that has been expanded by heating to 1800°F. It is light in weight (6 to 9 lbs/cu ft) and sterile, and is produced in many sizes. Be sure to use the agricultural grade of perlite, not the contruction grade, which has different properties.

Vermiculite is a micaceous material that has been expanded by heating to 1400°F. It weighs 6 to 8 lbs/cu ft and is sterile. The material does contain nutrients such as potassium and magnesium. It also has a high cation exchange capacity, unlike perlite, which has almost no cation exchange capacity. The cation exchange capacity means its ability to hold such cations as calcium, potassium, and magnesium in the medium rather than letting them drain away.

Perlite and or vermiculite usually make up about 50% of most artificial mixes. Peatmoss makes up the other 50%.

15

SOIL PASTURIZATION

Most floricultural crops are expensive to grow because of the intensive cultural conditions, and may sell for a high price compared to other horticultural products. Crop losses, therefore, are expensive. Growers can profit by taking extra precautions to avoid losses. Soil-borne diseases, nematodes, and weeds, the major causes of crop losses, can be greatly reduced by soil pasturization. Soil is usually pasturized with steam, aerated steam, or chemicals.

STEAM

Steaming is the preferred method of pasturization because steamed soil can be used as soon as it cools, whereas chemically treated soil has a long treatment and aeration period, lasting up to three weeks. Steaming is nonselective in that it kills almost everything, whereas chemicals may be limited in what they kill.

Steam kills by heating the soil to the thermal death point of the pathogen. The thermal death point is probably the protein coagulation or enzyme inactivation temperatures of the pathogen.

Various organisms in the soil are killed at different temperatures (Fig. 15.1). The exact thermal death point of any particular soil pathogen is dependent on its stage of development and state of growth. Moisture and temperature are among the primary factors that determine the state of growth. It will be easier to kill a pathogen in a warm moist soil, where it is in an active state of growth, than in a cold, dry soil. Experience has shown that 180°F (80°C) for 30 minutes will kill most of the common pathogens, and other soil organisms. The more resistant pathogens are killed with longer heating periods and higher temperatures.

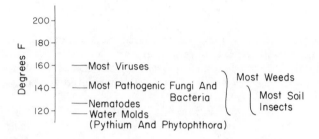

Figure 15.1 The thermal death points for various soil pathogens.

In Chapter 7 we discussed the advantages of a steam heating system over one using hot water. These advantages are even more important in soil pasturization. To raise one pound oı water from 50°F (10°C) to 212°F (100°C), or just to the boiling point, requires 162 Btu. To vaporize the pound of water (convert it to steam) requires 972 Btu, which will be released as the water cools back to 50°F (10°C). The important consideration in soil pasturization is the condensation point, for it is at that point that 972 Btu per pound of water is released. As soil is being steamed there is a condensation band on one side of which the temperature is 212°F (100°C) with steam and on the other side the temperature is the original soil temperature (Fig. 15.2). This condensation band moves from the source of steam outward. The speed with which the condensation band moves depends on a number of factors including, moistness and temperature of the soil, quality of the steam, and an exit for the air in the soil.

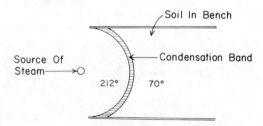

Figure 15.2 Soil mass showing the condensation band.

Water has a heat capacity of 1, i.e. one Btu will raise one pound of water 1°F, whereas soil particles have a heat capacity of approximately 0.2 or 20% that of water. Therefore, the wetter the soil the more Btu required to raise it to the required 180°F (80°C). This fact would appear to indicate that the soil should be dry before steaming, but this is not true. Dry soils cause many of the soil pathogens to enter into more resistant forms, which are more difficult to kill. Weed seeds should be in an active state of growth, preferably germination, to get the best kill. A soil moist enough to plant has the right moisture content.

A cold soil will require more Btu to heat and, therefore, slow down the steaming process. Frozen soils are very difficult and slow to steam. Remember that a large amount of heat is required to change water from solid to liquid form.

A boiler capacity that is too small for the area to be steamed will greatly prolong the operation and have all kinds of inefficiencies. A boiler capacity that is too large will cause blowouts, i.e. the steam will not be contained behind the condensation band. A blowout area will allow steam to take a path of least resistance, open a channel to the air and be very ineffective (Fig. 15.3).

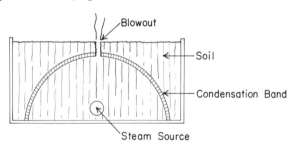

Figure 15.3 Soil steaming operation showing a blowout area.

If the steam source is above the soil, some provision must be made to allow the air contained in the soil pores to escape. If the air cannot exit or is slowed, the condensation band will not move rapidly and the steaming process will be greatly slowed. If it is stopped as shown in Figure 15.4 the rest of the soil will be heated by hot water from the condensation of the steam. If there were an exit for the air in the bottom of the bench, the condensation band would continue to the bottom (Fig. 15.5).

Computation of Steam Requirement

The objective of steam pasturization is to heat a unit of soil to 212°F (100° C). For calculation purposes we assume a temperature increase of

150°F (80°C), i.e. the starting soil temperature would be 62°F (17°C). A cubic foot of soil weighs about 50 pounds and if the soil contains 15% moisture there are 43.5 pounds of soil and 7.5 pounds of water. To raise the temperature of water requires 1 Btu/lb/°F: in this case 7.5 × 150 × 1 = 1125 Btu. To raise the soil temperature requires 0.2 Btu/lb/°F, or 43.5 × 150 × 0.2 = 1305 Btu. To raise both requires 1125 + 1305 = 2430 Btu.

A pound of steam contains 972 Btu plus the difference between the soil temperature and 212 (212 − 180 = 32) for a total of (972 + 32) 1004 Btu. Therefore, (2430 ÷ 1004) 2.4 pounds of steam will be required to steam 1 cubic foot of soil.

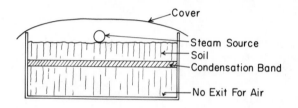

Figure 15.4   Bench of soil without an exit for the soil air.

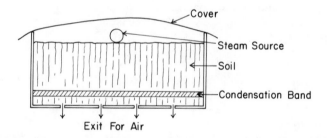

Figure 15.5   Bench with exits for the soil air.

Boiler Capacity and Efficiency

Boilers are rated in horsepower or Btu/hr or pounds of steam per hour. Table 15.1 shows the conversion of various sized boilers.

Unfortunately the efficiency of boilers and the piping system in the steaming process is poor. Experience has shown for calculation purposes an efficiency of 50% should be used. We note from the above example that 2.4 lb of steam would be required to steam one cubic foot of soil. Therefore, a general rule of thumb would be 5 pounds of steam per cubic foot of soil.

In our example greenhouse the benches were 3 feet wide, 65 feet long and 6 inches deep, therefore, there are (3 × 65 × .5) 97.5 cubic feet of soil in a bench. To pasturize the soil in that bench will require (5 × 97.5) 487.5 lb of steam.

Table 15.1   Horsepower, Btu output per hour, and pounds of steam per hour of various sized boilers.

Horsepower	Btu output/hr	pounds of steam/hr
½	16,737	17.3
1	33,475	34.5
5	167,375	86.3
10	334,750	345.0
50	1,673,750	862.5
100	3,347,500	3450.0

A steaming bin contains 25 bushels of soil (1 bu = 1.25 cu ft). Therefore, there are 31.25 cubic feet of soil to be pasturized. It will require (5 × 31.25) 156.25 lb of steam for the soil in the bin.

Volume of Steam

The amount of steam needed can be calculated, but the speed of delivery or volume is more difficult to measure. It is learned by experience. The volume should just be great enough to avoid blowouts, that is, the condensation band should be narrow, but not broken. This point is determined by the soil moisture, soil type, compaction, and soil temperature.

Amount of Soil to be Steamed

The volume of medium to be steamed at one time will depend on the size of the boiler and the efficiency of the system. If for example, steaming a certain volume of medium with an existing boiler required 1 hour to reach 180°F (80°C), 30 minutes to hold 180°F (80°C), and another hour to cool the equipment before it could be handled, the whole procedure would take 2.5 hours. Perhaps a slightly larger volume of medium could have been sterilized. The time to raise the soil temperature to 180°F (80°C), would have been longer, but if the efficiency of an 8-hour working day is considered, two larger volumes could be steamed per day. These types of considerations should be studied for each operation.

It is unwise to steam a volume of medium that is too large for the boiler capacity. A general rule of thumb is 2 to 3 hours to raise the medium to 180°F (80°C). A boiler with a capacity of 500 pounds of steam per hour should not steam more than 300 cubic feet of medium at one time.

Types of Steam Pasturization Systems

The pot plant or bedding plant grower is primarily interested in bulk pasturization. There are a number of types, mostly custom made for each operation. The mobile type includes carts, trailers, or truck bodies that have been constructed to hold the medium while it is being steamed, and to move the medium to where it is needed after pasturization. For stationary steaming, the medium is brought to these containers, pasturized, unloaded, and carted to where it is needed.

The methods of applying the steam are usually the same for either mobile or stationary steaming. The steam is usually applied through pipes buried in the soil or via a soil bin with a false bottom and holes in the bottom. The buried pipes should be 9 inches apart and 6 inches from the walls. The ⅛-inch steam outlet holes should be drilled 9 inches apart in the pipe (Fig. 15.6). The soil steaming bin with a false bottom has ⅛-inch holes every 4 inches (Fig. 15.7).

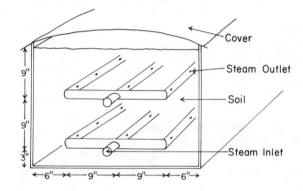

Figure 15.6   Soil steam bin with pipes buried in the soil.

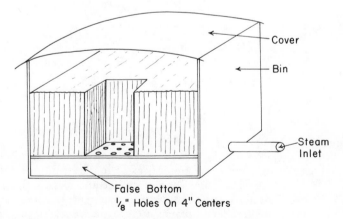

Figure 15.7   Soil steaming bin with a false bottom.

Either system works well. The buried pipe system is probably the cheapest to construct, but unloading the bin is more difficult because the pipes catch the soil. In both of these systems blowouts can be a problem and care must be taken not to apply too large a volume of steam. Once a blowout occurs the only way to prevent the steam from being lost is to dump and reload the bin. Experience is the best teacher in regulation of the volume of steam for each particular design.

Benches

Benches may be steamed in three different ways: from above, from below, or with movable steaming equipment. Each has advantages and disadvantages and the best system will depend on the particular operation.

The common system for steaming from above is called the Thomas method. A plastic or canvas cover is placed over the bench and the steam is injected under the cover. The steam inflates the cover, which serves as a distribution plenum over the whole bench (Fig. 15.8). The steam penetrates downward into the soil. Sometimes a porous pipe is laid on top of the soil under the canvas to speed up the distribution of steam from one end to the other. The advantages are that it is easy to install and requires very little special equipment. The disadvantage is that steam moves more rapidly upward than downward. The soil air must be pushed down by the steam and there must be an exit. A soil depth of about 8 inches is the maximum that can be effectively pasturized, and outside soil beds without titles or other methods of drainage to allow the soil air to escape cannot be steamed with this method.

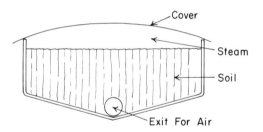

Figure 15.8 Thomas method of steam pasturization.

The original method of steaming was to inject steam into the drain tiles laid 12 inches or so below the soil surface and place a canvas cover over the bed. The advantages are that the system is permanent and easy to use, and no special equipment except the cover is needed. The disadvantage is the high initial expense for the tiles and installation, although they are usually necessary for the soil drainage (Fig. 15.9).

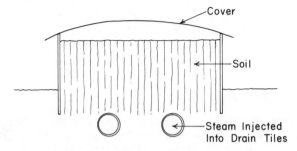

Figure 15.9   Drain tile steam pasturization system.

To speed up the steam pasturization process movable steam applicators have been designed. The first was the steam rake, which had some limitations. This was followed by the steam blade. They were both pulled through the soil either by a winch or by a self-propelled unit which included the boiler to produce the steam (Fig. 15.10).

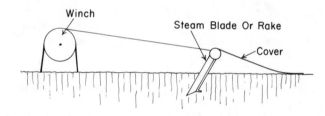

Figure 15.10   The winch and steam blade.

The steam rake got its name because it is shaped like a large rake. The tongs are about 11 inches apart, 12 inches long and, shaped like chisels. The header distributes the steam to small pipes that run down the back of the tongs and release the steam at the bottom (Fig. 15.11). The problem with the steam rake is the distance between the tongs. The area between the tongs for some soils cannot be properly heated at the 11-inch spacing. If the tongs were spaced any closer there was danger of soil build up between them and put too much load on the winch. If the steam volume were increased, blowouts would occur into the grooves cut by the tongs. In some soils, especially sandy soils, the steam rake worked very well.

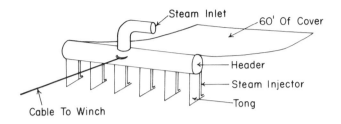

Figure 15.11   The steam rake.

To overcome the problem of the rake, the steam blade was designed. It consists of a wedge-shaped blade pulled through the soil. The steam was uniformly injected into the soil through a slit at the back end of the wedge. The problem of soil buildup was greatly reduced with this design (Fig. 15.12).

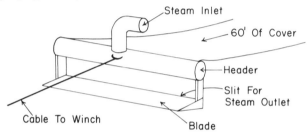

Figure 15.12   The steam blade.

The steam blade moves through the soil at the rate of approximately 1 foot per minute, depending on the steam volume, soil type, moisture content, and soil temperature. The plastic or canvas cover dragging behind the steam blade reduces the heat loss and keeps the soil at the desired temperature for 30 minutes. If the equipment is moving at the rate of 1 foot per minute, then at least a 30-foot cover will be needed.

AERATED STEAM

It was stated previously that 180° F (80°C) for 30 minutes was desired for the best soil pasturization. However, this high a temperature kills not only the pathogens, but desirable microflora as well. Steaming at a lower temperature, 140° to 160°F (60° to 70°C), is preferable. This will kill most of the soil pathogens but will not kill many of the desirable soil microflora such as the nitrifying bacteria or those that reduce the spread of plant pathogens that may, after pasturization, be inoculated into the sterile soil. Steam pasturization at temperatures of 140° to 160°F (60° to 70°C) can be accomplished by using aerated steam.

Aerated steam also has some other, more tangible, advantages such as speeding the pasturization process, cooling the medium quickly after the allotted time of pasturization, and preventing oversteaming.

When air is pumped into steam the temperature of the steam is reduced from 212°F (100°C) to some lower temperature without condensation of the steam. The exact temperature of the aerated steam is dependent on the air temperature, relative humidity, and temperature of the saturated steam. Table 15.2 gives the temperature of aerated steam when mixed with 70°F (21°C) air at 50% RH and saturated steam of 230°F (110°C). These are the basic figures used in calculations with aerated steam.

Table 15.2.   The steam-air and air-stream ratios and Btu/cu ft of various temperatures of aerated steam, in a mixture of 70°F (21°C), 50% RH air, and 230°F (110°C) saturated steam.

Aerated steam temp in °F (°C)	Steam-air ratio lb/cu ft	Air-steam ratio cu ft/lb	Btu/cu ft
140 (60)	.01124	89.0	12.9
150 (65)	.01574	63.5	18.1
160 (70)	.0225	44.5	25.7
170 (75)	.0318	31.4	37.3
180 (80)	.0487	20.5	56.8
190 (85)	.0850	11.8	94.9

Calculation for Aerated Steam

For these calculations we are interested in determining the number of pounds of steam (boiler size), the volume of air (blower size), and the duration of steaming. In the following example we will set 30 minutes as the time required to heat a unit of soil.

Using an aerated steam system, we want to raise the temperature of 1 cu yd of medium to 160°F. The medium weighs 50 lbs/cu ft and has a moisture content of 15%. Therefore, a cubic yard of this medium weighs (50 × 27) 1350 lb. There are (1350 × .15) 202.5 lbs of water in this cubic yard. To heat the yard of medium from 60° to 160°F we will need: for the medium (1147.5 × .2 × 100) 22,950 Btu and for the water (202.5 × 1 × 100) 20,250 Btu, for a total of 43,200 Btu to heat one cubic yard of this medium to 160°F (70°C). To accomplish this in 30 minutes the equipment should have an output of (43,200 ÷ 30) 1440 Btu/minute and aerated steam flow of 1440 ÷ 25.7) 56 cfm. Most systems assume 50% efficiency because of the heat losses; therefore, the aerated steam flow rate should be 112 cfm. Aerated steam at 160°F (70°C) contains .0225 lbs of steam per cubic foot (from Table 15.2); therefore in the above example (.0225 × 112) 2.52 lbs of steam per minute or 75.6 lbs. of steam for 30 minutes would be needed. If a conventional steaming operation had been used it would have required (5 × 27) 135 lbs of steam.

Equipment

The basic equipment for aerated steaming includes a blower and a steam valve. The steam is injected into the air flow which mixes the steam and air. In actual practice the temperature of the aerated steam is determined by reading a thermometer in the outlet and adjusting the flow of steam into the air flow (Fig. 15.13).

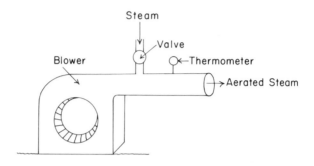

Figure 15.13   Aerated steamer with thermometer used to adjust the temperature of the aerated steam.

Control can also be obtained by varying the speed of the blower, but this is usually not as practical and would be more costly. The blower or fan has to force the air-steam mixture through the soil; therefore, it has to produce the cfm required at a certain amount of pressure. It has been shown by experience that 6 inches of static pressure is a good compromise for all types of soil mixtures. Therefore, the blower in the example above should produce 112 cfm at 6 inches static pressure.

Application Equipment

Aerated steam can be used with almost any conventional steam application equipment. There is more air pressure, which makes blowouts common if the aerated steam is applied from below. To avoid blowouts the aerated steam should be applied from above. There must be exits for the soil air to escape (Fig. 15.4).

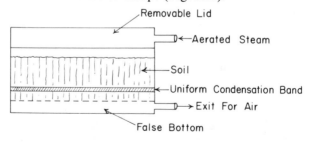

Figure 15.14   Cutaway of the treated aerated steam chamber.

For aerated steaming of benches the principle is the same. It is best to apply the aerated steam from the top, and to be sure there is adequate exit for the soil air.

Cooling

One of the advantages of an aerated steam system is speed. The time to get the medium to the desired temperature is usually quicker and as soon as the required 30 minutes of heating is completed, the steam is turned off and the blower is allowed to run. The medium cools rapidly, and it can usually be used within one hour. A conventional steaming system needs to cool overnight for the medium to reach a manageable temperature.

CHEMICAL STERILIZATION

Steam is the standard and best method to use for soil pasturization. However, there are many situations, such as pasturization of fields or other large areas, where steam cannot be used because a boiler to produce enough steam would be too costly. There are a number of chemicals, with various characteristics, uses, and formulations, that can be successfully used. All chemical sterilants are poisonous and special precautions should be taken. The time from application to when the soil can be used is often measured in weeks. The soil temperature should be above 50°F (10°C) for successful fumigation. Some floricultural crops are unable to grow in chemically treated soils.

There are five major chemicals used as soil sterilants: chloropicrin, methyl bromide, ethylene dibromide, dichloropropene-propane, and liquid carbonate.

Chloropicrin, or tear gas, is a very effective material that kills fungi, nematodes, insects, and weeds. It is packaged as a liquid, but it vaporizes rapidly and can cause discomfort to the operator unless he wears a gasmask. It is commonly applied with a hand applicator. Two to 2.5 cc of the chemical are injected on 1-foot centers. The area is immediately watered or covered with a gasproof material to keep the gas in the soil. The cover should be kept on for twenty-four hours and the soil aerated for 10 to 21 days, depending on the type and temperature of the soil. There should be no traces of chloropicrin smell in the medium before planting.

Methyl bromide is a very effective fumigant that kills all soil pathogens including weeds. It is manufactured in gas and liquid form. The gas form is packaged in small cans, 1 to 1½ lbs, and cylinders of 30 lbs. The cylinder is for tractor application and the small cans for hand applications. A special adaptor punctures the small can and releases the gas through a piece of tubing. The end of the tubing is place under a plastic sheet covering the soil. Four pounds of methyl bromide will sterilize 50 cubic feet of soil (Fig. 15.15).

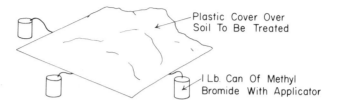

Figure 15.15   Fumigating soil with methyl bromide.

To apply methyl bromide from the larger cylinders special applicators are attached to tractors. The methyl bromide is carefully metered out according to the speed of the tractor. The methyl bromide is released through tongs that penetrate 8 to 10 inches into the soil. Special equipment on the back of the tractor covers the treated area with sheets of polyethylene. The plastic is rolled out and blades along the edge of the plastic throw up soil to anchor the polyethylene (Fig. 15.16). The plastic remains in place for a few weeks.

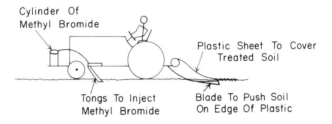

Figure 15.16   Tractor-drawn equipment for injecting methyl bromide and laying a plastic cover.

The liquid methyl bromide is made by mixing methyl bromide with a petroleum solvent. The liquid form can be applied with a tractor for large areas, or with a hand injector. The procedures for hand application are the same as those described for chloropicrin.

Ethylene dibromide and dichloropropene-propane kill only nematodes and insects. They are liquids applied with a hand injector or a tractor. Two to three weeks are needed for aeration before planting.

Liquid carbamate kills fungi, nematodes, and weeds. It can be applied with a watering can or can be proportioned into the irrigation system. A two- to three-week waiting period is needed before planting.

16
CONTAINERS

Containers are used for many of the stages of plant growth, from seeding to selling. Some crops are grown in just one container for their whole lifes and others are transplanted into larger and larger containers before going to their final location or sale. Because each stage and each crop has special needs, there are many types and shapes of containers. Growing crops in containers enable the greenhouse operator to move plants to different locations, to make optimum use of greenhouse space, and to transport the plants to the market.

TYPES OF CONTAINERS

Containers are made of a wide variety of materials including clay, plastic, styrofoam, wood fiber, wood, peat moss, and soil. Each has advantages and disadvantages.

Clay

Probably the first container used to grow plants was made of baked clay. It is still very popular and most people would agree it is the standard against which other containers are measured. The pot has a shoulder for strength, tapered sides which allow pots to be nested and one hole in the center bottom for drainage. Clay pots range in diameters from 1 inch to 8 inches. Larger sizes are expensive and usually must be specially ordered.

Clay pots can be reused after they have been washed and steam sterilized, but the cost of labor for this practice makes it uneconomical.

Clay pots are much heavier than pots made of other materials. A worker can hardly carry 100 four-inch clay pots, whereas the same number of four-inch pots made of the other materials can be carried easily. If stability is a consideration the weight of the pot may be an advantage. A lightweight medium used in conjunction with a lightweight pot can easily be blow or tipped over.

Clay pots are porous and some soil moisture is lost through the side of the pots. This has no real effect on plant growth, but more water is lost from a clay pot than from a plastic pot, where evaporation from the side does not occur.

Plastic

Polyethylene is the plastic used in plastic pots. Since polyethylene is sold by weight, the amount of plastic in the pot generally determines the cost and to some extent the quality. There are two thicknesses of plastic pots. Thin, pliable pots, used to grow plants that are to be transplanted, are frequently used in the nursery industry. Thick, rigid pots are generally used for finished plants that will be kept in the container after sale. In addition to having the advantage of light weight, plastic containers can be manufactured with multiple holes in the bottom for better drainage and are available in many colors and shapes.

Plastic pots cannot be steam sterilized; a chemical drench such as chlorox must be used. A major disadvantage is that they are nonbiodegradable. Pots larger than 4 inches must be thicker to prevent breaking during handling and are made from petroleum, which increase the cost.

Styrofoam

Styrofoam pots are manufactured in round or square forms and can be made in any color. The pots are light in weight and cannot be sterilized, and the large sizes break easily when not handled properly.

Wood Fiber and Wood

Wood fiber is molded and bound together to form either round or square pots of various sizes. The fibers can be stained to obtain any color desired. They have all the advantages and disadvantages of the plastics.

Wood, especially redwood, is used to make one-foot-diameter or larger tubs to hold large plants. They are decorative and are used to grow plants in offices and homes. The large wooden tubs are expensive and are commonly shipped knocked down to reduce the shipping cost, the grower must assemble them.

Peat Moss

Peat moss mixed with wood fiber and a binder is formed into various shapes of containers. The pots are lightweight and inexpensive. Containers of this material are useful for plants that require transplanting since the pot can be planted in the soil. Water is absorbed through the walls, roots can penetrate out, and the pot is biodegradable. The thickness of the walls determines the life of the pot; thin-walled pots last one to two months, thick-walled pots may last three months or more.

Soil

Soil blocks are formed by special machines that compact a soil mixture into a block. They are used mostly for internal use rather than for sale. The nursery industry and tomato growers have been the biggest users of this product and it is not commonly found in the florist industry.

SHAPES AND SIZES

The most common shape is the round, classic clay pot. Pots are defined by the measurement of the inside diameter across the top. A 4-inch pot, for instance, has a 4-inch diameter. Three basic depths of pots made are: standard (full), azalea (3/4), or bulb pan (1/2) (Fig. 16.1). Some areas of the country may use different terminology. Pots are also made square when manufactured from materials other than clay. These are measured by the inside width of the top edge of the pot.

Standard

Azalea (3/4)

Bulb Pan (1/2)

Figure 16.1 Three depths of pots.

The number of pots of various sizes, that can be filled with one cubic foot of soil is given in Table 16.1. This information is useful for determining the quality of soil to mix. For example, if a production program called for 100 6-inch pots of chrysanthemums per week then (100 ÷ 15) 6.6 cubic feet of mix would be needed each week or (6.6 × 52 = 343 cu ft) 12.7 cubic yards per year.

Table 16.1.   Number of pots filled per cubic foot of soil.

Pot size: standard	No. of pots per cu ft	Pot size: azalea (¾)	No. of pots per cu ft	Pot size: Bulb pan (½)	No. of pots per cu ft
2¼-inch	260	4-inch	60	5-inch	40
3-inch	110	5-inch	29	6-inch	32
4-inch	45	6-inch	16	7-inch	14
5-inch	26				
6-inch	15				
7-inch	9				
8-inch	6				

SPECIALIZED CONTAINERS

Packs

The bedding plant industry has created a great variety of containers. Important considerations of the bedding plant grower include growing, handling, and marketing. Many bedding plants are sold with 6 to 12 plants in a container. Not too many years ago the bedding plants were grown in large wooden flats and either the whole flat was sold or the 12 plants were dug out and wrapped in newspaper. Wooden grape baskets began to replace the flats because they were smaller units and easier to sell. Plastics and peat molds, which give the grower a large choice of shapes and sizes, are now on the market.

The pack is a small unit that holds 8 to 12 plants and is sold with the plants. These containers are available in a number of lengths and widths as well as depths. Packs (usually four) fit into a master flat, which simplifies handling (Fig. 16.2). Packs can be further divided into individual cells (Fig. 16.3). The possible variations on this theme are numerous and many different styles are available.

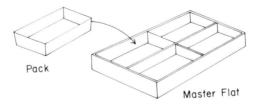

Pack

Master Flat

Figure 16.2   Market pack with master flat.

Hanging Baskets

The hanging basket has created another set of criteria for container design. The container must be decorative because the customer will hang it in a prominent position. It must have some device for hanging and usually has a saucer underneath to reduce the water drip. The basic form is shown in Figure 16.4.

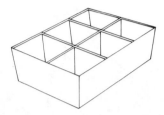

Figure 16.3   Market pack divided into individual cells.

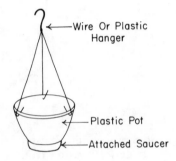

Figure 16.4   Hanging basket container.

Seed Plugs

Plugs have started some major changes in the bedding plant industry. A molded polyethylene sheet, 11 × 22 inches, with two sizes of indentations, 3/8 × 3/8 inches (648 plugs) or 9/16 × 1 inch deep (400 plugs) are filled with a peat-lite type media. Seeders, designed for each size sheet, automatically drop a seed in each plug. The seeders can dispense seed up to a rate of 60,000 seeds per hour. Special care is required during germination and early growth.

The biggest attribute is the ease of transplanting, which saves labor, and transplanting growth is very rapid. Salable plants can be achieved in less than four weeks with many cultivars. Transplanting equipment is being developed to speed up and replace the most labor-intensive part of the bedding plant culture. Plugs have allowed this process to occur.

17

FERTILIZING

The importance of a proper fertilization program cannot be over-emphasized. Over-or underfertilization reduces quality and quantity of the produce and causes a monetary loss. A well-managed operation should have a fertilization system designed to avoid problems. There is some excellent equipment on the market that greatly simplifies the fertilization system. The type of fertilizer dry, liquid, or slow release, dictates the mode of application.

The term dry refers to the insolubility of the fertilizer. Lime, including limestone, hydrated lime, and superphosphate are applied dry, usually when the soil is being prepared. In bulk soil preparation they are added to the mixer to get uniform distribution. In bed preparation they are broadcast evenly on the surface and rototilled or raked in to improve distribution.

Uniform distribution of dry fertilizers to growing plants is difficult. for example, visualize distributing one pound of fertilizer over 100 sq ft, or distributing one ounce to 6.25 sq ft. To improve distribution of a dry fertilizer, sand is mixed with the fertilizer, increasing the bulk to avoid an overdose. But of course, it is extra work to carry around the added weight.

A slow release fertilizer is a dry form of fertilizer that releases the plant nutrients over time. Slow release fertilizers are used both in the initial mixing of the media and later as a top dressing. There are three basic types available: microflora breakdown, slow solubility, and osmotic.

The best example of a slow release fertilizer controlled by the soil microflora breakdown is urea formaldehyde. This material is made up of chains of formaldehyde of various length attached to urea. The soil microflora consume the formaldehyde. The urea is not released until the formaldehyde is gone, because the chains of formaldehyde are different lengths, the urea is released gradually.

A good example of a slow solubility type of slow release fertilizer is Magamp, a nearly insoluble combination of magnesium ammonium phosphate and magnesium potassium phosphate. These fertilizer salts slowly dissolve in the soil solution and release nitrogen, phosphorus, and potassium for plant growth.

A good example of an osmotic slow release fertilizer in the soil solution is Osmocote, fertilizer granules coated with a plastic film. The plastic coat is porous to water and the dissolved fertilizer salts, by osmosis with the water in the soil, are slowly released into the soil solution.

Liquid fertilizer is the most common type used in floriculture. The fertilizer is soluble in water and is distributed through the irrigation system. This method insures uniform distribution of the fertilizer and quick availability to the plant roots.

FERTILIZERS

Fertilizers are chemical salts composed of one or more of the essential elements for plant growth. The salts must be soluble (i.e. dissolve in water), and must dissociate readily because most elements are absorbed by the plant roots in the dissociated form i.e. NO_3 rather than $CaNO_3$. The salts must not be greatly influenced by temperature or pH, and they must be inexpensive.

There are relatively few salts used as fertilizers. Table 17.1 lists the common fertilizer salts, percentage of essential elements, and solubility. The measure of solubility is the number of ounces that will dissolve in one gallon of water.

The percentage of the essential element in a fertilizer salt is used to determine the amount of fertilizer to apply to a given area and to compare the cost of different fertilizers. For example, if ammonium sulfate and ammonium nitrate both cost $10 per 100 pounds, then ammonium nitrate would be the better buy because there would be (33.6 – 20) 13.5 pounds more nitrogen per 100-pound bag. The cost per pound of nitrogen would be $.50 when buying ammonium sulfate and $.30 when buying ammonium nitrate.

Table 17.1 gives the solubility of the various fertilizer salts. Solubility of a salt means, for example, that 1163 oz or 72.6 lbs of ammonium nitrate could be dissolved in one gallon of water at 212° F, whereas, at the same water temperature only 138 oz or 8.6 lbs of ammonium sulfate could be dissolved.

Table 17.1.   Solubility of common fertilizer salts.

	Percentage of Essential element	Solubility (oz/gal)	
		Cold water	Hot water
Nitrogen Source			
Amonium sulfate (NH$_4$SO$_4$)	20	94	138
Ammonium nitrate (NH$_4$NO$_3$)	33.5	158	1163
Calcium nitrate (CaNO$_3$)	15.5	355	881
Potassium nitrate (KNO$_3$)	12–14	18	330
Urea	42–46	159	
Diammonium phosphate ((NH$_4$)$_2$PO$_4$)	21	57	142
Phophorus Source			
Superphosphate	18–20	insol	
Treble superphosphate	45	insol	
Diammonium phosphate ((NH$_4$)$_2$PO$_4$)	54	57	142
Potassium Source			
Potassium chloride (KCl)	50–60	37	75
Potassium nitrate (KNO$_3$)	44–46	18	330

Grades of Fertilizers

Fertilizer salts are manufactured in different grades. The fertilizer grade is the crudest and may contain impurities, whereas, the technical grade contains very few impurities. A good example of extremes is calcium nitrate, a very popular fertilizer. The fertilizer grade of calcium nitrate is obtained as a by-product of a manufacturing process and is relatively inexpensive, but contains some impurities, especially phosphorus. Calcium nitrate is a hygroscopic salt, and to reduce water absorption the fertilizer is coated with a waxlike material. Most of the fertilizer grade of calcium nitrate is used by farmers for outside crops and is applied in the dry form. When this calcium nitrate is used as a water soluble fertilizer a number of problems occur, including precipitation and a waxy scum on the surface of the water. The problem can be avoided by using technical grade calcium nitrate, but the cost is about four times greater.

The quality of the fertilizer salt used in a liquid fertilizer program must be carefully inspected and tested. There are a number of premixed fertilizers on the market for liquid fertilizer programs. They sometimes seem expensive, but the fertilizers will dissolve and not cause precipitation, which means they contain the more costly fertilizer salts.

FERTILIZER PROPORTIONER EQUIPMENT

Distribution of the dry fertilizer salts is difficult. Use of the liquid form can simplify the proceedings. The first systems included large tanks (1000 gallons or more) in which the fertilizer salts were mixed and that solution pumped via the irrigation lines to the greenhouse. The system works well but has little flexibility and is expensive. If we assume at each irrigation one quart of water was applied per sq ft, then the 1000 gallon tank would only cover 4000 sq ft of bench area. A range of one acre in size would need a 10,000-gallon tank just to water the whole operation once. In addition, a separate pump is needed to move the water from the tank through the irrigation lines (Fig. 17.1).

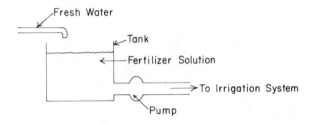

Figure 17.1 Fertilizer distribution system using a large tank.

To reduce the bulk of the equipment the fertilizer can be concentrated in a stock solution and small amounts proportioned into the irrigation lines. Two types of proportioning equipment are used: venturi and positive displacement pump.

Venturi

The venturi principle uses pressure differences to move the fertilizer solution into the water line (Fig. 17.2). This proportioner works by first restricting the flow of water in the line which causes a higher pressure, followed immediately by opening up of the line which causes a pressure drop. The pressure is lower than the outside atmospheric pressure, which forces the fertilizer solution in the bucket up through the tube into the area of low pressure. Control of the amount of fertilizer taken up depends on the orifice size and the pressure and uniformity of flow in the water line.

The simplest venturi type proportioner is the Hozon (Fig. 17.3). The Hozon has many limitations, especially a low proportioning ratio of approximately 1:15. The ratio means that for every 15 gallons of water going through the water line, one gallon of fertilizer solution is removed from the pail. One gallon of fertilizer stock solution would water only 60 sq ft (assuming one quart per sq ft).

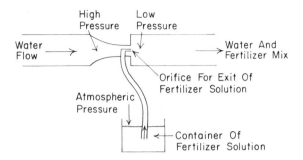

Figure 17.2 Schematic of the venturi proportioner.

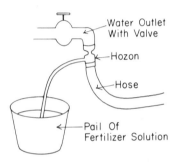

Figure 17.3 Hozon proportioner.

To avoid the pressure change problems and to obtain higher ratios, other equipment such as Gewa, MP, and Cameron Bucket is available. This equipment has no moving parts and wear is minimal. The orifice size is critical because this is where the wear occurs; it should be periodically checked. This equipment also is selfcontained. That is, in order to reduce the effects of line pressure changes, the stock solution is kept in a sealed container. The fertilizer solution is in a plastic bag inside the container. The area around the bag fills with clear water as the fertilizer stock solution is removed (Fig. 17.4). Equipment is available with ratios up to 1:1000 and tank capacity up to 25 gallons. This means that one 25-gallon tank filled with fertilizer stock solution assuming the 1:1000 ratio could cover 100,000 sq ft at the rate of one quart per sq ft.

Positive Displacement Pump

The positive displacement pump is connected to the irrigation line. The flowing water drives a piston which is connected to an outside fertilizer stock solution on the inlet and into the irrigation line at the outlet (Fig. 17.5).

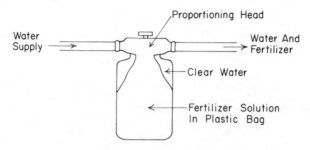

Figure 17.4 Self-contained venturi fertilizer proportioner.

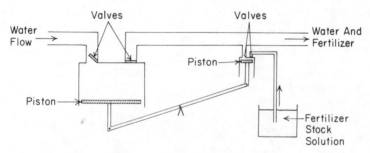

Figure 17.5 Positive displacement pump proportioning system.

There are a number of manufacturers of positive displacement fertilizer proportioning equipment including Commander, Fert-O-Jet, Smith Measuremix, and Viking. This equipment is manufactured in various sizes. A water pump has a minimum as well as a maximum flow rate in gallons per minute, and both numbers should be considered to determine the proper size. Table 17.2 shows the various sizes of equipment made by the Smith Precision Products Company and the minimum and maximum flow requirements.

For example, the R8 model of the Smith Measuremix has a minimum flow rate of 20 gallons per minute. If just one person were watering with one hose, ratios of fertilizer to water would not be accurate because the flow rate would be less than 20 gal. per minute. The same would be true if an automatic watering system with a flow rate greater than 100 gallons per minute was used.

Table 17.2.   The various sizes of Smith Measuremix fertilizer proportioners, flow requirements, and standard proportions.

Model	Water line size	Flow		Standard Proportions
		Max.	Min.	
R3	¾-inch	15	3	1:100
R8	2-inch	100	20	1:200
R12	3-inch	200	50	1:400–1:1000
R16	4-inch	350	100	1:400–1:1000
R24	6-inch	700	200	1:800–1:2000

Installation of Proportioner Equipment

The proportioner equipment should be installed in the water lines so it can be bypassed in case just water is desired at a watering and so it can be removed for repairs (Fig. 17.6).

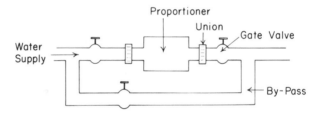

Figure 17.6   Proper installation of a fertilizer proportioner in the water line.

In some communities there is an ordinance against having a fertilizer proportioner directly connected to the municipal water system. To conform with the ordinance a back flow preventer or a break in the water line must be installed, to prevent the proportioner from serving as a syphon to drain the fertilizer and other materials back into the main water line. A break in the line is very effective but it means that a pump must be installed to maintain the water pressure (Fig. 17.7).

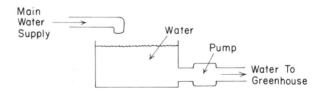

Figure 17.7   An installation showing a break in the water line.

A back flow preventer or check valve are sometimes acceptable and these have the advantage in that the municipal water pressure is not lost (Fig. 17.8).

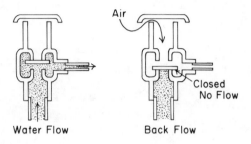

Figure 17.8 Schematic of a back flow check valve.

Calculating Fertilizer Proportions

Most fertilizer proportioner manufacturers and fertilizer companies publish charts, tables, etc. to indicate the number of ounces of fertilizer to add to a gallon of stock solution to obtain a certain number of ppm of an element in the irrigation water. The actual calculations are simple and a greenhouse manager should be able to calculate his own fertilizer programs. There are times in a "fine-tuned" fertilizer program when rates other than 100, 150, or 200 ppm of N, P, or K are needed.

Quick Calculations

For a quick calculation, a rule of thumb, the percentage of an element in the fertilizer multiplied by .75 equals the ppm concentration of that element when one ounce of that fertilizer is added to 100 gallons of water. For example, let us use Calcium Nitrate. From Table 17.1 note Calcium Nitrate has 15.5% N. Therefore, 15.5 × .75 = 11.6. If one ounce of Calcium Nitrate is added to 100 gallons the concentration will be 11.6 ppm N. If a 100 ppm N solution is desired, then 100 ÷ 11.6 = 8.6 and if 8.6 oz. of Calcium Nitrate is added to 100 gallons, the concentration of N will be 100 ppm.

To use this information for a stock solution, we must know the ratio of the proportioner. If it is a 1:100 proportioner and 100 ppm N is desired, then 8.6 oz. Calcium Nitrate is put in one gallon of stock solution. If the proportioner is a 1:200, then 2 × 8.6 = 17.2 oz. of Calcium Nitrate is put in one gallon of the stock solution.

Calculations

A more precise method to determine ppm of a fertilizer solution is to use some basic chemistry. Table 17.2 shows the atomic weights of the elements and Table 17.3 shows the chemical formula and weights of some of the common fertilizer salts. This tells us what proportion (or percentage) of the salt is the actual element. For these calculations, the metric system is better because milligram per liter (mg/l) is actually ppm. Now using simple proportions, the problems can be solved.

$$\frac{\text{mg of fertilizer}/l}{\text{mg}/l \text{ desired of element}} = \frac{\text{formula wt. of salt}}{\text{atomic wt. of element} \times \text{no. of units of element}}$$

$$\text{or,} \quad \text{mg of fertilizer}/l = \frac{\text{mg}/l \text{ desired of element} \times \text{formula wt. of salt}}{\text{atomic wt. of element} \times \text{no. of units of element}}$$

Table 17.2.   The atomic weight of various elements commonly found in fertilizer salts.

Element	Symbol	Atomic weight
Boron	B	10.8
Calcium	Ca	40.1
Carbon	C	12.0
Chlorine	Cl	35.5
Copper	Cu	63.6
Hydrogen	H	1.0
Iron	Fe	55.8
Nitrogen	N	14.0
Manganese	Mn	54.9
Molybdenum	Mo	95.9
Oxygen	O	16.0
Phosphorus	P	31.0
Potassium	K	39.1
Sodium	Na	23.0
Sulfur	S	32.0

Table 17.3.   The formula and formula weights of common fertilizer salts.

Fertilizer Salt	Formula	Formula weight
Ammonium nitrate	NH_4NO_3	80.0
Ammonium sulfate	$(NH_4)_2SO_4$	132.0
Calcium nitrate	$Ca(NO_3)_2$	164.1
Diammonium phosphate	$(NH_4)_2PO_4$	131.0
Potassium chloride	KCl	74.6
Potassium nitrate	KNO_3	101.1

For example, we would like 100 ppm of N using Calcium Nitrate. From Table 17.2 and 17.3 we obtain the formula wt. (164), the atomic wt. (14) and note there are 2 units of the element ($Ca(No_3)_2$). Therefore,

$$\text{mg of fertilizer}/1 = \frac{100 \times 164.1}{14 \times 2} = 586.1 \text{ mg}/1.$$

or, 586 mg of Calcium Nitrate in one liter will be a 100 ppm N solution.

Convert to ounces and gallons

To convert to gallons, multiply the result by 3.78 (the number of liters in a gallon) or 3.78 × 586.1 = 2215 mg/gallon or 2.215 gm/gallon. This can be converted to 100 gallons by 100 × 2.215 = 221.5 gm/100 gallons. This solution will contain 100 ppm N.

To convert the gm to ounces divided by 28.4 (the number of gm in one ounce), or $\frac{221.5}{28.4}$ = 7.8 oz. of Calcium Nitrate in 100 gallons of water is a 100 ppm N solution.

Note the difference between the quick and accurate methods, 7.8 vs 8.6.

Calculations using mixed fertilizer salts

Commonly, it is desired to use a commercially mixed soluble fertilizer and the exact fertilizer salts are not known. The fertilizer formulations are given as N, P_2O_5 and K_2O. To calculate the number of ounces to put into 100 gallons use the following

$$\text{mg of fertilizer}/1 = \frac{\text{ppm N} \times 100}{\%\text{N in fertilizer}}$$

For example, we will use a 20-20-20 fertilizer and want a 100 ppm N solution.

Then, $\frac{100 \times 100}{20}$ = 500 mg of fertilizer/1

and   500 × 3.78 = 1890 mg/gal or 1.89 gm/gal

and   1.89 × 100 = 189 gm/100 gal

and $\frac{189}{28.4}$ = 6.7 oz/100 gal

Therefore, if we add 6.7 oz of 20-20-20 fertilizer to 100 gallons of water, it will contain 100 ppm N. If 6.7 oz of 20-20-20 fertilizer is added to 1 gallon of a stock solution in a 1:100 fertilizer proportioner, the irrigation water will contain 100 ppm N.

Potash and phosphorus calculations can be confusing, because it must be clear whether P or P_2O_5 is desired. Remember the fertilizer formulations are given in P_2O_5 and K_2O. Let us use an example where we want 100 ppm K using a 20-20-20 fertilizer. Note K is 83% of K_2O, i.e., the atomic weight of K is 39.1 and O is 16. The formula weight is 94.2 and the two K atoms are $\dfrac{2 \times 39.1}{94.2} = \dfrac{78.2}{94.2} = 83\%$. Therefore,

$$\text{mg of fertilizer}/1 = \frac{\text{ppm K} \times 100}{\% \text{ of } K_2O \text{ in fert.} \times \% \text{ of K in } K_2O} = \frac{100 \times 100}{20 \times .83} = 415 \text{ mg}/1$$

and $415 \times 3.78 = 1569$ mg/gal or 1.57 gm/gal

and $1.57 \times 100 = 157$ gm/100 gal

and $\dfrac{157}{28.4} = 5.5$ oz of 20-20-20/100 gal would produce a 100 ppm K solution.

Let us use an example where we want 50 ppm P using a 20-5-30 fertilizer. Note that P is 44% of P_2O_5, i.e., P atomic weight is 31, O is 16, the formula weight of P_2O_5 is 142; therefore

$$\frac{2 \times 31}{142} = \frac{62}{142} = 44\%.$$

Therefore,

$$\text{mg of fertilizer}/1 = \frac{\text{ppm P} \times 100}{\% \text{ of } P_2O_5 \text{ in fert.} \times \% \text{ of P in } P_2O_5} = \frac{50 \times 100}{5 \times .44} = 440 \text{ mg}/1$$

and $440 \times 3.78 = 1663$ mg/gal or 1.66 gm/gal

and $1.66 \times 100 = 166$ gm/100 gal

and $\dfrac{166}{28.4} = 5.85$ oz/100 gal of 20-5-30 will be a 50 ppm K solution.

In the above example, to determine the ppm of N and K in this fertilizer solution use the following:
For N

$$5.85 \times 28.4 = 166 \text{ gm}/100 \text{ gal}$$

and $\dfrac{166}{100} = 1.66$ gm/gal or 1660 mg/gal

and $\dfrac{1660}{3.78} = 439$ mg/1

$$\text{ppm N} = \frac{\text{mg of fert.}/1 \times \%N}{100}$$

and $\dfrac{439 \times 20}{100} = 87.8$ ppm N

For K

$$\text{ppm K} = \frac{\text{mg of fert.}/1 \times \%K_2O \times \%K \text{ in } K_2O}{100}$$

and $\dfrac{439 \times 30 \times .83}{100} = 109.3$ ppm K

The 5.6 oz of 20-5-30 fertilizer per 100 gallons would contain 87.8 ppm N, 50 ppm P, and 109.3 ppm K.

Calculations for Minor Elements

There are situations when small amounts of specific minor elements Boron (B), Copper (Cu), Iron (Fe), Manganese (Mn), or Molybdenum (Mo) need to be added in a fertilizer program.

The atomic weights are given in Table 17.2 and the formula weights and formula for the common minor element salts are given in Table 17.4.

Table 17.4.   The formula and formula weights of common minor element salts.

Minor Element Salt	Formula	Formula weight
Boric acid	H_3BO_3	61.8
Sodium tetraborate	$Na_2B_4O_7 \cdot 10\ H_2O$	381.2
Copper sulfate	$CuSO_4$	159.6
Iron sulfate	$FeSO_4 \cdot 7H_2O$	277.8
Manganese sulfate	$MnSO_4$	150.9
Ammonium molybdate	$(NH_4)_6Mo_7O_{24} \cdot 4H_2O$	1235.3
Sodium molybdate	Na_2MoO_4	205.9

For example, we want to add 0.1 ppm Mo to the irrigation system. The greenhouse uses a 1:100 fertilzier proportioner. How much Ammonium Molybdate should be added to the stock solution?

The procedures are similar to those used for the major elements, just the amounts are much smaller.

$$\text{mg of fert.}/1 = \frac{\text{ppm Mo desired} \times \text{formula wt.}}{\text{atomic wt of mo} \times \text{no. units of Mo}}$$

and $\dfrac{.1 \times 1235.3}{95.9 \times 7} = \dfrac{123.53}{671.3} = .184$ mg/1

and $3.78 \times .184 = .696$ mg/gal or $.00696$ gm/gal

and $.00696 \times 100 = .696$ gm/100 gal

and $\dfrac{.696}{28.4} = .025$ oz/100 gal

or to convert to a stock solution .025 oz of Ammonium Molybdate per 1 gal for a 1:100 fertilizer proportioner. It is very difficult for most growers to weigh .025 oz. They can weigh one ounce. The problem would be easier if a gram scale was available and if miximg of fertilizers or growth regulators is contemplated, then a gram scale should be purchased. In this particular problem the one ounce of Ammonium Molybdate can be added to 1 gallon of water and 1 quart of this solution removed and added to 9.75 gallons of stock solution for the 1:100 fertilizer proportioner.

If the recommendation had been 1 ppm Molybdenum, then add 1 ounce to 1 gallon of water and place 1 quart of this solution into 3 quarts of water to make a 1 gallon of stock solution for the 1:100 fertilizer proportioner.

SOIL TESTING

An experienced manager knows what macroelements have been added to the soil and perhaps more important knows what the plants should look like. Experience is important, but it is gained through trial and error, which is expensive. Soil testing can indicate the levels of N, P, and K. If this information is integrated with all the other known factors — weather, crop appearance, fertilizer program and temperature — a good management decision can be made.

Many states have soil testing laboratories and in many areas with high concentrations of greenhouses there are private soil testing laboratories. These labs all do a good job of accurate testing. It is unfortunate that all soil testing laboratories do not use the same method. Care should be used in comparing the results from different laboratories.

Problems can occur if there are delays in testing, for the soil microflora can change the nutrient composition of the soil, especially if it is moist and warm. The delay could cause inaccurate test results because of changes between sampling and testing.

There are soil test kits on the market. Experience has shown that consistent results with these soil test kits are difficult to obtain. It is generally not the kit, but rather the operator that is not consistent. Most kits use a color matching technique, and without experience and a good standard to compare, color matching is very inconsistent. It is best to use one of the commercial or state soil testing laboratories.

Soil testing by itself, however, can have some limitations including sampling error, no minor element test, and changes in the sample between sampling and testing. Care should be taken to avoid these problems.

In an average 100-foot by 4-foot bench there are 200 cu ft of soil or about 1000 pounds of soil and water. The soil sample, which is just a few ounces, must be representative of the whole bench. The upper quarter-inch of soil should be scraped away because high concentrations of fertilizer salts can collect there. The whole length of the bench as well as the width of the bench should be sampled. Figure 17.9 shows a good sampling procedure for a bench.

The availability of minor elements is not routinely tested in a soil analysis. The minor elements are difficult to test because they are present in very small quantities. Minor element availability is determined by foliar testing. In most fertilizer programs a complete minor element fertilizer is added. Minor element mixes such as Peters Compound 111 and, Stem contain all of the minor elements in a soluble form. In a majority of cases minor element problems can be avoided by regular application of fertilizer.

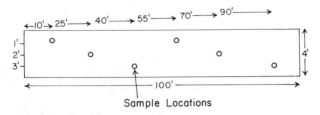

Sample Locations

Figure 17.9   Soil sampling sites on a bench.

Interpretations of Results

The best person to interpret the soil test results is the manager. He can look at the plants and he knows exactly what has been done. If there is a regular fertilizing program it is best to wait until the next month's results before making major changes unless an element is very far out of line. If the fertilizer program is changed every month, conclusions will be difficult to make.

For example, if after two months of soil testing the nitrogen level is below the desired level, the amount of N can be raised from 200 to 250 ppm for a couple of months to see how much the level changes. Another method used to change the nutrient levels in the soil is to apply more or less water at each watering. Generally, more water reduces the levels and less water raises the levels.

Soluble Salts

There is always a concern with the level of soluble salts, which can be harmful. A soluble salt reading can be used very successfully to determine how the nutrient levels are holding in the soil, after a few years of soil testing and a regular fertilizing program, the nutrient levels have settled down and there is a good history of soluble salts readings. When the N, P, and K levels are correct there will be a certain soluble salt reading for that soil. A soluble salts reading can give quick confirmation of a potential problem if the other readings are astray.

The solubridge is a relatively inexpensive piece of equipment and easy to operate. Soil samples should be regularly checked for soluble salts and with a history of soil testing, a regular fertilizing program, and careful observations of the plants the frequency of soil testing can be greatly reduced.

18

WATERING

Water is essential for plant growth for up to 95% of a plant may be water. In a hand-watered greenhouse operation, watering is a major labor item. In any greenhouse operation, however water quality, water measurement, and various methods of application and control must be taken into consideration.

WATER QUALITY

In many areas, especially the west coast of the United States, water quality is poor. Ideal water, which is very rare, would contain no dissolved materials. Usually water picks up impurities as it percolates through and over the soil. The major problems in water quality are high soluble salts, high pH, and high iron content. Recently high nitrates have been found in the water on Long Island. The water should be tested every two years to be sure the levels have remained the same. The state agricultural Stations can perform a satisfactory test. Health Department water tests are generally not relevant.

High Soluble Salts

If the irrigation water contains high salts, special precautions must be taken or growth will be reduced. A solubridge reading of water is used to determine the salts level. The reading is in mohs, a measure of electrical conductivity. Table 18.1 shows various soluble salts levels in water and a water quality rating.

Table 18.1.   The rating of irrigation water of various soluble salts levels.

Solubridge reading (mohs x 10^{-5})	Rating
less than 25	excellent
26–59	good
60–150	fair
above 150	poor

If the soluble salts level of the irrigation water is high, an alternative water source should be sought. If an alternative source cannot be found, the manager should seek additional advice. There is no easy solution. The quantity of water used for most greenhouse operations makes use of a deionizer, which would remove the salts, impractical. The most common method of coping with the problem is to change the water management procedures so that the soil is kept wet all the time; plants are able to grow very satisfactorily in high salt situations if the moisture levels are kept high.

Alkalinity

A water source that contains many carbonates and bicarbonates is usually very alkaline and has a high pH. Alkalinity may cause some elements to be unavailable for plant growth because they are in an insoluble form. Azaleas watered with high pH water, for example, would show iron chlorosis because the iron, although present, is in an insoluble form.

The high pH problem can be alleviated by the addition of phosphoric acid (H_2PO_4) to the water. A food grade of phosphoric acid is recommended to avoid any toxic substances. The phosphoric acid is proportioned into the water lines using the same type of equipment as the positive displacement fertilizer proportioners. The equipment should be acid resistant. Equipment is available that constantly monitors the pH of the water, and the amount of H_2PO_4 added is controlled by the pH readings of the water (Fig. 18.1). The pH can control the solubility of the fertilizes and the water should be adjusted before being mixed with the fertilizer stock solution.

High Iron

In some areas the water source has passed over and through iron-bearing rock and soil. Ferrous bicarbonate is the common form of iron that is dissolved in the water. As the water is aerated and takes up oxygen the iron form changes to ferric hydroxide, which becomes a rusty precipitate. The red precipitate forms over everything, cuttings in the propagation bench, the glass, and the floor. A deionizer would be practical only for special needs such as mist propagation water, drinking water, and water for flower vases. An alternative device is an oxidizing system. Water is sprayed into the air (oxidized) and falls onto a sand filter. The iron precipitates out and collects on top of the sand, and clear water percolates through the sand (Fig. 18.2).

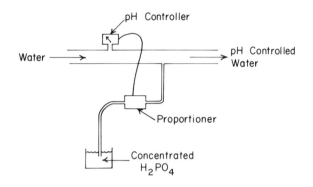

Figure 18.1   Schematic of a pH controller.

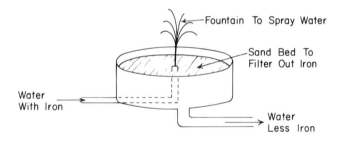

Figure 18.2   An oxidizing system to remove iron from the irrigation water.

WATER MEASUREMENT

How much water and when to add it is difficult to prescribe. Most decisions are based on experience rather than empirical readings. Water, like many of our other natural resources, is becoming in short supply, so more precision in irrigation to avoid waste will be demanded. The present water measuring systems include experience, weight, electrical, and pressure.

Measuring by Experience

Experience is the least accurate system, but the most common. A good manager can look at the plants and soil and decide when to water.

Fortunately, plants are very tolerant and grow rather successfully over a wide range of soil moisture contents. Although imprecise, we should trust our experience, and if the plants are wilting something should be done, no matter what more exact measuring systems indicate.

Measurement by Weight

Every soil mix has a different relationship of water in the soil with the availability of the water to the plant. Every soil must be calibrated by taking moisture samples of a soil and observing the condition of the plant. To calibrate the drying cycle of a soil mix, place it in a pot and establish a succulent plant such as a tomato or a bean. Irrigate the soil once and take a sample two times a day until the plant is well wilted. Weigh each soil sample immediately, dry it in an oven at 175°F for at least twenty-four hours, and weigh again. The difference between the wet and dry weights of the soil is the amount of water in that soil. A graph can be drawn showing the drying curve with the observations of the condition of the plant (Fig. 18.3).

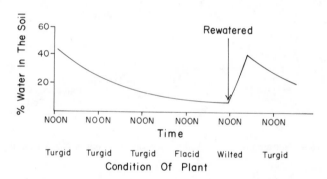

Figure 18.3 The moisture content of a soil during a drying cycle, with plant observations.

The limitation of this system is the time required to calibrate the soil, but it can be used in conjunction with other methods, especially the electrical method.

Electrical Measurement

Since water conducts electricity, a measure of conductivity can be used to determine the relative quantity of the water in the soil. The problem with this system is there are varying amounts of fertilizer salts dissolved in the soil water and they improve the conductivity of electricity. To reduce the variance in salt concentration, Professor Bouyoucos used a saturated solution of salt; therefore, only the water variation was measured. The Bouyoucos system includes a block of gypsum or plaster of paris, which is a saturated salt, in which are imbedded two electrodes (Fig. 18.4) and a modified wheatstone bridge to measure the conductivity (Fig. 18.5).

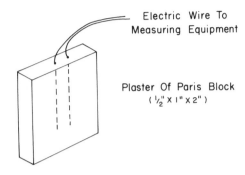

Figure 18.4   The Bouyoucos block.

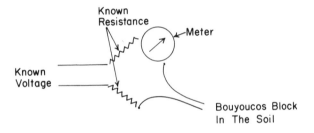

Figure 18.5   Schematic of the Bouyoucos block measuring equipment.

The ohmmeter reads some arbitrary number, which will be meaningful only when correlated with the actual soil moisture measurements and plant observations. For example, we will use the information from Figure 18.3 and show typical electrical readings in Figure 18.6.

From this example soil we can make readings and determine the soil moisture content. If a Bouyoucos block buried in the example soil gave a reading of 4000 ohms, the plant would be showing signs of flagging and the moisture content would be about 12%. Frequent measurements (which are instantaneous) and irrigation when the reading was 5000 would avoid letting the plants flag.

There are electrical moisture measuring probes on the market that do not use the saturated salt block. They are very prone to error. A dry soil with a high salt level will show a high moisture content on the meter. This equipment can be used, but the limitations must be clearly understood.

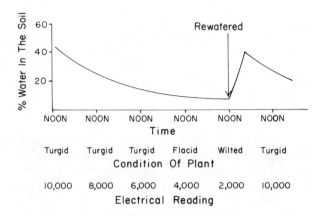

Figure 18.6   Typical readings in relation to a soil drying curve.

Measuring Pressure

The water used by plants is found in the soil pores. These tiny pores hold water by capillary action. The drier the soil the greater the force holding the water. Plant roots must take water from the soil by a force that is greater than that exerted by the soil pores. The drier the soil the less water the plants are able to extract. An instrument called a tensiometer measures this force (Fig. 18.7).

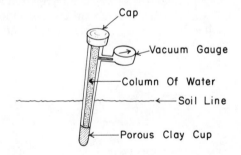

Figure 18.7   Tensiometer.

In the tensiometer there is a continuous column of water from the diaphram of the vacuum gage to the capillaries in the porous clay cup. The water at the surface of the porous clay cup makes contact with the soil water and as the water in the soil is reduced it exerts a greater tension which pulls on the capillaries in the porous cup. Because water is not expandable, the pull is exerted on the diaphragm in the vacuum gage and a needle moves on the dial.

The tensiometer works well in moist soils. When the soil exerts a tension greater than one atmosphere, many of the capillaries on the surface of the porous clay cup are broken and air enters the system. Air is expandable, and the readings are no longer valid. Fortunately the moisture levels maintained in floricultural crops (pots and beds) are less than one atmosphere.

The major limitation of this equipment is the operator's lack of understanding of the principle. He may not take the precaution of removing the air from the instrument when it enters. The instrument does not give instantaneous readings, requires 24 hours to equilibrate with the soil, and cannot be moved or else air will enter the system.

METHODS OF APPLICATION

There are many methods of applying irrigation water to crops. For our discussion we will divide the irrigation systems into overhead, surface, and subirrigation and further subdivide them to pots and benches.

Overhead Watering

Overhead watering inside the greenhouse is not very common because it wets the foliage which is not desirable especially during the dark winter months. Under these conditions, diseases can become difficult to control. Overhead irrigation is primarily used during the summer months in greenhouses, in cloth houses, and out of doors. It is used to irrigate large areas for a relatively low cost.

One of the major problems with overhead irrigation is uniformity of application. Any spray nozzle delivers a variety of droplet sizes. Droplet size and pressure determine the spray pattern and winds or drafts alter this pattern (Fig. 18.8).

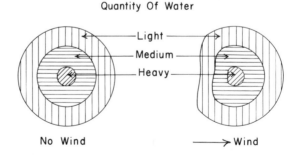

Figure 18.8 Distribution of water from a spray nozzle with and without wind.

To calibrate an overhead irrigation system for uniformity of coverage, containers are uniformly placed in the area to be irrigated. The containers should have straight sides to simplify the readings. One-pound or 5-

pound coffee cans can be used successfully. The cans should be spaced as shown in Figure 18.9.

If the cans were numbered as shown in Figure 18.9 and the irrigation system turned on for 30 minutes we could expect the typical reading shown in Table 18.2.

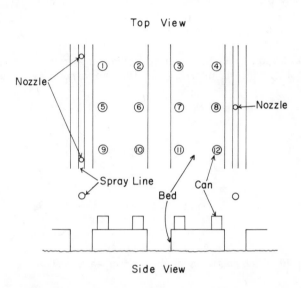

Figure 18.9 The placement of cans to calibrate an overhead irrigation system.

Table 18.2.   Water in each can from an example overhead irrigation system

Position	oz of water	Position	oz of water
1	2	7	1.5
2	1.5	8	2
3	1.25	9	2
4	1.5	10	1.5
5	1	11	1.25
6	1.5	12	1.5

It is clear that there is variation in the distribution of the water. A compromise will have to be made when irrigating. If 1.5 oz of water were the desired rate, the benches should be irrigated long enough to apply 1.5 oz to the median group of cans (cans no. 2, 4, 6, 7, and 12). The other areas will receive less or more water. If we used cans 1, 8, and 9 to determine the time, most of the area would receive less than 1.5 oz of water and if we used cans 3 and 11, the area would be overwatered. The can calibration method can be used to improve uniformity of irrigation by measuring the water after changing irrigation nozzles, nozzle spacing, or water pressure.

Most overhead irrigation systems apply a lot of water at one time and timing is critical. Each irrigation should be timed to produce the desired quantity of water. If a section of potted plants is to be irrigated with 4 oz of water per container and the system requires 6 minutes to apply one oz of water to the median pot, the irrigation system is turned on for (6 × 4) 24 minutes.

The common types of overhead irrigation nozzles are fixed nozzles (Fig. 18.10), whirling nozzles (Fig. 18.11) and rotating impact nozzles (Fig. 18.12).

Figure 18.10   Fixed nozzles in the line for overhead irrigation.

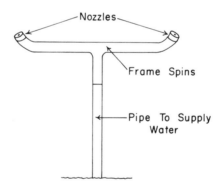

Figure 18.11   Whirling nozzle for overhead irrigation.

The spacing of the nozzles is usually 65% of the diameter of the spray pattern. For example, if the spray pattern were 20 feet, then the nozzles would be 13 feet apart. Adjustments may have to be made for wind and water pressure.

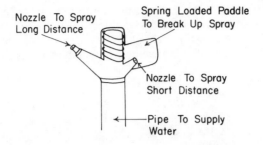

Figure 18.12 Rotating impact nozzle for overhead irrigation.

One of the major disadvantages of overhead irrigation is the inefficiency of watering. Only a percentage of the water applied to an area actually gets to the plants, especially if they are in containers. Table 18.3 shows the percentage of an area covered by 6-inch containers at various spacings.

Table 18.3.   The percentage of area covered with 6-inch containers.

Spacing	area covered
6″ × 6″ (pot-to-pot)	78.5%
9″ × 9″	39.3%
12″ × 12″	19.6%

Therefore, using a 12 × 12 spacing (common) and applying 4 oz of water per container to 1000 containers, it would be necessary to apply (5 × 4) 20 oz per sq ft or 156.25 gallons per 1000 sq ft. Of the total only 31 gallons would be used by the plants.

Surface Watering

Surface watering has the advantage in most systems of not wetting the foliage and of applying water to the soil immediately around the plant.

Bench. There are a variety of systems used to apply water to the bench including hose, perimeter, and poly tubing.

A man applying water with a hose to each plant is still common. This system has the advantage of allowing spot watering, and enabling the operator to regulate the application of water from one area to another. The disadvantages are it is expensive in terms of labor and hose watering generally causes more compaction of the soil than the automatic systems.

Perimeter irrigation consists of rigid plastic pipe placed on the perimeter of the bench and flat spray nozzles spaced along the pipe (Fig. 18.13). This system applies water rapidly, and therefore, a large volume of water should be available. A 100-foot bench requires about 20 gallons per minute. Table 18.4 shows the maximum flow in gallons per minute for various size pipes and Table 18.5 shows the pressure loss through 100 feet of pipe as the flow is increased. This information is used to calculate the pipe requirement for a greenhouse irrigation system.

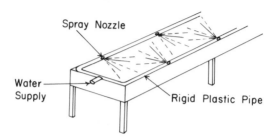

Figure 18.13   Perimeter watering system.

Table 18.4.   The flow of water through various size pipes. (The velocity of water is 10 ft/sec.)

Pipe size (in)	Flow (gpm)
½	10
¾	22
1	36
1¼	70
1½	90
2	155

Table 18.5.   The loss in pressure of water flow through 100 feet of pipe.

gpm	Pipe size (inches)					
	½	¾	1	1¼	1½	2
5	22.4	6.0	1.8	—	—	—
10	66.6	20.5	6.3	1.7	0.8	—
15	—	43.5	13.4	3.5	1.7	—
30	—	—	48.3	12.8	6.0	1.8
40	—	—	—	21.6	9.2	3.0
80	—	—	—	—	38.6	10.9
120	—	—	—	—	—	23.1
140	—	—	—	—	—	30.8

The flow rates given in Tables 18.4 and 18.5 are greatly affected by elbows and tees in the line. Any obstacle in the water line reduces the flow.

In the design of a perimeter system a safety factor is included to avoid problems, i.e. the system is underdesigned to insure uniformity of distribution.

The following are a few general rules for designing a perimeter irrigation of distribution.

1. Use 1 water inlet for benches up to 42 inches wide and 100 feet long.
   Use 2 water inlets for benches up to 42 inches wide and 200 feet long.
2. Use 2 water inlets for benches over 42 inches wide and up to 150 feet long.
3. The poly pipe size should be ¾-inch.
4. Nozzles should be spaced as shown in Fig. 18.14.

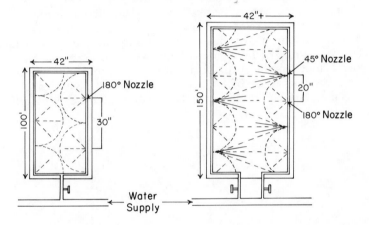

Figure 18.14   The spacing of flat spray nozzles according to the bench widths.

The polyethylene plastic fittings necessary for perimeter irrigation are readily available from a plumbing supply house or from horticultural jobbers. The nozzles are available through horticultural jobbers (Fig. 18.15).

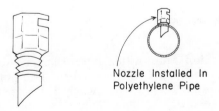

Nozzle Installed In
Polyethylene Pipe

Figure 18.15   Nylon flat spray nozzle used in the perimeter irrigation system.

Calibration of the amount of water used is difficult. If the greenhouse is using municipal water supply there is probably a water meter that can be read, although these are hard to interpolate for a relatively few gallons of water. The second alternative is to use a fertilizer proportioner if it is installed in the main line and if the amount of stock solution is carefully noted. If watering a 100-foot bench, for example, took 10 minutes and used exactly one gallon of stock solution and the proportioner ratio was 1:100, then 100 gallons of water was applied to that bench. The bench was 48 inches wide, or 400 sq ft of bench area, so one quart of water was applied per sq ft. From that calibration the watering should be done by timing. If one pint of water per sq ft. were required, the irrigation system would be on for 5 minutes.

There are three systems that use polyethylene tubing for bench watering: Gro-Hose®, Chapin Twin Wall® hose, and Via-Flow®.

A 2-inch diameter extruded black polyethylene tube with small pin holes every three or four inches is the main feature of the Gro-Hose system. Three lengths of tubing are used for a 4-foot wide bench. (Fig. 18.16). The limitations of the system are that the maximum length of tubing must be less than 100 feet and regulation of the pressure is difficult.

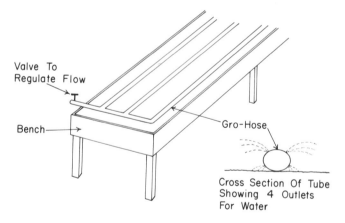

Valve To Regulate Flow

Bench

Gro-Hose

Cross Section Of Tube Showing 4 Outlets For Water

Figure 18.16 Gro-Hose system on the bench.

A unique system of a tube within a tube Chapin Twin Wall hose has fewer limitations than the Gro-Hose system. Two polyethylene tubes (3–12 mil black polyethylene) approximately 2 inches in diameter and up to 250 feet long are used. The outlets in the outer tube are 4 inches or 8 inches apart. The spacing of the holes on the inner tube depends on the spacing of the outer holes (Table 18.6).

Table 18.6.   The ratio used to determine the spacing of the holes, the thickness of the plastic, length and gpm/100 ft of tube

Ratio	Mil poly	Pressure (psi)	gpm	Outer tube outlet spacing (in)	Inner tube outlet spacing (in)	Length (ft)
1:4	3	4	1.54	4	16	120
1:4	3	4	.77	8	32	220
1:5	4	6	1.54	4	20	150
1:5	4	6	.77	8	40	250
1:6	8	8.5	1.54	4	24	170
1:6	8	8.5	.77	8	48	280

Source: Chapin Watermatics, Watertown, N.Y.

The water squirts from the outlets in the outer tube as a stream 2 inches to 3 inches high. From the main water line of polyethylene pipe a number 3 or 4 polyethylene spaghetti supply line is connected to the inner tube (Fig. 18.17). The end of the twin-wall tube is folded over and held closed to prevent the water from running through.

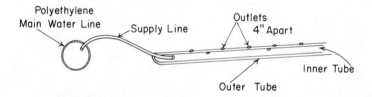

Figure 18.17   The supply tube from the main water line to the Chapin Twin Wall tube system.

A similar system called the ooze tube is made by sewing a plastic thread along the edge of a single thickness of polyethylene tube. A continuous drip along the length of the tube occurs at each thread hole (Fig. 18.18).

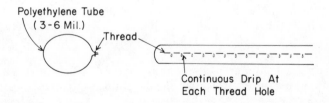

Figure 18.18   The ooze tube.

The Dupont Company has developed a porous sheet structure ViaFlo®, that allows water to flow slowly through it. The porous material is incorporated in a polyethylene tube to form a continuous surface on either one or both sides. The flow rate is higher for the tube with two porous sides.

This system must be run at a low water pressure of 3 to 4 psi. At this pressure the single porous side waters at the rate of a tenth of a gallon per 100 lineal feet of tubing per minute, whereas the two-sided ViaFlo® uses two tenths of a gallon per 100 lineal feet per minute. The water must be very clean and if any sediment is expected, a filter should be used or the pores of the ViaFlo® will clog. A pressure-reducing valve must be installed in the water line to keep the pressure at 3 to 4 psi. For large installations a stand pipe 10 feet high prevents the water pressure from going over 4 psi and bursting the tube (Fig. 18.19). The length of the ViaFlo® tube can be 600 feet (1-sided) and 400 feet (2-sided) long when fed from one end.

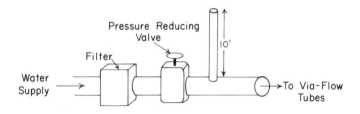

Figure 18.19   Schematic of the arrangement of a filter, pressure-reducing valve, and stand pipe for a ViaFlo watering system.

Pots. Richard Chapin of Watertown, New York should be credited with many of the innovational ideas in pot watering. It was his idea of using spaghetti tubing that caused the Chapin System to become a very common word in floricultural terminology.

The system is simple and relatively inexpensive. Small diameter polyethylene tubing (called spaghetti tubing) can be pressed into prepunched holes in large polyethylene pipe to form a watertight connection. The quantity of water that can flow through the spaghetti tubing depends on the diameter and length (Fig. 18.20). To hold the spaghetti tubing in the pot, lead or plastic weights are attached to the ends (Fig. 18.21).

There are many modifications available for specific crops or situations. This watering system is flexible and the uniformity of watering from pot to pot is very good, even with a large number of spaghetti tubes from one main water line. For example, using the smaller diameter spaghetti tubes (.036-inch inside diameter), 1600 pots can be watered with just a ¾-inch water supply line. The number of pots that can be watered is reduced to

700 for the .060-inch ID and 400 for the .076-inch ID spaghetti tubes. The largest tube is used if the water is dirty or if large containers are to be watered.

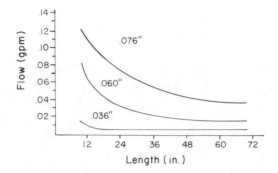

Figure 18.20 Water flow through three diameters (inside diameter) and various lengths of polyethylene tubing at 4 psi. (From Chapin Watermatics.)

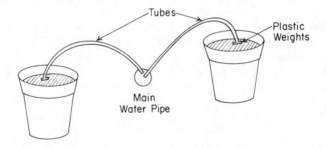

Figure 18.21 Tubes with weights at one end and the water main at the other.

Subirrigation

The capillary action of soil makes possible the use of subirrigation systems. The medium, however, plays an important role in the success of this method. The size of the average capillary determines how high the water will rise in a soil. The smaller the capillary the higher the water will rise (Fig. 18.22).

Therefore, a course sand medium does not work well because the capillary action is poor and the upper part of the medium is dry. Conversely, a clay medium is too wet, as all of the capillaries are full of water and there is no air. Adjustments in the air-water relationships can be made by altering the various components of the medium and some adjustments in moisture content can be made with some of the subirrigation systems. The most satisfactory method is to use a medium that accomplishes the desired result. An equal mixture of peat moss and vermiculite has been used successfully for the subirrigation systems.

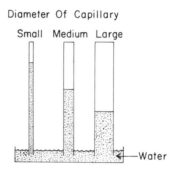

Figure 18.22   The height of water in three capillary tubes.

Benches. Subirrigation for bench crops was very popular in the 1940s and 1950s. In the next two decades automatic watering systems were produced that were very satisfactory and replaced subirrigation watering. A subirrigation system for bench crops requires a special expense in bench construction and special care in preparation. Figure 18.23 shows a cross section of subirrigation bench system. As water in the soil is lost by evaporation from the soil surface and transpiration by plants, the water moves by capillary action from the free water in the gravel to the soil. The water level in the bench and reservoir is lowered, which causes the float to turn on the water supply and the level is raised back to the original position. The bench must be level and the gravel in the V bottom must be level, which requires time for proper preparation. In addition, the bench must be waterproof, which becomes a problem after a few years of steam pasturization and normal uses.

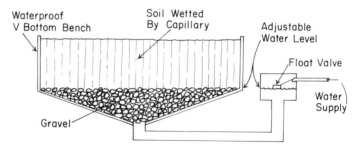

Figure 18.23   Constant water level subirrigated bench.

Pots. Most pot plant crops are well suited for subirrigation. They are rapidly growing plants in a limited soil volume and require frequent respacing. There is at least one drain hole in the bottom of the pot that water can enter. Two systems have been devised: constant water level and capillary watering.

The constant water level system uses the same basic concept as that used for the bench. It also has the same problems. The one advantage is the amount of moisture in the container can be altered by adjusting the water level or the depth to which the containers are plunged in the sand (Fig. 18.24). The deeper the pots are pluged in the sand or the higher the water level, the wetter the pots can be maintained.

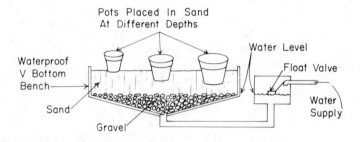

Figure 18.24   Constant water subirrigation system for pot plants.

The European floricultural industry stimulated innovation in capillary watering. The first system was a sand bed followed by the capillary mat.

The sand bed in principle is very simple and requires very little capital investment. A bed of sand is kept close to saturation and the pots are placed on the sand and watered by capillary action between the sand to the soil in the pots (Fig. 18.25).

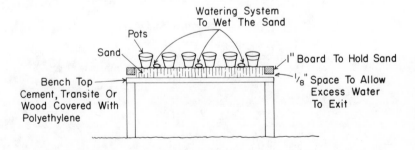

Figure 18.25   Sand bed capillary watering system.

There are no limits, other than practical, to the length and width of the bench. Several sizes of pots can be placed on a single bench, which is not possible with other automatic pot watering systems because of unevenness of watering. The containers should be well watered from overhead the first time they are placed on the bench to establish the capillary action. The pots can subsequently be lifted for spacing and reset without any particular precautions and without losing capillary action.

The problems of capillary watering are excessive growth, salt buildup on the soil surface, and algae growth on the sand. The excess growth in most cases is a positive problem and can be controlled by starting the plants later or using growth retardants. Salt buildup on the surface of the soil can be a problem for crops grown longer than 3 months. Because the direction of water flow is up, salts in the soil solution also move up, and when the water evaporates from the surface the salts remain, accumulate, and show up as a white deposit. To reduce this problem the containers should be watered overhead once a month to wash the salts back down.

Algae on the surface of the sand is a major problem. It can be reduced by using clean sand, by not applying fertilizer in the watering system, by sanitation, and by removing the sand every year. Many sources of sand contain organic matter that is conducive to the growth of algae. The fertilizer for the plants should be incorporated in the mix at the time of medium preparation and enough added to last the life of the crop. Magamp and Osmocote are examples of fertilizer that have successfully been added; they eliminate the need for liquid fertilization. Removing fallen leaves and flowers, and removing the sand annually also help to eliminate the algae problem. Algaecides, unfortunately have not been successful because at the rates of application that control algae, there has been severe stunting of the plants.

A synthetic fiber mat, called a capillary mat, was substituted to avoid the problems of sand. The principle of watering is the same, but the mat has the advantages of light weight and easy installation (Fig. 18.26).

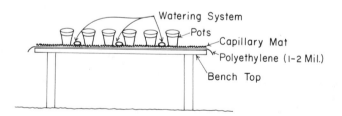

Figure 18.26 Capillary mat subirrigation system.

The limitations are the same as those of the sand bed except for the annual removal of the sand. Everett Green of Belmore, Long Island, has devised a system to alleviate the algae problem with the mat. A thin sheet of black polyethylene with pin holes punched every inch covers the mat. The innovation has worked well and does eliminate the algae. Holes the size of the base of the pot could be cut into the black polyethylene sheet, but they do not allow respacing.

Any watering system that wets the sand or mat is satisfactory. ViaFlo®, Gro-Hose, Twin Wall tubing as well as a Chapin System of tubes have worked very satisfactorily. The system is usually controlled by a timeclock and solenoid valve and is activated two or three times a day. Each "on" period should be long enough to saturate the sand or mat, with some excess run off (Fig. 18.27).

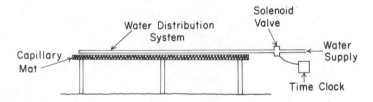

Figure 18.27   Control system for water distribution on a capillary mat.

Hydroponics

Hydroponics has been used to grow plants in scientific research and commercial applications for years, dating back to the 1920's. In the past it had not been successfully used commercially. Allen Cooper, a plant scientist in England, in 1973 described a system called Nutrient Film Technique (NFT). This system was successfully used and today there are acres of NFT in greenhouses in England and Europe. The crops grown are mostly tomatoes, cucumbers and lettuce. It is slowly arriving in the United States.

The Hygro-flo Company of Panama City, Florida has developed an NFT system especially for tomatoes and lettuce. Their package includes everything needed from the greenhouse to the seeds plus a training program.

The NFT system basically differs from the general concept of hydroponics in that a thin film of water is constantly passing by the roots of the plant instead of the plant being grown with its roots submerged in water. The advantages of NFT are: ease of setup, ease of control of nutrient levels, less water to handle, and crop changes are quick. The disadvantages are: it is costly to set up, especially if an existing system must be removed, and constant attention is needed to monitor the pH and salt levels.

A basic schematic of how the NFT operates is shown in Figure 18.28. The water and nutrients are pumped to one end of the trough which holds the growing plants. The slope of the trough is approximately 1 in 75 or a 1-inch fall for every 75 inches of trough length. The water and nutrients flow from one end to the other. Troughs are usually not longer than 50 feet. Longer troughs have had problems of poor aeration, especially at the end. The flow rate of solution is about 2 quarts per minute per trough. An adaptation to this system is to place rock wool in the troughs, which gives plant support, improved water holding and aeration.

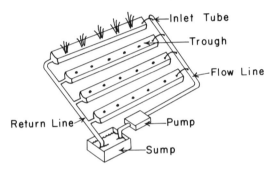

Figure 18.28.   A basic schematic of the NFT system.

The nutrient and pH levels must be carefully monitored. There is automatic equipment available that measures the pH (should be between 5.5 and 6.5) and will add an acid or base when the pH begins to rise or fall. Another instrument, conductivity meter or salinity controller, regulates the nutrient concentrations in the solution. The conductivity meter measures the salt concentration and adds more fresh nutrient solution as the level is lowered by the plants removing the nutrients. It is possible to measure and regulate the major ions in the solution (N and K) by special electrodes.

A well-balanced nutrient solution is very difficult to obtain. The nutrients are not absorbed by the plants equally, water uptake is not uniform over time and there is a build-up of chlorides and sulfates in the solution. Experience interpreting the conductivity readings can be very preceptive of the solution status.

To avoid minor element deficiency or toxic build-ups, many systems are drained and refilled with fresh solution every two or so weeks, depending on the crop and season.

There are a number of nutrient formulations that have been devised for NFT. A basic example is one published by the Greenhouse Crops Research Institute in 1975, and it includes: in ppm 208 Nitrogen, 332 Potassium, 62 Phosphorus, 49 Magnesium, 168 Calcium, 12 Iron, 2.2 Manganese, 0.32 Boron, 0.065 Copper and 0.007 Molybdenum.

CONTROL

The degree of automation is a management decision. A completely automatic system removes the human element from any day to day decisions about watering because the decisions have already been made. It is not feasible, however, to eliminate inspection. Although a system may turn on and off automatically, someone must have the responsibility to see that the equipment is working and that the proper amount of water is being applied. Some safeguards must be built in. A semi-automatic system is one where the manager makes some of the daily watering decisions.

There are controllers on the market today that can be programmed to determine when and how much to water.

When to Water

The question when to water can be answered by measuring the environmental conditions or by predetermined managerial decisions using devices such as a time clock.

The environmental conditions determine the loss of water from the plant and soil so a monitor of these conditions measures water loss. Sunlight, evaporation of water, or soil tension are environmental conditions that are readily measured.

There is a close correlation between the amount of sunlight and the transpiration rate from plants. The brighter the day the more water a plant will lose. Equipment is available that records the amount of sunlight. The manager must correlate the amount of sunlight recorded with the appearance of his crop. He will learn that when a certain amount of sunlight is recorded, the watering system should be turned on. This system is easy to run electronically.

The evapometer measures water loss from a wetted surface. The hotter and drier the day, the greater the water loss. The instrument produces a relative number and the manager has to decide that after a certain amount of water is lost from the evapometer the watering system should be turned on. A potted plant placed on a sensitive scale can be used as an evapometer.

As indicated earlier in this chapter, a soil tensiometer measures the force with which the soil holds the water. The actual dial on the vacuum gage can be altered to make electrical contact when the needle reads a certain predetermined tension, and thus to turn on the watering system.

Most irrigation systems use a series of clocks and timers. The decision must be made by the manager to start the watering process at some predetermined regular time, for example, every other day at 10 o'clock. This determination must come from experience and compromise. The time clock system does not compensate for cloudy or rainy days, while the environmental controls do. The biggest asset of the clock system is it is less expensive and more reliable than the other control systems.

How Much to Water

The quantity of water added to the soil is very important. One of the greatest assets of the automatic watering system is that a uniform amount of water added each time. Hand operated systems can be quite variable, which in turn can cause problems. Too great a quantity of water leaches the fertilizer salts, keeps the fertility level low, and affects the pH. Too little water does not leach out the salts, and high soluble salts become a problem. The manager must decide how much water to add. Since in most cases the controllers use time clocks, the answer will be in terms of time.

As a rule of thumb, about 10% of the irrigation water should be leached through the soil to maintain the soluble salts at a satisfactory level. This is not much excess water and most systems greatly exceed this amount. For example, if one quart of water is added per sq ft to a 4-foot by 100-foot bench, then just 10 gallons of water should be leached. The quantity of water to add will depend on how dry the soil got between waterings. If the watering interval were 3 or 4 days, the soil would be drier than if the watering interval were one day. The manager must make a number of trials, use judgment and experience to be sure to set the controls properly. For example, if a watering system takes 10 minutes to apply one quart of water per sq ft to an area and one qt per sq ft is the desired amount, the controller is set to turn the water on for 10 minutes.

Usually the whole greenhouse operation cannot be watered at one time because of the limitation of water mains. The water mains are not large enough to deliver sufficient water; therefore the watering system is divided into units depending on the size of the water main or of the greenhouse range. A solenoid valve is placed at the head of each unit and a controller is selected with one station for each solenoid.

For example, the controller activates the timer and stepping device at 10 a.m. every other day. The timer cycle is 10 minutes, the predetermined time necessary to water one unit. The stepper moves from one station to the next until all the units have been watered, and is activated again by the controller 2 days later at 10 a.m. (Fig. 18.28).

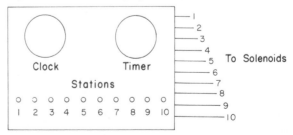

Figure 18.28 Clock controller with automatic stepping system.

Leaching

It is sometimes necessary to reduce the soluble salts in the soil. This is usually done by adding an excess amount of water. As a rule of thumb, one quart of water per square foot leached through the soil will reduce the salt reading (MOHS 10^{-5}) by approximately 66. For example a 100×4 foot bench had a soluble salt reading of 250 and it was recommended to reduce the level to 150. About 1.5 qts/sq.ft. or 150 gallons of water added to this bench will reduce the salt level to about 150. (Note, the soil should be moist so all of the 150 gallons leaches through.)

19

PEST CONTROL

Insect-infested or diseased crops have no market value, so the greenhouse manager must be vigilant in the effort to control these problems. There are two schools of thought on pest control programs: (1) spray on a regular basis to prevent an infestation or (2) spray only when the problem is observed. Good arguments can be made for both. The second philosophy is becoming more popular, especially with increasing costs for labor of application, increased cost of pesticides, and improved pesticides.

Biological control, an alternative to chemical spraying for pest control, is being studied and used in European greenhouses.

Whichever program is used the manager must know what pests may attack the crop and must make frequent, careful observations for detection. There are a number of decisions a greenhouse manager must make about the pest control program including equipment, safety, pesticides, and pesticide storage. Other management decisions such as purchasing only clean stock, ensuring proper sanitation, controlling temperature and humidity, play a major role in reducing the potential for pest problems.

EQUIPMENT

There are a number of methods of applying pesticides: spray, mist blowers, fog, dust, smoke, aerosol, and granular. Each method has advantages and disadvantages and each requires special formulations of the pesticides.

Spray

Water is the carrier and there are two types of equipment to disperse the chemical: the compressed air sprayer, which is useful for spot applications; and the hydraulic pump sprayer.

The compressed air sprayer is a small hand-carried sprayer up to 5 gallons in capacity. It is pressurized by the operator's energy on the pump (Fig. 19.1).

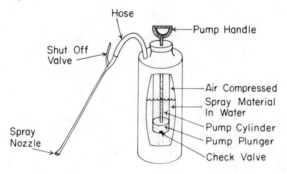

Figure 19.1   Portable compressed air sprayer.

The hydraulic pump sprayer varies in capacity from 10 gallons to 100 gallons or more. The motor and pump produce pressures up to 400 pounds per square inch. The pump and tank may be movable or stationary depending on the size. Many operations have one large, centrally-located sprayer that pumps the liquid at high pressure through high pressure pipe to the various greenhouses (Fig. 19.2).

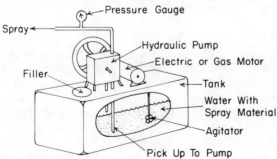

Figure 19.2   Hydraulic sprayer.

The pipe, fittings, and hoses for the hydraulic sprayer should be rated to withstand the high pressures. Most piping is designed for 100 or 150 psi rather than the 300 or 400 psi required for the hydraulic sprayer system.

The spray pattern is controlled by the nozzle and the pressure. The nozzle should be selected for the desired spray shape, particle size, and volume delivery. Most nozzles are composed of the housing, strainer, swirl plate, orifice plate, and cap (Fig. 19.3). Water is very abrasive at high pressures and the orifice wears quickly. The larger orifice not only increases the amount of spray material used, but increases the droplet size, which may reduce the effectiveness of the spray. The nozzle should be taken apart and cleaned after every 10 hours of service. The orifice should be checked and replaced if worn.

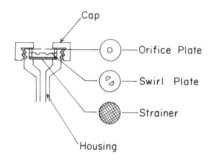

Figure 19.3 Typical spray nozzle.

The size of the orifice and the pressure determine the amount of spray delivered. The orifice size for most greenhouse spray nozzles varies from .05 to .125 inches in diameter. Manufacturers number the nozzle orifice plates in increments of 1/64th of an inch; a number 3 plate has a 3/64-inch or .045-inch orifice and a number 10 plate has a 10/64-inch or .156-inch orifice. As a general rule of thumb the number of gallons delivered per minute per nozzle increases 20% for each 100 pounds of pump pressure increase and the droplet size decreases.

Mist Blower

Mist blowers are most useful for outside field operations or for the application of dust. This equipment uses high velocity air to break up the liquid into fine spray particles and blow them into the air for distribution onto the plants (Fig. 19.4).

The mist blower uses a concentrated mixture of pesticide and water. If the recommendation for the hydraulic sprays were one quart of the pesticide per 100 gallons of water, the mist blower would use one quart per 7.5 gallons of water. The spray is obviously more concentrated and care must be taken not to overspray. The same amount of pesticide should cover the same number of plants regardless of spray method.

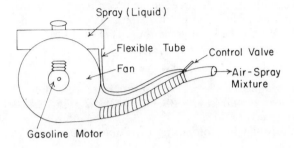

Figure 19.4   Portable mist blower.

Fog

A special formulation is used for the fogging applicator. The pesticide is dissolved in a petroleum solvent. This formulation, during application, is carefully metered onto a hot surface, for example the manifold of a small gasoline engine, which produces a fog of the pesticide (Fig. 19.5). The disadvantage of this equipment is that only a limited number of formulations can be used.

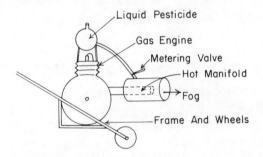

Figure 19.5   Fogging machine.

Dust

The mist blower can be converted to blow dust, or a duster with a hand-cranked fan can blow the dust into the air. The dust is usually talc mixed with the pesticide. This method is not very useful in the greenhouse.

Smoke

For smoke application, a special formulation of a pesticide is prepared to include a combustible material. The formulation is packed in small containers (less than one pound capacity) and each will smoke or fumigate a certain volume of greenhouse, usually 10,000 or 20,000 cubic feet. The volume of the greenhouse is computed by multiplying the total surface area of one end by the length. The formula for computing the volume of an even span greenhouse is (Fig. 19.6).

$$He \times W + \frac{W \times Hr}{2} \times L = \text{vol in cu ft.}$$

The volume of a 35-foot by 75-foot greenhouse 16 feet high with 7 feet at the eaves would be: $7 \times 35 + (35 \times 9) \div 2 \times 75 = 245 + 157.5 \times 75$; or 30, 187.5 cu ft.

The formula for computing the volume of a quonset greenhouse is

$$\frac{3.14 \, Hr^2}{2} \times L = \text{vol in cu ft}$$

Therefore, the volume of a quonset house, 35 feet by 75 feet and 16 feet high is $3.14 \times 256 \div 2 \times 75 = 30,144$ cu ft.

A.   B.

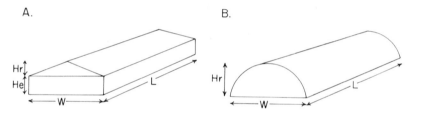

Figure 19.6 Even span greenhouse (A); and quonset greenhouse (B).

If the roof is vaulted as shown in Figure 19.7, the volume would be computed using the formula.

$$He \times W + 2(A \times Hr) \times L = \text{vol. in cu.ft.}$$

This type of house is usually covered with polyethylene and A is known. In this 35×75 foot greenhouse example, A is 20 feet and Hr is 4 feet.

$$7 \times 35 \times 2(20 \times 4) \times 75 = 30375 \text{ cu.ft.}$$

In the examples cited, if the smoke containers were to fumigate 10,000 cu ft each then three containers would be used. The containers should be spaced evenly in the greenhouse, opened, and lit with a sparkler that is supplied with each container.

The disadvantage of the smoke method is that the number of pesticides available in the smoke formulations is limited.

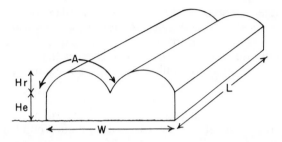

Figure 19.7.   Multi-vaulted roof greenhouse.

Aerosol

The pesticide in the aerosol method is dissolved in a liquid, which is subsequently placed in a special cylinder and pressurized. The liquid vaporizes upon release from the cylinder, thereby carrying the pesticide into the air (Fig. 19.8). The disadvantage of the aerosol method is the limited number of pesticides available in this formulation.

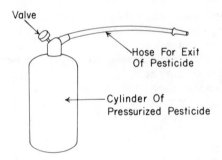

Figure 19.8.   Aerosol bomb.

Granular

The pesticide is impregnated onto an inert granular material, which can be easily spread on the soil. The pesticide dissolves in the soil water and is subsequently absorbed by the plant roots. The pesticide is transported throughout the whole plant and an insect that feeds on this plant ingests the pesticide and dies. At present only one insecticide is in granular form.

SAFETY

Many of the pesticides used in the floricultural industry are poisonous, some of them very poisonous. There are thousands of people poisoned each year and some die from pesticide poisoning.

The federal and state governments have placed restrictions on the use of many pesticides. In addition, the more poisonous materials can be purchased only with government approval, i.e. a license is required. Each state operates differently, so one should check with the county agricultural services to obtain the full restrictions and requirements.

Label

The label on a pesticide container has a great deal of information and should be read. The following is a list of information found on a pesticide label.
1. Brand name
2. Formulation (i.e. wettable powder, emulsifiable concentrate, dust, granular)
3. Common name
4. Ingredients (active and inert)
5. Manufacturer
6. Environmental Protective Agency registration number
7. Signal words (i.e. high toxicity, moderate toxicity, or low toxicity)
8. Use and application directions including: a) pests controlled (b) crops to be used on (c) rate of application (d) where, when, and how to apply
9. Precautionary statements: (a) hazards to humans (b) hazards to the environment
10. Storage and disposal directions
11. Medical treatment: (a) first aid (b) notes to physicians
12. Misuse statements

Poisons

Pesticides are rated in four classes of toxicity; highly toxic, moderately toxic, slightly toxic, and relatively nontoxic. This rating is based on tests run on laboratory animals fed various quantities of the pesticide. When one-half of the lab animals die, that particular dosage is called the LD50 (lethal dosage for fifty percent). The dosage is based on the number of milligrams of pesticide per kilogram of body weight of the test animal. Therefore, a material that has an LD50 of 1 is very toxic compared to an LD50 of 5500 which is nontoxic. This dosage is called the oral LD50. The dermal LD50 is established with lab animals, but the pesticide is absorbed through the skin and not fed. The dermal LD50 is usually higher. Table 19.1 shows the four classes of pesticides and their related LD50s.

There are relatively few pesticides used by greenhouse operators. Table 19.2 is a list of the more common pesticides with their oral and dermal LD50s.

Table 19.1.   The range of oral and dermal LD50s for the 4 classes of pesticides.

| | | | LD50 mg/kg | |
Class	toxicity	label word	Oral	dermal
1	high	Danger-Poison	1–50	1–200
2	moderate	Warning	50–500	200–2000
3	slight	Caution	500–5000	2000–20,000
4	nontoxic	none	over 5000	over 20,000

Table 19.2.   The oral and dermal LD50s of the common pesticides.

Pesticide	Oral LD50	Dermal LD50
Insecticides		
Aldicarb (Temik)	.93	2.5
Carbaryl (Sevin)	500–850	4,000
DDVP (Vapona)	58–80	75–107
demeton (Systox)	2–6	8–14
Diazinon	300–400	455–900
dicofal (Kelthane)	1000–1100	1000–1230
Guthion	11–13	220
malathion	1000–1375	4,444
Meta-Systox R		
(Oxydemeton methyl)	65–75	250
Zectran (meracurbate)	83	285
nicotine	83	285
parathion	4–13	7–21
Pentac	3,160	>3,160
Pirimor (pirimicarb)		500
Resmethrin		3,040
Tedion (tetradifon)	14,700	>10,000
Fungicides		
Benlate (benomyl)	9590	low
Botran	4040	medium
captan	9000–15000	low
ferbam	17,000	low
Karathane	980–1190	low
maneb	6750–7500	low
Parnon	5000	low
Pipron	2529	low
sulfur	17,000	low
zineb	5200	low

Safety Equipment

It is clear that many of the common materials used in the pesticide program are toxic. These materials can enter the skin and it is possible to be poisoned without actually drinking the pesticide. Protective clothing for the skin and protection of the air we breathe is very important.

The more toxic the material the more protective clothing should be worn. No pesticides should be handled with bare hands. Rubber gloves should always be used. If the spraying operation is to be above the shoulders then a full rubber rain coat or suit should be worn, with rubber boots and rain hat to protect the head and feet. If, however, the spray is at a level below the shoulders, coveralls are more comfortable to wear.

If the pesticide is very toxic and the operator will be in the fumes, a full gas mask should be worn. If the operator will not be working in the fumes, a cartridge type respirator will be sufficient. The cartridge should be the proper one for the pesticide being used.

PESTICIDES

Pesticides are generally formulated as wettable powder, emulsifiable concentrate, and dust. Not all pesticides are found in all three forms.

Wettable powder (WP) is a dry powder that is mixed with water. The powder stays in suspension, i.e. does not dissolve, and the liquid must be well agitated in the spray tank to prevent settling. Wettable powders leave a slight residue (usually white), which may be objectionable, but are generally less phytotoxic than emulsifiable concentrates.

Emulsifiable concentrate (EC) is a liquid; usually the pesticide is dissolved in a petroleum distillate such as xylene. The pesticide forms a milky white spray mixture when mixed with water, but does not leave a residue. It probably does the best job of eradication, but may cause phytotoxicity.

To make a dusting powder, the pesticide is mixed at a low concentration with talc or similar material. Dust leaves an objectionable dusty film on the plants and is generally believed by entomologists to be the poorest method of application.

Wetters and Spreaders

Most WP pesticides contain some wetter spreader. If the powder does not mix readily with water some wetter may be added. In some locations the water is hard and a poor spray (uneven wetting of the upper and lower surface of the leaves) is achieved. Additional spreader improves the spread and uniformity of coverage. To determine the appropriate rate, continue to add 2 ounces of spreader per 100 gallons of water until the desired results are obtained. The amount of spreader should be recorded and used each time with that pesticide. There are specially prepared materials such as Dupont Spreader Sticker, Triton B-1956 or Ortho X-77 for this use.

Compatibility of Pesticides

There would be an obvious saving in time if various fungicides and insecticides could be applied at the same time. Most pesticides can be mixed together. The pesticide label will usually mention compatibility problems. The Meister Publishing Company of Willoughby, Ohio, publishes a compatibility chart of the common pesticides.

Mixing of different formulations, e.g. EC with WP, will probably not work. Mixing pesticides with fertilizers, especially lime mixtures, will probably not work.

STORAGE OF PESTICIDES

Because pesticides are poisonous, special precautions should be taken with storage. If possible the storage should be in a separate building. In case of fire, the source would be noted and the smoke could then be avoided. The area should be ventilated, locked, and a note placed on the door to indicate that the room contains poisons.

Most pesticides remain active for at least two years if kept properly closed in a dry and heated (above 32°F (0°C) room. If there is any doubt about the effectiveness of the pesticide, it should not be used. All pesticides should be dated when they are purchased. Some of the symptoms of loss of effectiveness of a pesticide are described in Table 19.3.

Table 19.3.   Symptoms of loss of effectiveness of pesticides.

Formulation	Symptoms
Emulsifiable Concentrate (EC)	No milky formation, insoluble sludge or layers in the mixture.
Wettable Powder (WP)	Lumping and not all material will go into suspension.
Dust	Excessive lumping.
Granular	Excessive lumping.
Aerosols	Obstruction in opening.
Smoke	Difficult to light, lumping.

BIOLOGICAL CONTROL

There is on the horizon an alternative to chemical pest control. The reasons for looking to other ways to control pests are expense, danger to humans and the environment and damage to the plant. At the present time, Biological Control is being used successfully in greenhouses in Europe. A grower in England can buy *Encarsia formosa* — a white fly parasite; *Mycotal* — a natural fungus of the white fly; *Phytoseiulus persimilis* — a red spider predator; *Bactospeine* — a bacteria of caterpillars; and *Vertalec* — a natural fungus of aphids. Unfortunately, it is not so simple to just spread these organisms around the greenhouse. Timing is critical, the stage of the pest and crop, temperature and level of infestation all must be carefully considered. Perhaps the major criticism of Biological Control is the pest is always present. A low level of the pest is necessary to keep the Biological Control organism alive. For most of our floricultural crops, this is not satisfactory. At the present time a combination of Biological Control and chemical control appears to have potential.

20

GROWTH REGULATORS AND WEED KILLERS

Growth regulators serve very useful purposes in the management of floricultural crops. There are eight basic areas of plant control by growth regulators.

Growth regulators can be used to control flowering. Three examples are the flowering of Bromeliads by Ethrel, the flowering of azaleas by Alar, and the flowering of Clerodendrum by A-Rest.

Pinching of many floricultural crops is a very tedious job. Growth regulators can be applied that cause a pinching reaction. The best example is the use of OFF-SHOOT-O for the pinching of azaleas.

A number of floricultural crops must be disbudded. Attempts are being made to use growth regulators for disbudding but success is not good. An example would be the disbudding of chrysanthemums by alkyl-naphthalenes.

Some of the floricultural crops have a dormancy period and to flower out of season they must be artificially treated, usually with cold, to break the dormancy. Growth regulators can be used to substitute for some of the cold period. The best example is the use of gibberellins to replace some of the cold requirement of azaleas.

To reduce plant loss it is sometimes important to delay bud break. Growth regulators are being used for this purpose. An example would be abscisic acid delaying the bud break of roses.

Height control of pot crops is very important. If plants are too tall their marketability is reduced. A number of growth retardants are being used including A-Rest, Cycocel, Florel, B-Nine, and Alar to retard floricultural crops such as poinsettias, lilies, chrysanthemums, geraniums, petunias, and some others.

To facilitate handling it is necessary to defoliate plants prematurely. A growth regulator such as Ethrel to defoliate hydrangea is a good example.

There have been a number of reports indicating that growth retardants such as Alar reduce plant susceptibility to white fly and A-Rest makes plants less susceptible to air contaminations such as ozone and SO_2.

CHEMICALS

There are seven groups of growth regulators recognized and used in floriculture: auxins, gibberellins, cytokinins, growth inhibitors, abscisic acid, growth retardants, and ethylene. Table 20.1 gives a list of the common growth regulators and their uses.

Table 20.1.   Growth regulators and their uses in the floriculture industry.

Group	Growth Regulator	Use
Auxin	IAA (indole acetic acid)	rooting
	NAA (naphthalene acetic acid)	rooting
	IBA (indole butric acid)	rooting
Gibberellins	GA₃ (gibberelic acid)	substitute for some of the cold period for azaleas
	Gibberellin	" "
Cytokinins	BA (N₆Benzyladenine)	inhibits senescence of green leaves and increases breaks on geraniums and poinsettias
Growth Inhibitors	Maleic hydrazide	retards growth of roses
	Morphactins	pinching and disbudding
Abscisic Acid	ABA (abscisic acid)	not readily available, causes dormancy
Growth Retardants	Alar–B-Nine (succinic acid)	height control on azaleas, hydrangeas, and chrysanthemums
	A-Rest (ancymidol)	height control on poinsettia and Easter lilies
	Cycocel (chlormequat)	height control on poinsettias and azaleas
Ethylene	Ethrel	defoliation of hydrangeas, stimulation of bottom breaks on roses

METHOD OF APPLICATION

All of the growth regulators are formulated as liquid or soluble powders (SP) and are generally sprayed on the foliage. Spraying on the foliage is quick, but not accurate. To improve accuracy either dilute the concentration of the chemical and apply at two or three intervals, still achieving the total amount of material per plant or, for some growth retardants, apply as a drench, and the chemical will be absorbed by the roots. Drenching is the most accurate, because an exact amount of chemical can be added per pot.

The timing and rate of application should carefully follow the recommendations. A typical recommendation for pot mums will read "Amount of B-Nine (5%) per 1 gallon of solution, 9 oz for average varieties, 9–12 oz for vigorous, tall varieties or during high temperature, black cloth periods." (From 1977 Cornell Recommendations for Commercial Floriculture Crops, Part I p. 37). There is obviously some leeway and the operator must use his judgment. Using this recommendation, one gallon of growth retardant would cover about 150 six-inch pots of chrysanthemums.

Calculations for dilutions

To measure and mix growth retardants accurately use the metric system. The only measures really needed are grams (gm), milligrams (mg), liters (l) and milliliters (ml). To emphasize its usefulness: one milligram of a material mixed in one liter is one part per million (ppm). Two common growth retardants are B-Nine and A-Rest. B-Nine is a soluble powder (SP) and A-Rest is a liquid formulation. We will use these as examples to illustrate how to calculate various dilution rates or application rates.

B-Nine SP is usually sold as an 85% a.i., which means 85% of the material is the "active ingredient" and 15% is "inactive." B-Nine is usually sprayed on the plant at rates of 2000 to 3000 ppm. If we want to make a 2000 ppm solution then we must add 2000 + .15 (2000) = 2300 mg of 85% B-Nine SP to one liter of water. The resulting solution will be 2000 ppm, which is sprayed on the plants until runoff.

A-Rest is usually sold as a liquid and contains .0264% a.i. or 264 mg per liter or 264 ppm solution. This growth retardant can be applied as a spray in the range of 10 to 150 ppm or as a drench in the range of .25 mg a.i. to .50 mg a.i. per plant or pot.

To calculate the spray concentrations we know the .0264% a.i. A-Rest is a 264 ppm solution and just a dilution process with water is necessary to obtain the desired concentration. For example, we want one liter of a 25 ppm A-Rest solution. A ratio can be set up to determine the amount of A-Rest and water to add.

$$\frac{1}{264} = \frac{x}{25} \text{ or } x = .094 \text{ l or } 94 \text{ ml}$$

Therefore, 94 ml of A-Rest added to 906 ml of water will produce a liter of a 25 ppm solution. This solution is sprayed on the plants.

When used as a drench a certain quantity of material is applied to each plant or pot. We want to drench with .25 mg a.i. A-Rest per plant. A-Rest is usually sold by the quart and there are .946 l in a quart. A liter of A-Rest .0264% would have 264 mg a.i. The quart, therefore, contains .946 (264) = 250 mg a.i. A-Rest. A ml from this quart contains .25 mg a.i.

The next step is to determine the amount of water to add to the pot so the medium is uniformly watered and yet not allow excessive drainage. Let us use an example of ½ pint of water. If there are 100 pots to be treated then 100 ml of A-Rest should be put in 6.25 gallons (25 quarts) of water. Each pot is watered with ½ pt of solution and will receive the required .25 mg a.i. A-Rest.

WEED KILLERS

Weeds in and around the greenhouse are not only unsightly but may harbor insects and disease. Hand pulling is not always possible or convenient. There are a few weed killers that can be used successfully in the greenhouse. Extreme caution should be used. The wrong material or sloppy applications can destroy a crop and in some cases, leave enough residue to keep the greenhouse unusable for a long period of time.

The weed killer, all of the spray equipment, and mixing containers should be kept together and stored in a location where a spillage or mixup could not cause a problem

There are two types of weed killers: nonresidue and residue. The nonresidue type of weed killer kills the weeds present, but new weeds are not affected. This type has the advantage of being safer in that pots and flats could subsequently be placed on the area that has been treated. Examples of nonresidue weed killers are paraquat, Diquat, and Stoddard solvent.

The residue type of weed killer remains in the soil for 2 to 3 years depending on the amount applied. It should only be used in an area where crops will not be grown and where pots, flats, or plants will not be in contact in any way. Examples of residue weed killers are monuron (Telvar), diuron (Karmex, Karmex DW), and simozine (Princep).

Most weed killers are applied as a spray. The labels on the containers are very specific about the dilution rates to use and the method of application. These recommendations should be followed very carefully.

When applying these weed killers care must be used to avoid any spray on the heat pipes. These materials will fumigate off the pipes when the heat is turned on and cause plant damage.

A spill or miscalculation can cause a great deal of damage. If the error is discovered quickly an application of activated charcoal mixed into the surface of the soil will help reduce the problem. The charcoal apparently absorbs the chemical. Use 100-200 lbs of activated charcoal per lb of active weed killer applied.

REFERENCES

Aldrich, R. A. 1969. *Design of systems for aerated steam treatment of soil and soil mixes.* Mimeographed. Pennsylvania State University, State College, PA.

Aldrich, R. A. and P. E. Nelson. 1969. Equipment for aerated steam treatment of small quantities of soil and root mixes. *Plant Disease Rept.* 53(10):784-788.

Baker, K. F. and C. M. Olson. 1960. Aerated steam for soil treament. *Phytopath.* 50:82.

Baker, K. F. ed. 1957. The Univ. of California system for producing healthy container-grown plants. *Univ. of Calif. Experiment Station Manual 23,* Berkeley, CA.

Baker, K. F. and C. M. Olsen. 1959. *Soil steaming.* Mimeographed. Dept. of Plant Pathology, University of California. Los Angeles, CA.

Boodley, J. W. and R. Sheldrake. 1973. Cornell peat-lite mixes for commercial plant growing. *Cornell University Information Bulletin 43.* Ithaca, N.Y.

Boodley, J. W., C. F. Gortzig, R. W. Langhans, and J. Layer. 1966. Fertilizer proportioners for floriculture and nursery crop production Management. *Cornell Information Bul. 129.* Ithaca, NY.

Cathey, H. M. 1972. Chemical growth regulators. *Horticulture* 50(12): 42, 50, 52, 54.

Chapin Watermatics, Inc. 1976. *Design for profits.* Watertown, NY.

Chapin Watermatics, Inc. 1974. *Pioneers in drip irrigation.* Watertown, NY.

Cooper, A. 1973. Rapid crop turn-around is possible with experimental nutrient film technique. The Grower. May 5.

Cornell University. 1977. Cornell recommendations for commercial floriculture crops. Part I. Cultural practices and production programs. Part II. Disease, pest and weed control. Ithaca, NY.

Cornell University. 1976. Cornell recommendations for pest control for commercial production and maintenance of trees and shrubs. Ithaca, NY.

Dimock, A. W. and K. Post. 1956. An efficient, labor-saving method of steaming soil. *Cornell University Bulletin 635.* Ithaca, NY.

Dupont. 1975. DuPont ViaFlo. Porous plastic tubing for trickle and subsurface irrigation. *DuPont General Technical Bul.,* Wilmington, DE.

Fulton, R. A., F. F. Smith, and R. L. Busbey. 1964. Respiratory devices for protection against certain pesticides. *USDA ARS Bul. 22,* Washington, DC.

General Sprinkler Corp.   1972.   *Sprinkler irrigation Manual.*   Fresno, CA

Industrial Instruments.   RD-B15 soil tests.   Industrial Instruments Brochure.   Cedar Grove, NJ.

Karmeli, D. and J. Keller.   1975.   *Trickle irrigation design.*   Rain Bird Sprinkler Manufacturing Corporation, Glendora, CA.

Koths, J., S. R. Judd, and J. Marisano.   1976.   *Greenhouse crop nutrition.*   Cooperative Extension Service, University of Connecticut. Storrs, CT.

Koths, J., R. Judd, J. Marisano, G. Griffin, J. Bartok, and R. Ashley. 1976.   *Nutrition of greenhouse crops.*   University of Connecticut Cooperative Extension Service.   Storrs, CT.

Meister Publishing Co.   1978.   Toxicity of certain pesticides: in *1971 Farm chemical handbook.*   Willoughby, OH.

Newhall, A. G.   1955.   Disinfestation of soil by heat, flooding and fumigation.   *Bot. Review XXI*   (4):189-250.

Newhall, A. G. and B. Lear.   1948.   Soil fumigation for nematode and disease control.   *Cornell University Bul. 850.*   Ithaca, NY.

Pennell, J.   1966.   Cornell Multidirectional sprayer.   *NY State Flower Growers Bul.*   248:1, 4-5.

Peters, R. B.   1971.   *A system of greenhouse soil fertility control.* Robert B. Peter Co.   Allentown, PA.

Sheldrake, R. and J. W. Boodley.   1974.   Commercial production of vegetable and flower plants.   *Cornell University Information Bulletin 82.*   Ithaca, N.Y.

Smith Precision Products Co.   1961.   *Smith measuremix liquid fertilizer injectors.*   Catalog K162.   South Pasadena, CA.

Stratton, C. L.   1959.   New evaluation in soil fumigation.   *Vo-Ag teacher* 15(2):63.

Tsujita, M. J.   1976.   Growth regulators in ornamental crops. Mimeographed.   Dept. of Hort. Sci., University of Guelph, Guelph, Canada.

Winsor, G., R. Hurd and D. Price. 1979. Nutrient Film Technique. Grower's Bulletin No. 5, Glasshouse Crops Research Institute, Littlehampton, England.

SECTION IV

Crop Programming and Business Analysis

21
RECORDKEEPING AND ANALYSIS

The term accounting was avoided in the title of this chapter because it is not the purpose to teach accounting. Every greenhouse business should have an accountant, at least in an advisory capacity. The accountant knows the tax laws, financing, and business analysis and is an excellent person to consult about the feasibility of any financial venture. The accountant can also help to set up the books to keep the day-to-day financial records of the business. There are many reasons why and many times when accurate records of the business are needed, yet it is safe to say that a majority of the greenhouse operations do not have good records. The minimum records to cover the business for tax purposes, are not enough for an analysis of the business.

Recordkeeping is difficult because each operation is different and no standard system seems to be adaptable. Many greenhouse operations handle many types of plants for various lengths of time so each plant has different costs. In addition, perhaps the major reason for a lack of good records is the managers themselves. Most managers are not trained to keep them, do not understand their use, and unfortunately are not interested.

What kind of records are needed? The basic records needed for tax purposes are sales and costs. The sales receipts will cover the sales and the bills will cover the costs. This information will not allow any analysis, except perhaps to show an overall profit or loss. There are any number of good bookkeeping systems available. These range from formal ledgers with daily entries to computers that are given information of the daily transactions via telephone. Each has advantages and disadvantages, and an accountant can usually advise you on the best system to use.

Electronic Spread Sheet

Most growers keep their records on spread sheets that list the check and cash amounts, income and also place the dispersals under various categories. A spread sheet should have the following categories: salaries, payroll taxes, unemployment insurance, workmen's compensation, utilities, heating fuel, electricity, telephone, depreciation, interest, insurance, repairs, property taxes, advertising, dues and subscriptions, travel and entertainment, office expenses, professional fees, travel expenses, land rental, contributions, miscellaneous and bad debts. Most spread sheets do not have these categories because they are limited by the size of the paper. Most spread sheets are filled out once a month or when the checks are written. This sheet is given to the accountant and he fills out the tax forms.

A home computer and an electronic spread sheet software package, such as Visicalc or Supercalc, can make this task almost fun. The electronic spread sheets have over 50 columns (50 categories) and about 250 lines per sheet (250 separate entries), which is usually sufficient. A second sheet can be used if more than 250 entries per month are needed. The two major advantages are the accuracy of the math and the expanded number of columns which translates into obtaining more details. The programs are written to do all of the math calculations. For example, when the salary is placed in a column, the computer will then calculate the withholding tax, social security tax, etc. to be paid by the employer and employee and any other calculations. At the end of the month when all the columns are added up, there are no mistakes. Many handwritten spread sheets will not have enough columns to obtain the details necessary for proper evaluation or monitoring of expenditures. For example, a column of utilities may contain telephone, heating fuel and gas so there would be no way to determine telephone costs per month or even heating costs per month. A detailed spread sheet is necessary for a proper analysis of the business.

COSTS

The economist divides the cost incurred in the business into overhead and direct. The overhead costs include those incurred for the whole operation and not specifically for one crop. They are further broken down into variable and nonvariable or fixed overhead costs.

The variable overhead costs vary with the crops and the season, occur because the business is operating, and include: water and sewer, electricity, telephone, advertising, truck operation, truck maintenance, office supplies, fertilizer and pesticides, freight, fuel, and miscellaneous expenses.

The nonvariable overhead costs are stable and are incurred whether the business is operating or not. They include: depreciation, insurance, taxes, interest, and salaries.

The direct costs are directly traceable to a particular crop and include: plants (seeds, bulbs, cuttings, plants), pots, medium, growth retardant, packaging (sleeves, boxes), additional labor (for disbudding, tying, etc.), and miscellaneous expenses.

SUMMARY OF THE RECORDS

Once the system for recordkeeping has been devised, how can it be used? First an accountant should be retained to advise the manager on the interpretation of the records. There are, in addition to the business records for billing and tax purposes, a balance sheet and an income statement.

The balance sheet, sometimes called the statement of financial position, reports the business' financial position at a given point in time. The balance sheet is divided in half, the left side indicated the business' assets, i.e. the resources owned, and the right side the business' liabilities and owner's equity, i.e. the money owed (Table 21.1). The assets must equal the liabilities. An example of a balance sheet is shown in Table 21.2.

Table 21.1.   Outline of a balance sheet.

BALANCE SHEET	
1. *Current Assets* (short term)	1. *Current Liabilities* (short term)
Cash	Accounts payable
Marketable securities	Estimated taxes
Accounts receivable	Expenses payable (wages)
Inventory	Deferred income
Prepaid expenses	Short-term debt (less than 1 year)
2. *Fixed Assets*	2. *Other Liabilities*
Land	Long-term debt
Buildings	Mortgages
Equipment	3. *Owner Equity*. Owner investment,
3. *Other Assets*	usually stockholder's equity.
Investments (Securities)	Paid-in capital. The amount the
Intangible assets	owners have invested.
Good will	Retained Earnings. Profit from the
Patents	business (the entire amount the
Leases	owners have invested since the
	business started).

The income statement is a summary of the business' revenues, costs and expenses over a period of time, usually one year (Table 21.3). The cost of production for the operation described in these statements would be reported on a schedule of costs of production. An example is shown in Table 21.4.

D. ANALYSIS OF THE RECORDS

There are some so-called quick tests that can be used to determine the

Table 21.2   Sample balance sheet.

Langhans' Greenhouses
Balance Sheet
December 31, 1979

ASSETS

Current assets

Cash		4,500
Accounts receivable	36,000	
Less allowance for bad debts	(1,000)	
Less allowance for sales discount	(500)	34,500
Inventories		
Merchandise	2,000	
Supplies	10,000	12,000
Prepaid insurance		1,000
Total current assets		$ 52,000

FIXED ASSETS

Buildings & equipment	126,000	
Less accumulated depreciation	(51,000)	75,000
Land		8,000
Total fixed assets		83,000
TOTAL ASSETS		$135,000

LIABILITIES AND OWNER EQUITY

Current liabilities

Accounts payable	5,000	
Notes payable (1 year)	3,000	
Total current liabilities		8,000

OTHER LIABILITIES

Mortgages	22,000	
Long-term debt	–0–	
Total Other Liabilities		22,000

OWNER EQUITY

Owner equity		105,000
TOTAL LIABILITIES AND OWNER'S EQUITY		$135,000

Table 21.3.   Income statement.

<table>
<tr><td colspan="3" align="center">Langhans' Greenhouses
Income Statement
December 31, 1979</td></tr>
<tr><td>SALES</td><td></td><td>$200,000</td></tr>
<tr><td>Less: Plants on hand, end of previous year</td><td>$ 2,500</td><td></td></tr>
<tr><td>   Cost of production</td><td>95,000</td><td></td></tr>
<tr><td>   Cost of plants available for sale</td><td>97,500</td><td></td></tr>
<tr><td>   Plants on hand at end of this year</td><td>(3,500)</td><td></td></tr>
<tr><td>Cost of plants sold</td><td></td><td>94,000</td></tr>
<tr><td>GROSS MARGIN</td><td></td><td>106,000</td></tr>
<tr><td>Less: selling and administrative expenses</td><td></td><td>34,000</td></tr>
<tr><td>NET INCOME</td><td></td><td>$ 72,000</td></tr>
</table>

Table 21.4.   Schedule of costs of production.

<table>
<tr><td colspan="3" align="center">Langhans' Greenhouses
Schedule of Costs of Production
December 31, 1979</td></tr>
<tr><td>DIRECT COSTS</td><td></td><td></td></tr>
<tr><td>Inventory of material on hand, end of last year</td><td>$ 9,000</td><td></td></tr>
<tr><td>Purchase of material</td><td>41,000</td><td></td></tr>
<tr><td>Cost of material available</td><td>50,000</td><td></td></tr>
<tr><td>Less: inventory of material on hand, end of year</td><td>(10,000)</td><td></td></tr>
<tr><td>Total</td><td></td><td>$40,000</td></tr>
<tr><td>DIRECT LABOR</td><td></td><td>20,000</td></tr>
<tr><td>OVERHEAD COSTS</td><td></td><td></td></tr>
<tr><td>Overhead labor</td><td>7,500</td><td></td></tr>
<tr><td>Office supplies</td><td>5,000</td><td></td></tr>
<tr><td>Heat, light, power</td><td>11,000</td><td></td></tr>
<tr><td>Depreciation of buildings</td><td>5,000</td><td></td></tr>
<tr><td>Depreciation of equipment</td><td>3,000</td><td></td></tr>
<tr><td>Micellaneous</td><td>2,000</td><td></td></tr>
<tr><td>Total</td><td></td><td>33,500</td></tr>
<tr><td>PRODUCTION COSTS, this year</td><td></td><td>93,500</td></tr>
<tr><td>Work in progress, end of last year</td><td></td><td>3,500</td></tr>
<tr><td>Work in progress, end of this year</td><td></td><td>(2,000)</td></tr>
<tr><td>TOTAL COST OF PRODUCTION</td><td></td><td>$95,000</td></tr>
</table>

financial health of a business. The balance sheet shows the relationship of the assets and liabilities and from them the analyst can determine the liquidity and solvency of a business.

Liquidity is the ability of the business to meet the current obligations, and it is revealed by a comparison of the current assets with the current liabilities. Liquidity is measured in three ways: the quick test ratio, the current ratio, and the working capital.

The quick test ratio is the ratio of current assets (cash and accounts receivable) to current liabilities. The ratio should be greater than one and measures the ability to pay off the current liabilities immediately. From the sample balance sheet (Table 21.2) we find a quick test ratio (40,500 ÷ 8000) of 5.1 which indicates a healthy firm.

The current ratio is the ratio of current assets to current liabilities and should be greater than one. This is the most commonly used ratio and measures the liability of the business. From Table 21.2 we find a current ratio (52,000 – 8,000) of 6.5, which also indicates a healthy business.

The working capital is the current assets less the current liabilities, giving the amount of capital that is available for immediate use by the business. The assets should be larger than the liabilities. From Table 21.2 we find the working capital is (52,000 – 8,000) $44,000.

Solvency is the ability of the business to meet its interest costs and long-term obligations. The business analyst generally measures solvency of a business in two ways: the debt/equity ratio and the days needed to pay off current debt.

The debt/equity ratio is the ratio of total liabilities to owner's equity. The lower the ratio the better, for it measures the ability of the business to meet the payments on mortgages. The bank or other lenders carefully note this ratio. From Table 21.2 we find a debt/equity ratio of (135,000 ÷ 105,000) 1.3. The ratio is low and the sample business should be able to borrow money easily.

The number of days needed to pay off current debt is computed using two formulas. First, the average daily net sales is the annual net sales divided by 360 days. The annual net sale for the sample business is found on the income statement (Table 21.3) and was $200,000. The average daily net sales for Langhans' Greenhouses would be (200,000 ÷ 360) $556/day. Second, to determine the number of days needed to pay off the current debt the average pay-off period would be total liability minus current assets, divided by average daily net sales. Using the example of Langhans' Greenhouses we compute ([135,000 – 52,000] ÷ 556) 149 days. In other words, it would take 149 days to pay off the current debt on Langhans' Greenhouses.

The income statement gives information about the profitability of the business. The business analyst uses three ratios in this analysis: the profit margin, investment turnover, and the average collection period for accounts receivable.

The profit margin is the net income as a percentage of net sales. This ratio measures the overall profitability of the business. From the income statement of Langhans' Greenhouses (Table 21.3) we find the profit margin is (72,000 ÷ 200,000) 36%.

Investment turnover is the ratio of net sales to investment. This ratio should be greater than one. It measures the sales generated for each dollar invested. From the income statement and balance sheet of Langhans' Greenhouses (Tables 21.2 and 21.3) we find the investment turnover is (200,000 ÷ 105,000) 1.9.

The average collection period for accounts receivable is calculated by dividing the average balance of accounts receivable by the average daily net sales. The average daily net sales was computed above and for the sample business was $556/day. From the balance sheet of Langhans' Greenhouses (Table 21.2) we find the average collection period for accounts receivable is (34,500 ÷ 556) 62 days.

These are the kinds of tests bankers and other business analysts apply to the financial statements the greenhouse operator submits when he asks for money or advice. They help to determine the health of the business, and its ability to pay back borrowed money.

22

CROP PROGRAMMING

The objective of crop programming is to utilize the greenhouse space and other specialized skills to produce maximum profit or self-satisfaction. That rather complex statement is an attempt to include all of the considerations that a manager must review. Many managers are more concerned with reputation, continuation of the business, and other personal considerations, than with maximum profit. The largest flowers that gain the widest reputation may not produce the greatest profits. If the operator realizes this and is satisfied, then his crop programming schedule is good. It is probably true, however, that most managers have maximum profit as their primary objective. Careful planning is as important to greenhouse management as to any other endeavor.

Most crop programming is based on past experience; for example last year we grew 1500 lilies and were a little short, so this year when the salesman comes around we will order 2000 lily bulbs. Planning is done by remembering what was done last year and making an adjustment. This method works best when there are accurate records of sales, crop quality, and previous problems. This method is not very flexible, and changes are slow to occur, which can be both good and bad.

Experience alone will not allow the manager to evaluate the profitability of all the feasible alternatives. Linear programming, however, enables him to use computers to look at a large number of crop programs. The computer can handle many variables, such as the number and size of plants, costs, and prices, at the same time. The use of linear programming will be discussed in more detail later.

DETERMINING CROP COSTS

Before any decisions can be made there is a great amount of detailed information that must be obtained. Some of this information can be very exact, such as the square footage of available bench area. Some of the information, unfortunately, can only be an educated guess, such as the cost of a 4-inch geranium next spring or the quantity that could be sold at a particular price. This information is frustrating to obtain, but a review of the selling price over the past five years and some idea of the quantities sold in that time will make the estimated price next year very realistic. Experience has shown the accuracy of these estimates can be very good if some care has been taken in making them.

We must make an assumption that the purpose of crop programming will be primarily maximum profit. It then becomes necessary to determine the cost and selling price of each unit, for it is the difference between these two that is profit.

Overhead Costs

The overhead costs in a greenhouse were discussed in Chapter 21. The overhead costs can be determined by reviewing a year's worth of bills and records. The costs shown in Table 22.1 are modified from an actual greenhouse operation.

Table 22.1.   Overhead costs for Langhans' Greenhouses.

Overhead Variable Costs		
Water and sewer	315	
Electricity	1,199	
Telephone	1,090	
Advertising	439	
Truck operation	3,515	
Truck maintenance & repairs	1,406	
Office supplies	193	
Fertilizer & pesticides	2,263	
Freight	1,576	
Miscellaneous	2,315	$14,309
Overhead Nonvariable Costs		
Depreciation	8,000	
Insurance	8,985	
Taxes	7,050	
Interest	1,207	
Salaries	20,800	$46,042
		$60,351

Note that the cost of fuel was not included among the overhead variable costs. Because fuel is a high cost and variable over the year — low during the summer and high during the winter — we treat it separately. From records of temperatures and fuel use, we know that about 50% of the fuel is used during the months of December, January, February, 40% during October, November, March, April, and 10% May through September. The fuel bill for Langhans' Greenhouses was $9,854. The greenhouse range was 22,000 sq ft of covered area with an actual bench area of 17,000 sq ft (77% efficient). All costs will be calculated per square foot of bench area. The overhead variable costs were (14,309 ÷ 17,000) $.84/sq ft/year. The overhead nonvariable costs were (46,042 ÷ 17,000) $2.71/sq ft/year. The fuel costs were (9,854 ÷ 17,000) $.58/sq ft/year. The total overhead cost was $4.13 per sq ft of bench area per year.

Weekly Costs

Since crops are grown for a period measured in weeks, the weekly designated cost per square foot of bench area per week is an important figure. The overhead variable costs were (.84 ÷ 52) $.016/sq ft/week. The overhead nonvariable costs were (2.71 ÷52) $.052/sq ft/week. Fuel costs for December through February were ([.58 × .5] ÷ 12) $.024/sq ft/week; for October, November, March, April ([.58 × .4] ÷ 16) $.015/sq ft/week; and for May through September ([.58 × .1] ÷ 24) $.002/sq ft/week.

The overhead costs for a square foot of bench area per week, therefore, from December through February, were (.016 + .052 + .024) $.092; during October, November, March, April (.016 + .052 + .015) $.083; and during May through September (.016 + .052 + .002) $.070. This is the cost of operation per square foot of bench area per week during the various months of the year.

Direct Costs

The direct costs of a greenhouse operation were discussed in Chapter 21. The direct costs for a 6-inch pot chrysanthemum are shown in Table 22.2.

Table 22.2.   Direct costs for a 6-inch pot mum with 5 cuttings per pot.

Cuttings	@ $.10 × 5	$.50
Pot		.10
Medium		.04
Growth retardant		.02
Sleeve		.03
Disbudding		.15
		$.84

The direct cost for a 6-inch pot mum is $.84. To compute the total cost we must add the variable costs. These depend on the time of year, the length of time the plant is grown, and the number of pots per square foot of bench. For example, this crop was planted November 1 and grown for 13 weeks. The crop was spaced pot-to-pot for two weeks and then placed at the final spacing of 12 inches by 12 inches.

To determine the overhead costs we use the following formula:

$$\frac{\text{wks} \times \text{variable costs}}{\text{pots/sq ft}} = \text{overhead/pot}$$

Therefore: Nov., weeks 1 & 2 $(2 \times .083) \div 4 = .04$
            Nov., weeks 3 & 4 $2 \times .083 = .16$
            Dec.–Jan., weeks 5–13 $9 \times .092 = .83$

The total overhead cost for this crop was $1.03 per pot. The direct and overhead costs together are (1.03 + .84) $1.87.

The cost can be subtracted from the proposed or actual selling price and the difference is the profit. For example: the cost is $1.87, the selling price is $2.25, and the profit is $.38 or 20%.

USING CROP COSTS

Crop cost figures can be used to determine selling price and the feasibility of making alternatives in cultural programs, to reduce overhead costs, and to change spacing.

Determining Price

If the crop cost is known and a 20% profit is wanted then the price of the pot mum would have to be [(1.87 × .20) + 1.87] $2.24. A proposed profit of at least 20% in the planning stage is not too unrealistic. If any quantity of pot mums are grown, a 10% loss can be expected. This would mean if we grew 100 pot mums and 10 were lost, the total return would be $201.60 rather than $224.00. Since both the direct and overhead costs included all 100 pots, the return was actually $2.02 per pot or a 7.8% profit.

Reducing Overhead Costs

What effect would a 10% reduction in overhead costs have on profit? In most operations a 10% reduction in overhead costs would not be possible. Note also that only the variable costs could readily be reduced; the nonvariable overhead costs such as taxes, interest, and insurance are not under the manager's control. For the greenhouse in our example the overhead variable cost was $14,309. If we reduced this 20% it would be $12,879. The overhead costs per sq ft of bench per week would be $.0145 instead of $.016, for a savings of $.0015, which would amount to only a penny for our pot mum.

Altering the Cultural Program

There appear to be some substantial changes that could be made in the cultural procedures. For example, the number of cuttings per pot could be reduced from 5 to 4, which would not drastically reduce the quality, but would reduce the direct cost $.10, from $1.87 to $1.77. Some growers avoid disbudding by selecting proper cultivars and are able to obtain market acceptance for them. If the pot mum was not disbudded the direct cost would be reduced $.15 from $1.87 to $1.72. If the growth retardant was not used a savings of $.02 could be accomplished. A 5-inch pot instead of a 6-inch pot could save .$02 on pot and medium costs. If the crop was handled so that no sleeves would be needed another $.03 could be saved. It appears possible by altering the cultural program to reduce direct costs as much as $.32, to $1.55, but the quality would be lower. A tough management decision would have to be made.

Changing the Spacing

When determining the proper spacing of the crop on the greenhouse bench at least three items must be considered: the labor needed to move the pots, the quality of the plants, and the cost per square foot of bench per week. It requires labor to move and space a crop. The actual costs depends on how far the plants have to be moved and the ease of movement. A well-planned operation should be designed so that this task can be accomplished efficiently, and quickly. For our pot mum program let us assume that a person paid $3 per hour moves 100 pots per hour or $.03 per pot per move.

The quality of the plant is important. If the plants are crowded, quality will be reduced. The ideal would be to have the leaves from one pot just touching the leaves in the next pot. This way there would be no crowding or shading and at the same time no open space.

It is probably obvious that the overhead cost of a square foot of bench per week is expensive, from $.07 to $.09 per sq ft per week, and occurs whether a crop is growing or not. To show the relationship between the overhead costs and the total cost of the product we will use the following example. In our first pot mum program, the spacing was pot-to-pot for 2 weeks and then 11 weeks at 12 inches by 12 inches. Let us use 100 pot mums and move them 2 inches farther apart every 3 weeks until the final 12 by 12 spacing is achieved (Table 22.3).

The savings between the two spacing systems would be (1.03–.65) $.38. The extra labor to move the pot would have been $.06 or a difference of $.32 per pot. Another benefit is the added bench space made available, as shown in Table 22.4.

Table 22.3.   The overhead costs involved in moving the pots every 3 weeks.

Week*	Spacing	Pots/ sq ft	Cost/ Pot/wk	Total cost/pot
1-4	6 × 6	4	.02	.08
5-7	8 × 8	2.25	.04	.12
8-10	10 × 10	1.44	.06	.18
11-13	12 × 12	1	.09	.27
				.65

* Weeks 1-4 overhead cost = .083
  Weeks 5-13 overhead cost = .092

Table 22.4.   Total area of bench needed to produce 100 6-inch pots at different spacing methods.

	Spacing	Weeks	Space
1 move	6 × 6	2	50 sq ft
	12 × 12	11	1100 sq ft
		Total	1150 sq ft
3 moves	6 × 6	4	100 sq ft
	8 × 8	3	133 sq ft
	10 × 10	3	208 sq ft
	12 × 12	3	300 sq ft
		Total	741 sq ft

There would be a total savings of (1150 – 741) 409 sq ft. This area could be utilized to grow another crop.

SPACE PROGRAMMING

The manager must determine what crops to grow for what periods and then must plan to utilize space as efficiently as possible. To illustrate some of the planning problems we will follow up on our pot mum program. It was decided to produce 100 pot mums per week year round. We will use the 3-move program. From Table 22.4 note that a total of 741 sq ft would be needed, therefore 13 weeks of crops will require during any one week 741 sq ft of bench. Two 100-foot by 4 foot benches (800 sq ft) will hold this crop with some space between the photoperiod treatments for light barriers and black cloth. Figure 22.1 shows graphically the spacing of the crops and the moves necessary week by week.

This is a simple program but it does show the technique and how a well-planned program can account for the space in the greenhouse each week of the year. If we return to the production costs we can evaluate the yearly costs and the potential profit of this crop. For example, let us assume we obtained a year-round contract to sell the pot mums for $2.15 and our loss was only 5%. There were (52 × 100) 5,200 pot mums produced on 800 sq ft of bench. Less our loss, 4,940 pots were sold for a price of $2.15 each, for a total of $10,621. The direct costs were $.84/pot or (5,200 × .84) $4,368, and the overhead costs were $4.13/sq ft or (800 × 4.13) $3,304 for a total production cost of $7,762. The profit was ($10,621 − 7,672) $2,949 (38%).

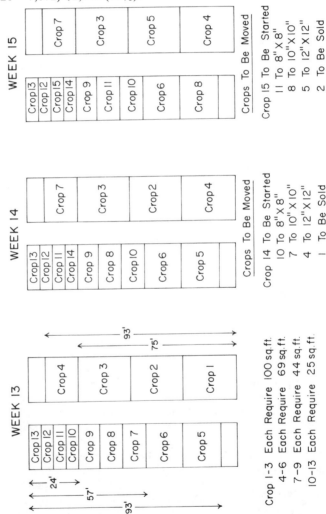

Figure 22.1   The spacing and moves for a year-round program.

To illustrate again how crop programming and space scheduling can give the manager working tools to make decisions let us look at this same pot mum program without the two additional moves. A common practice is to put the containers pot-to-pot for two weeks and then to their final spacing. This program would require 1150 sq ft of bench area or 287.5 linear feet of a 4-foot-wide bench. In practice three 100-foot benches would be used. Assuming all other factors, i.e. losses and selling price, were similar, the production cost and profit would be:

Selling 4940 pots @$2.15		$10,621
Direct costs (5200 × .84)	$ 4,368	
Variable costs (1200 × 4.13)	$ 4,956	(9,324)
Profit		$ 1,297

The difference between the two programs is dramatic and becomes even more so when the extra bench is used to grow another crop. To emphasize this point (which is not totally fair); if more pot mums had been grown on the extra bench with the same costs and selling price, then the total difference between the two programs in terms of profit would be (2949 + 1474) $4,423 instead of $1,297.

USING LINEAR PROGRAMS

As an operation gets larger and more crops are grown and more sizes of crops are grown, programming and evaluating different programs become more difficult. We looked at a simple example of spacing just one crop. Suppose there were ten crops and three different pot sizes.

Linear programs are available through computer businesses and some state agricultural schools, and soon in small programable desk-type computers. Using a linear program is a skill a manager should have, for as we have seen, the efficient use of space and the profitable selection of crops are important.

We will describe a simple problem of the type that linear programs are typically used to solve.

We wish to grow 3-inch and 4-inch geraniums in three greenhouses. We have found that because of bench configurations and some watering problems only a certain number of pots can be grown in the benches in these houses. Table 22.5 gives the limits on the number of pots per square foot and total square footage of bench per house.

Table 22.5.   The capacity of three greenhouses.

	Pots/sq ft		Total sq ft bench area
	3-inch	4-inch	
GH I	4	6	2400
GH II	8	4	2400
GH III	2	3	1500

The selling price of the 3-inch geraniums is $.60 and of the 4-inch geraniums, $.75. We want to determine the optimum numbers of 3-inch and 4-inch pots to grow and the number of each that should be grown in each greenhouse.

Total sales can be expressed by the formula: $.60 (X) + $.75 (Y) = total dollar sales, where X and Y are the numbers of 3- and 4-inch geraniums, respectively. The problem, then, is to solve this equation for X and Y so as to maximize total dollar sales, either mathematically or graphically as shown in Figure 22.2.

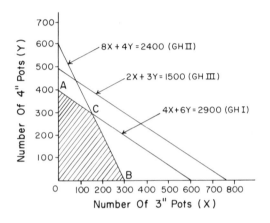

Figure. 22.2 Graphic solution.

The area outside the shaded area does not fit the restrictions we have placed on the problem. The solution lies at points A, B, or C. Points A and B indicate growing only a single size. If we solve for A, the maximum number of 4-inch pots one can grow is 400 and the maximum dollars would be (.75 × 400) $300. If we solve for B, the maximum number of 3-inch pots we can grow is 300 and the maximum dollars would be (.60 × 300) $180. If we solve for C, a mixture of the two pot sizes, then Y is 300 for a dollar value of (.75 × 300) $225, X is 150 for a dollar value of (.60 × 150) $90, and the two together total $315. Therefore, the number of pots that should be grown in each of the greenhouses is as shown in Table 22.6.

If for example under the limits given we grew only 4-inch geraniums we would have grown 28,500 pots in the three greenhouses for a value of (28,500 × .75) $21,375. The net gain using the combination suggested by the graph is (22,860 – 21,375) $1485

Graphic solutions to the problems of greenhouse programs require one dimension for each variable and are impractical for problems with three or more variables. Linear programming allows rapid solutions to such problems- using a computer to solve the equations mathematically for maximum results.

Table 22.6.   The number of pots for maximum sales.

Greenhouse	Pot size	Formula	Sq ft/ greenhouse	Pots	Selling Price
GH I	3″	4 × 150	600	2,400	$ 1,440
	4″	6 × 300	1,800	10,800	8,100
GH II	3″	8 × 150	1,200	9,600	5,760
	4″	4 × 300	1,200	4,800	3,600
GH III	3″	2 × 150	300	600	360
	4″	4 × 300	1,200	4,800	3,600
				Total	$22,860

23

LAWS

The purpose of this chapter is to make the manager aware of his responsibilities, and not to cover each state, county, town, and city regulation. Laws are generally complex enough that consultation with a lawyer and an accountant is advisable. The major areas of involvement by greenhouse managers appear to be zoning, sales taxes, and employee-employer responsibilities.

ZONING

To ensure orderly development of urban areas more and more towns and counties are initiating zoning laws. Zoning Laws designate the area to be zoned, define the categories of land use, and provide for enforcement and interpretation of the regulations. Zoning is basically a community project; one of the many frustrations with zoning appears to be the variations in the law and enforcement from area to area.

The land area of a community to be zoned is generally divided into districts for residential, agricultural, business, industrial, public, marine, and special use. Each of the districts has a special set of regulations pertaining to such things as storage areas, advertising signs, parking areas, size of buildings, proximity to property lines, and so forth. To modify and interpret the regulations a zoning board of appeals hears individual requests for variances.

New Structures

If a new structure is desired, a complete site plan including the relationship to property lines, public streets, topography, and existing structures is presented to a planning board. The planning board approves or disapproves the proposal. If it disapproves, there is usually a grievance procedure before the zoning board of appeals. If the project is approved, a building permit is issued to start construction. Upon completion of the building, the structure is inspected and issued a certificate of occupancy which certifies compliance with the ordinance.

SALES TAX

Many states, counties, and cities have sales taxes, and it is the manager's responsibility to obtain information regarding these taxes. The manager must record the sale, collect the tax, and forward the tax to the appropriate governmental agency. Products that are sold wholesale, for further sale to a consumer, are not taxed. Many retail sales, however, must have a sales tax collected. The distinctions between retail and wholesale in each area should be clarified for the employees by the manager.

EMPLOYEE-EMPLOYER RESPONSIBILITIES

The manager must register with the Internal Revenue Service to obtain a federal identification business number and with the state department of labor to determine the amount of state unemployment insurance he must pay. The amount varies from 1.7 to 5% of the employee's salary and the exact figure depends on the experience factor for that business.

The manager must post in a prominent position for the employee to see and read: the state minimum wage and hour law, workmen's compensation notice of compliance, disability benefit law notice of compliance and the state unemployment insurance notice to employees.

If adults are hired, no permits are needed other than for handicapped workers who, with a special permit, can be paid 25% less than the minimum wage. If young people are hired, the employer should have a certificate of age. Work permits are required for workers under 16 and it is advisable to keep this information on file. Child labor laws are generally very strict.

Income Taxes

The employee files a withholding exemption status form. With the appropriate tax tables or by calculation, the federal tax is computed and withheld from his pay. Depending on the number of employees and the quantity of federal tax withheld, this tax must be sent to the IRS weekly, monthly, quarterly, or yearly. The employee must be informed each pay period of the amount of federal tax withheld. The first of each year he must be issued a federal wage and tax statement for the previous year. If the state does collect income tax it usually parallels the procedures for the federal tax.

Social Security

Social Security tax is more complicated because the employer matches the amount of FICA tax paid by the employee. The rate paid by each is 5.8% of the employee's wage up to a maximum wage of $16,500. The amount withheld for FICA must be reported to the employee. The employer must deposit the FICA tax at the end of each month, if the accumulated amount is greater than $200. The tax can be deposited in a Federal Reserve Bank or authorized commercial bank. In addition, a quarterly report is filed with the FICA.

FICA benefits are available to all retired and qualified employees. In addition many organizations have retirement programs to which the employee can contribute on a regular basis.

Unemployment Compensation

There apparently is not a great distinction between quitting and being discharged in reference to unemployment benefits. During the time the employee is working, the employer has to pay unemployment insurance. This is a federal law administered by the individual states. The rate is based on that employer's experience rating, i.e. the number of employees that have filed for benefits. The rate varies from a minimum of 1.7% to a maximum of 5% of the first $4200 of wage and is determined by the state department of labor. The payments are made quarterly.

When an employee quits or is discharged he is given a record of employment. He will use this information when filing for unemployment benefits. The state unemployment office sends to the employer a request for employment and wage data which includes detailed information about this employee over the past year. This information is used to judge the employee's qualifications for unemployment benefits.

Disability

If an employee is injured and unable to work he is eligible for disability benefits. The employer must have a disability benefit plan, generally with a private insurance company. The plan must be approved by the workmen's compensation board and a notice of compliance must be posted. The cost depends on the type of program. The employee sometimes make a small contribution to the program, but it is basically paid for by the employer.

REFERENCES

Baumback, C. M. and K. Lawler.   *How to organize and operate a small business.*   Prentice Hall, NY.

Beneke, R. and R. Winterbeer.   1973.   *Linear programming applications to agriculture.*   Iowa State University Press.   Ames, IA.

Brumfield, R., P. Nelson, A. Contu, D. Willits, and R. Sovell.   1981.   *Overhead costs of greenhouse firms differentiated by size of firm and market channel.*   North Carolina Agric. Research Serv. Tech. Bull. No. 269.

Fisher, G. A.   1971.   *Greenhouse flower production in Ontario.*   Ontario Dept. of Agriculture and Food.   Toronto, Canada.

Good, D. L. and R. L. Pease.   1975.   *Lake Ontario fruit farm business summary and analysis.*   Cornell University A. E. Extension 75-21. Ithaca, NY.

Hosmer, R. T., A. C. Cooper, and K. H. Vesper.   1977.   *The entrepreneurial function.*   Prentice-Hall.   Englewood Cliffs, NJ.

Lilies, P. and R. Irwin.   *New business ventures and the entrepeneur.* Homewood, IL.

Loomis, C. W., A. C. Lowry, and S. F. Smith.   1974.   Cornell agricultural management information system.   *Cornell University A. E. Extension 74-21.* Ithaca, NY.

Perry, D. and J. Robertson.   1980.   *An economic evaluation of energy conservation investments for greenhouses.*   Ohio Agric. Research and Development Center, Research Bull. 1114.

Stathacos, C. and G. White.   1981.   *An economic analysis of New York greenhouse enterprises.*   Cornell Univ. Agric. Economics Res. 81-21.

State of New York.   *State of New York Employer's Instructions Booklet IT-2100.*   Aibany, NY.

State of New York.   *Handbook for employers.*   State of New York Dept. of Labor, Division of Employment.   Albany, NY.

U.S. Dept. of Labor Wage and Hour Division.   *Child Labor Bulletin No. 101.*   Washington, DC.

Weston, J. F. and E. F. Brigham.   1977.   *Essentials of managerial finance.*   Dryden, Hinsdale, IL.

APPENDIX

Metric-English Conversions

English Units   Metric Units

Length Units

1 inch	25.4 millimeters	0.039 inches	1 millimeters
1 inch	2.5 centimeters	0.39 inches	1 centimeter
1 foot	30.48 centimeters	0.032 feet	1 centimeter
1 foot	0.31 meters	3.28 feet	1 meter
1 yard	0.914 meters	1.09 yards	1 meter
1 mile	1.61 kilometers	0.621 miles	1 kilometer

Area Units

1 sq inch	645.16 sq millimeters		
1 sq inch	6.45 sq centimeters	0.155 sq inches	1 sq centimeter
1 sq foot	928.8 sq centimeter		
1 sq foot	0.093 sq meters	10.76 sq feet	1 sq meter
1 sq yard	0.836 sq meters	1.196 sq yards	1 sq meter
1 sq mile	2.59 sq kilometers	0.386 sq miles	1 sq kilometer
1 acre	0.405 hectares	2.47 acres	1 hectare

Volume Units

1 cubic inch	16.387 cubic centimeters	0.061 cubic inches	1 cubic centimeter
1 cubic foot	23.60 cubic centimeters		
1 cubic foot	0.283 cubic meters	35.3 cubic feet	1 cubic meter
1 bushel	0.352 cubic meters		
1 cubic yard	0.765 cubic meters	1.308 cubic yards	1 cubic meter

Capacity Units

1 U.S. fluid ounce	29.57 milliliters	1.034 U.S. fl oz	1 milliliters
1 U.S. quart	946.33 milliliters		
1 U.S. quart	0.946 liters	1.057 U.S. quarts	1 liter
1 U.S. gallon	3.785 liters	0.264 U.S. gallons	1 liter

Energy Units

1 BTU	107.5 kilogram meters	0.0093 BTU	1 kilogram meter
1 Joule	0.102 kilogram meters	9.81 Joules	1 kilogram meter
1 gram calorie	0.427 kilogram meters	2.34 gram calories	1 kilogram meter

Pressure Units

| 1 pound per sq inch | 70.31 grams per sq centimeter | 0.015 pound per sq inch | 1 gram per sq centimeter |
| 1 pound per sq foot | 4.88 kilograms per sq meter | 0.205 pounds per sq foot | 1 kilogram per sq meter |

Mass Units

1 ounce (Avoirdupois)	28.35 grams	0.035 ounces (Avoir.)	1 gram
1 ounce (Troy)	31.3 grams	0.032 ounces (Troy)	1 gram
1 pound (Avoirdupois)	453.59 grams	2.21 pound (Avoid.)	1 kilogram

Temperature

To convert degrees Fahrenheit ($°F$) to degrees Celsius ($°C$) subtract 32 from the reading and multiply by 5/9.

example: $45°F = (45 - 32)\ 5/9 = 7.2°C$

To convert degrees Celsius ($°C$) to degrees Fahrenheit ($°F$) multiply the reading by 9/5 and add 32.

example: $10°C = 10\ (9/5) + 32 = 50°F$

Abbreviations

Metric Units		English Units	
millimeter	mm	inch	in
centimeter	cm	foot	ft
meter	m	yard	yd
kilometer	km	mile	mi
milliliter	ml	fluid ounce	fl oz
liter	l	pint	pt
cubic centimeter	cc	quart	qt
cubic meter	m^3	gallon	gal
gram	gm	cubic inch	in^3
kilogram	kg	cubic foot	ft^3
hectare	ha	cubic yard	yd^3
		ounce	oz
		pound	lb
		bushel	bu
		acre	a

INDEX

NOTES

NOTES

NOTES

NOTES

NOTES

NOTES

Robert W. Langhans, professor of floriculture, arrived at Cornell University in 1952 with a Bachelor of Science from Rutgers, obtained his Masters and Ph.D. degrees under Kenneth Post and remained on the faculty. Professor Langhans has taught the "greenhouse management" course since 1970, and the beginning course in floriculture before that for 14 years. He has received a number of honors, among them election to the honorary societies of Pi Alpha Xi, Sigma Xi, and Phi Kappa Phi. In 1979 he received the W. A. Blake Award for Distinguished Graduate Teaching from the American Society for Horticultural Science and was elected a Fellow to ASHA in 1981.

Professor Langhans has visited the major floricultural production areas and research stations in the United States, Europe, Israel, South America, Japan and Australia.

Langhans has written and collaborated with his students and colleagues to publish more than 200 articles. He edited the New York State Flower Growers Bulletin for 14 years and edited the Carnation Manual, Snapdragon Manual, Chrysanthemum Manual, and co-edited with D. C. Kiplinger of Ohio State the Lily Manual and with J. Mastalerz of Penn State, the Rose Manual. He also edited "A Growth Chamber Manual" published by Cornell University Press in 1978.